School Security

This Book
Belongs To

School Security

How to Build and Strengthen a School Safety Program

Paul Timm, PSP

ELSEVIER

AMSTERDAM • BOSTON • HEIDELBERG • LONDON
NEW YORK • OXFORD • PARIS • SAN DIEGO
SAN FRANCISCO • SINGAPORE • SYDNEY • TOKYO

Butterworth-Heinemann is an imprint of Elsevier

BH

Acquiring Editor: Brian Romer
Editorial Project Manager: Keira Bunn
Project Manager: Priya Kumaraguruparan
Designer: Alan Studholme

Butterworth-Heinemann is an imprint of Elsevier
The Boulevard, Langford Lane, Kidlington, Oxford OX5 1GB, UK
225 Wyman Street, Waltham, MA 02451, USA

Library of Congress Cataloging-in-Publication Data
Application submitted

British Library Cataloging-in-Publication Data
A catalogue record for this book is available from the British Library

ISBN: 978-0-12-407811-6

For information on all Butterworth-Heinemann publications visit
our web site at http://store.elsevier.com/

Working together
to grow libraries in
developing countries

www.elsevier.com • www.bookaid.org

Contents

About the Author

Paul Timm is a board-certified Physical Security Professional (PSP), president of RETA Security, Inc., and a nationally acclaimed expert in school security. In addition to conducting numerous vulnerability assessments and his frequent keynote addresses, Paul is an experienced School Crisis Assistance Team volunteer through the National Organization for Victims Assistance (NOVA). He holds a patent on a vulnerability assessment methodology known as ALPHA™ and is certified in Vulnerability Assessment Methodology (VAM) through Sandia National Laboratories. He is a member of ASIS International, where he serves as vice-chairman of the School Safety and Security Council, and the Illinois Association of School Business Officials (IASBO), where he serves on the Risk Management Committee. Nearing the completion of his M.Div. at Moody Theological Seminary, Paul holds a degree in speech communications and a certificate in business administration from the University of Illinois.

Acknowledgments

First and foremost, I thank God for seeing me through the writing process.

This book has been a true family effort. Most of the groundwork, the "rigor and discipline," was developed by my dad, the late Ron Timm, CPP. Both of my sons, David and Joshua Timm, made significant contributions, especially to the social media chapter. My mom, Karen Timm, was helpful in editing. Both of my daughters, Bethany and Amanda Timm, cheered for me along the way.

I also valued the contributions of those whom I consider family—Sheri Jacobs and Bairet Bazemore. Brian Moore, Mike Fickes, and Mike Guido also deserve credit. Kudos to Keira Bunn, Mike Johnson, Barbara Hoskins, and Steve Hughes for keeping me on track.

What Is School Security?

Introduction – Security Is Not CSI

Chicago boasts two major airports—O'Hare Airport and Midway Airport. As a frequent traveler, I benefit from both an economic and a scheduling standpoint to have air travel options. I prefer Midway Airport to O'Hare Airport. Due to its smaller size, Midway experiences fewer delays and cancellations. On the other hand, Midway's airlines do not offer flights to as many places as O'Hare. I encountered that reality after being asked to provide a security seminar for a school district in West Virginia a couple of years ago. The only direct flight to my destination was through O'Hare. When I arrived at the airport in the late afternoon on the day before the seminar, weather reports were calling for severe thunderstorms. Shortly before boarding the plane, O'Hare's public address system announced that the National Weather Service had issued a tornado warning for the airport vicinity. Although we did not have to wait in the designated tornado shelter area much longer than 60 minutes before the warning was lifted, all flights in and out of the airport that evening were cancelled. I called the school district contact in West Virginia and informed him that I had been rebooked for the first flight the next morning. Any delay to that flight could result in a late arrival to my own seminar. Not surprisingly, the flight the next morning was indeed delayed. In fact, by the time I actually walked into the auditorium filled with hundreds of staff members, I was 15 minutes late.

I rushed into the auditorium with my own laptop and began to set up the PowerPoint presentation. With all eyes upon me, that few minutes of pushing buttons, plugging cords, and syncing systems began to feel like an eternity. In the midst of my panicked efforts, one of the teachers in the audience approached me with the hope of engaging me in a conversation. As you can imagine, I was not feeling very talkative at that moment. Her part of the dialogue went something like this: "Oh, Mr. Timm, I'm so glad to have you here to speak on this topic. Our district has lots of security problems. I've been telling them what to do, and, even though I know more about security than anyone else in the county, no one will listen to me. So, maybe they'll listen to somebody from the outside." My part of the dialogue consisted mostly of preoccupied head nods and saying "uh huh". Pretty soon, my lack of participation frustrated her to the point that she finally demanded, "Mr. Timm, don't you want to know why I know more about security than anyone else in the county?!?" Now, quite frankly, at that moment I was not very interested to know, but I diplomatically invited her to tell me anyway. Without hesitation, she stated, "Because I've never missed an episode of CSI!" That true story illustrates the fact that many stakeholders involved in the school security discussion may not have an accurate frame of reference, understanding, or concept of school security.

Security is also not…

People can have the wrong idea about the meaning of security. In addition to the humorous introductory example, I have encountered several other vantage points that miss the mark to varying degrees. The following groups demonstrate additional misconceptions regarding school security.

The Safety Activists

Safety activists tend to possess strong personalities and persuasively advocate for oversimplified beliefs. They make assertions such as "All school security problems are the result of mental health issues" and "Schools would be safe if staff members had the right to carry firearms." Typically well intentioned, these stakeholders want their ideas adopted now. While there is definitely a place for personal beliefs to be shared and discussed, an effective security program depends on knowledge, collaboration, accountability, and prudence. If strong opinions alone lead the decision making process, the result will be a security program that is—at best—less than comprehensive or—at worst—ineffective.

The Security Relativists

Security relativists have seen or heard about security measures adopted by other entities and assume those measures must be universally effective. They make confident declarations, such as "District X decided to mandate student uniforms, so we should adopt the same practice" or "Airports use metal detectors on everyone; schools should use them too." Security relativists can also wield strong personalities and frequently want immediate action. Do not yield to this kind of pressure. Specific applications and circumstances determine the effectiveness of security measures and practices. Research and implement best-practice solutions conducive to your needs. Collaborate with nearby districts and related entities, but make your own determinations on how to reduce risk and prepare for emergencies. If granted permission to lead the charge, security relativists can blaze a trail toward financial and operational regrets.

The Quick-Fixers

Beware of persons possessing a reactive mentality that demands "quick fix" solutions such as cameras, metal detectors, or bullet-resistant glass. These quick-fixers want something tangible implemented now, no matter the cost. But haste can lead to buyer's remorse. It is important to understand that effective school security is never accomplished through product-driven solutions alone. The value of security products and systems is determined by people and practices. In fact, products and systems play a complementary role to the real star of the show: people-driven solutions. Do not buckle under pressure. Maintain a course that is comprehensive and collaborative.

The Officer Advocates

Officer advocates believe that school security rests solely on the shoulders of local police, a school resource officer, in-house safety monitors, or contract security personnel. This group wants to place exclusive responsibility for providing a safe learning environment on those assigned to that task. Police/security officers, however, cannot be omnipresent and often operate in a responsive or reactive mode. When an alarm sounds after a break-in, for instance, officers are dispatched to investigate the scene. Without slighting the importance of police/security officer activities or disputing their primary involvement in school security matters, an effective security program depends on a school-wide culture of awareness and ownership. Routinely express appreciation for the efforts of officers, but do not imagine that they can successfully carry the security program without the assistance of others.

The Crisis Confused

The crisis confused have adopted the mistaken notion that the term "school security" refers to possessing an emergency plan. Members of this crisis confused club might have helped in the development of emergency procedures or participated in crisis team meetings. To continue underscoring the importance of a preventative approach, however, it should be noted that a crisis management plan is *not* a security plan. Most states require schools to maintain a crisis management plan comprised of written emergency procedures. These procedures can greatly assist in mitigating or lessening the impact of crises. In fact, chapter 7 of this book ("Managing Emergencies") details ways to significantly enhance the emergency preparedness component of your security program. But emergency plans alone do not sufficiently address the protection of students and staff. The following chapters will demonstrate a comprehensive approach to school security that relies on contributions from proactive components such as violence prevention programming and staff training.

The Past Performers

Past performers believe that yesterday's school security solutions also apply today. They will utter phrases such as, "We used to make the boy that started the fight wear a pink shirt in school all day" and "After a theft, we would require all the students to stay after school until someone confessed or snitched on the thief." While some crime prevention principles are timeless, today's school security issues cannot be oversimplified. Past performers can also romanticize historical tactics as being more effective than they were. Instead, school administrators should seek collaborative, evaluation-based solutions. Some of the most effective solutions will be recommended by those that have no knowledge of the past—students!

Security Is Loss Prevention

Security is loss prevention. How can we protect (i.e., prevent harm to) students, staff and visitors? The purpose of this book is to establish a clear foundation for school security and build on that loss prevention foundation with appropriate measures and practical strategies. There will also be a section devoted to helpful resources.

The term "loss prevention" is most often associated with the retail sales industry. Retail companies attempt to preserve profits by reducing preventable losses. Preventable losses include theft, vandalism, and other criminal behaviors. "Four elements are necessary for a successful loss prevention plan: 1) Total support from top management, 2) A positive employee attitude, 3) Maximum use of all available resources, 4) A system which establishes both responsibility and accountability for loss prevention through evaluations that are consistent and progressive."[1] Effective school security also depends on those four elements, as well as some additional components. Chapter 2 ("How Safe is Your School?") will provide a more detailed view of loss prevention as it applies to the school arena.

As a means of whetting your appetite for the upcoming chapters, please take the following security "pop quiz." Once completed, consider asking staff members to do the same.

1. What is your primary means of emergency communication?
2. Excluding code-driven requirements such as fire extinguishers, first aid kits, and automated external defibrillators (AEDs), what emergency supplies does your school have?
3. How many registered sex offenders live in the community surrounding your school?
4. What is an ICS structure?
5. What are the main tenets of your documented dating violence policy?
6. Outside of the classroom or school building, how do teachers and staff correspond with students?
7. Which exterior door in your school is most often propped open?
8. What does your documented social media practice address?
9. What is the most important security product?
10. How effective is your bullying prevention program?

Answer key:

1. Acceptable answers include landline telephones, two-way radios, and intercom systems. Interestingly enough, cellular phones are probably not an acceptable answer. Most staff members feel so attached to personal cellular phones that they assume these devices would be the best option in an emergency. Cellular phones, however, have numerous potential drawbacks: phones may not be powered on, signal strength may be poor, batteries might not be adequately charged, etc. Even if none of those issues occur in an emergency situation, phones must be unlocked, individual numbers must be dialed, and calls must be answered by another individual. Contrast the functionality of a cellular phone with that of the best answer—a two-way radio. These devices offer one-button, instant communication with a number of individuals who are already in the vicinity. Because it can be impractical to provide all staff members with two-way radios, other acceptable answers include landline telephones and the intercom system call buttons.
2. Emergency supplies consist of those items that may be essential during an incident that results in an evacuation or extended shelter-in-place. Specific items include flashlights, Mylar blankets, and drinking water. Some schools refer to the bundling

of these supplies in one container as "Go Kits" or "Emergency Backpacks." Consider the quantity of supplies that will be sufficient and determine where the kits or backpacks will be kept. Obviously, an emergency supply container that is kept in one location presents a level of risk that containers kept in multiple locations effectively reduces.

3. Even though sex offender laws vary from state to state, most dangerous levels of offenders are legally prohibited from accessing school grounds without predetermined restrictions. Since security personnel alone may not be sufficient to identify a registered offender, consider posting your state's registry in a staff-only or intranet section of the school website. Registries typically provide names, addresses, photos, and types of offenses committed. As an alternative to state registries, one of the more helpful nationwide registries is http://familywatchdog.us/.

4. ICS in an acronym for Incident Command System. The ICS structure is a basic component of the National Incident Management System (NIMS). The Federal Emergency Management Agency (FEMA) developed an online 100-level course that can be accessed at http://training.fema.gov/EMIWeb/IS/IS100SCA.asp.

5. The policy should have components such as a statement that dating violence will not be tolerated, violence reporting procedures, instruction for school employees, prevention education for students, parents'/students' rights, discipline procedures for students that commit violence at school, and contact information for and resources available through domestic violence programs and rape crisis programs.

6. Outside of the classroom, it has become increasingly more common and socially acceptable for teachers to text, "friend," and correspond with students via social media. Many parents are understandably concerned about private communication between their children and school staff members. Allegations of inappropriate correspondence are rising rapidly. As a result, the state of Virginia was the first to enact a law banning all electronic correspondence between staff and students that is not school sanctioned. In other words, staff utilizing e-mail that runs through the school's system to correspond with students is permitted, but staff utilizing a privately chosen system, such as Gmail or Yahoo, is strictly prohibited. The state of Missouri attempted to pass a similar law that banned social networking such as Facebook between staff and students, but the law was overturned when the teachers' union protested the restriction.

7. The access control practice of keeping exterior doors closed and locked often gets defeated by students and staff who prop doors open for the sake of convenience. Granted, most individuals would never rationally decide to trade building security for personal convenience, but this is exactly what takes place when exterior doors are propped and left unmonitored. Common responses include recess/PE door, delivery door, and parking lot door.

8. A documented social media policy should address components such as prohibiting the online sharing of student information and data (i.e., test scores), maintaining separate professional and personal e-mail and Facebook accounts, instruction

regarding appropriate online behavior, monitoring of professional social media sites, and guidance regarding personal social media sites.

9. This answer is not subject to debate. The most important security product is a functional communications device. Murphy's Law dictates that without a functional communications device, an emergency will occur when there is no way to contact assistance or receive the warning announcement.

10. An effective bullying prevention program observes students throughout the day; tracks bullying behaviors; performs surveys with teachers, students, and parents; reviews current policies with administrators and staff; and promotes a positive culture.

If you were able to answer the majority of these questions confidently and correctly, you are doing well. Now administer the quiz to teachers and staff members.

Which of these questions reveal the need for short-term instruction? Collaboratively pursue methods for addressing gaps in knowledge. The point of the quiz is not to get a passing grade as much as it is to test and improve security awareness. Consider utilizing this quiz on an annual basis. Establish benchmarks. Strive to improve continuously.

Today's Student

Reorient your perspective on school security. School is different today. Students are different. Anxiety among the student population is increasing. "The average high school kid today has the same level of anxiety as the average psychiatric patient in the early 1950's."[2] A higher level of anxiety translates into a higher level of risk.

Today's students face new threats. Social media risks abound. Never before have students been more connected and more isolated. The Pew Research Center reported in February 2014 that Facebook is used by 73 percent of US teens aged 12–17. In March 2013, the Pew Research Center found that 78 percent of that age group had a cell phone, almost half (47 percent) of which were smartphones. That translates into 37 percent of all teens who have smartphones, up from just 23 percent in 2011.[3] The prevalence of social media and handheld electronic devices has introduced unprecedented, immediate, and far-reaching problems.

Consider the following statistics from the Kaiser Family Foundation. "Over the past five years, young people have increased the amount of time they spend consuming media by an hour and 17 minutes daily, from 6:21 to 7:38—almost the amount of time most adults spend at work each day, except that young people use media seven days a week instead of five. Moreover, given the amount of time they spend using more than one medium at a time, today's youth pack a total of 10 hours and 45 minutes worth of media content into those daily seven and a half hours—an increase of almost two and a quarter hours of media exposure per day over the past five years."[4] The Kaiser Family Foundation released these findings in 2010. Can there be any question that the numbers have grown significantly since?

Issues that Students Face: Immediacy

For generations, students have cared too much about social standing relative to their peers. They will go to great lengths to avoid feeling inferior. The pressure to compete socially is nothing new, but the battlefield has changed dramatically.

Just a few short years ago, the drive to "keep up" was expressed in terms of hardware. Students wanted the latest phone, the latest music player, and the latest television. In today's world, the technology arms race is expressed in terms of software. A constant wave of new apps that can be downloaded immediately over Wi-Fi to a phone, tablet, or hand-held electronic device make it nearly impossible to compete with peers. Impossibility does not seem to deter students. They simply live in a different, faster world. Students' lives are ruled by immediacy.

When something exciting happens to a student, the first response is to document it. A photo is taken and shared, a status is posted, and texts are sent. The moment itself is not fully appreciated until the student's ecosystem of social networks is made aware of it. The moment itself is not truly a success until it is liked and "favorited." This may seem strange and foreign to adults, but it is simply a reality for today's students.

Teachers and administrators would love for all students to put their phones away and pay attention at all times. We have reached a point where that expectation is no longer realistic.

Issues that Students Face: Single-Tasking

The current generation of students may be the best multitaskers to have ever walked the planet. Stop and observe students in their daily routine. They are reading e-mails while they are watching TV. They are responding to a party invite while they are ordering lunch. When students are talking to you, they are probably talking to someone else, too. Today's generation multi-tasks with ease because they are programmed that way.

Prohibiting students from multi-tasking in a classroom setting presents a significant challenge. The traditional classroom environment is designed for single-tasking. Teachers face significant obstacles in attempting to address this tension. They face a room full of students that have full-time access to any form of entertainment they could possibly imagine and, at the same time, must focus the attention of those students on a single subject such as biology for an entire class period.

Many people have framed the discussion of multi-tasking as an addiction. While that may be a bit extreme, the concept makes sense. Students need to be doing something while they are doing something. Their output will likely suffer if they do not.

Issues that Students Face – Permanence

Today's students are famous. They are very similar to the A-list movie stars seen on television and in magazines. Students get photographed nearly every day; their pictures are posted online and discussed by many different people. While this reality may not fall under the traditional definition of fame, consider the similarities. Students are treated like celebrities.

In the past, compliments and insults were special. They were initially expressed and, after that, the specific comments were remembered only through memory. Today's compliments and insults are permanent. Prior to the advent of social media, a student might have heard that a classmate said that she thought he was cute. Now, that information is posted on an Instagram page. Prior to the advent of social media, if a student dropped her lunch tray in the cafeteria, students in the immediate vicinity laughed. Now, a video of the incident gets posted on YouTube for all to see just moments after it occurs.

Students have learned the reality of permanence, and they live their lives in anticipation of it. They almost act as their own publicists. Students must think about the ramifications of certain actions and consider, ahead of time, how those actions might be received. They get dressed with this in mind, they order lunch with this in mind, and they interact with their friends with this in mind.

Today's Security Program

School security is more complicated than ever. Consider the increasing part that technology plays. How much power does the director of information technology (IT) wield? Security products and systems purchased today can be antiquated tomorrow. School stakeholders resist new security practices but simultaneously demand a safer learning environment. The "do more with less" mentality seems to apply to people and funding.

Security Coordinator for IT

Security today comes with technology to enable security directors to expand the capabilities of staffs that are often too small. The school or district IT department can help plan, budget, and make decisions about acquisitions. IT can help with installations and make sure that the overall IT system has enough capacity to carry out security's needs as well as the school's educational and operational needs. Technology tools include mass notification systems, public address systems, and two-way radio systems on the communications side. They include video cameras, access control systems, and visitor management technology to help organize that part of security.

Program Development

Security programs emerge, grow, change, and evolve all the time. Right now, for instance, key programs address bullying, workplace and school violence, visitor management and access control, and fire and life safety. Detecting these issues as they emerge, studying them, and finding the security solutions as they become available are part of every security director's job.

Security's Impact on School Culture

The security measures schools implement—and do not implement—affect the culture of the facility and the community. The part products and systems play pales in comparison to the role people play. People determine the value of products and systems. A staff member that props a door open renders useless a perfectly good locking mechanism. Those who murmur about the security program plant seeds of fear and discontent. On the other hand, a good attitude begets more good attitudes. People who take ownership of school security set an invaluable tone. Those who make concerted efforts to follow security practices plant seeds of confidence and preparedness.

Negative Impact

Why begin with how security can negatively impact school culture? Because the sad reality is that the majority of schools look at security as a second class program. Security personnel rarely garner respect. They do not usually possess cheerful dispositions. They are not perceived as advocates. Negative consequences greet those who engage in behaviors that violate security practices. Students, staff, and visitors do not usually welcome discipline and rule enforcement. These patterns often produce an adversarial tone toward the security program.

One high school student expressed a commonly held view of school security by stating, "I don't mind the police officer. He's just doing his job. The safety monitors are grouchy and old. They just sit around. They don't like students. We know all the ways to get around stuff they have in place (security measures) to catch kids. We make fun of them."

If you can relate to school security's negative impact, it is time to change the culture.

MAKING A POSITIVE IMPACT

Brian N. Moore, Public Safety Director of the Red Clay Consolidated School District in Delaware, exhibits a fresh and positive attitude toward school security. He describes his responsibilities in the following way.

The primary mission of a school district public safety director is to place as many barriers, either real or perceived, between students and those who would do harm to students. That sums up the mission, but the skill sets and methods used to accomplish that task can be very daunting, if not confusing. Focus on employing the following skill sets and methods to accomplish the mission.

Skill Set: Administrator. A public safety director cannot be effective without resources. Good administration of your department is vital. Part of the task revolves around funding. In order to ensure a solid budget, a good director strives to make school board members aware of what they receive for their investment. Unlike traditional education programs, which can supply actual data to support success in student achievement, public safety directors must rely on a different matrix when looking at K–12 security. We have to document how many issues we have prevented. That can be accomplished by documenting what programs we have in place and

---

(Continued)

how well they are received by the teaching community. Customer service is an important aspect of this undertaking. Ensure that when the public safety department provides services, we do it in a way that makes the school and staff members feel safer or better equipped to manage an emergency.

Skill Set: Liaison. The liaison role is also important. Schools must have a good working relationship with partners in the public safety community. Create a strong communications program. Reach out regularly to contacts in the local police, fire, emergency management and emergency medical services (EMS) community. Offer your schools as sites for emergency training opportunities. The more time spent working on pre-planning with these groups, the less "getting to know you" time will be required during an actual response. Drills are a great way to work with these partners. Every agency regularly seeks opportunities to train. Attempt to sponsor a full-scale drill or even a tabletop exercise. Local responders will appreciate your efforts and permit you the opportunity to work with them in a comfortable, pre-planning setting.

Skill Set: Public Relations and Crime Prevention. Often overlooked, the role of public relations and crime prevention is imperative for gaining the support of the parent community. Consider hosting a few school PTA/PTO crime prevention nights. Bring in speakers from the crime prevention community and present work sessions for parents. Plan some fun activities for students, and provide food and door prizes for everyone. As a result of these forums, parents learn that the public safety department is active in protecting their children. Make sure school board members are aware of these parent outreach programs and document their attendance. It can go a long way to ensuring that stakeholders know how hard you are working.

Skill Set: Intelligence Analyst. Stay current on the most recent trends in school incidents and emergencies. Pay attention to the outcomes of recent school events and attempt to find the lessons learned. Share these lessons with key stakeholders. If you have school resource officers, meet with them to discuss discipline and crime trends. Talk about issues and patterns in the schools. In the community at large, public safety has found great value in intelligence-led policing. Schools can benefit and become more productive in the same way. Timeless issues, such as petty theft, and newer crimes, such as the "knockout game," can be analyzed and discussed from a preparedness perspective in schools. Trends in drug trafficking in your local community have a natural nexus with the school community. If, for example, your community is experiencing a heroin outbreak, work with local law enforcement agencies to educate staff and students on the effects of heroin abuse. Information is a key resource for anyone in the role of a public safety supervisor.

Skill Set: Educator and Trainer. Provide instruction on a routine basis. Train your staff to maintain a high level of security awareness and think about emergency preparedness in their everyday operations. Remind staff members to look for visitor and staff identification. Review visitor management practices and incident reporting procedures. Foster a culture of security awareness. Hold regular internal drills and tabletop exercises for school-based incident command teams to ensure that they are ready to perform their roles in the event of an emergency. Simply being visible in schools and at events can be just as important as conducting training. When visiting schools, speak to staff members about relevant "what if" scenarios. While

MAKING A POSITIVE IMPACT—cont'd

observing a school lunch period, ask staff on duty how they would respond if someone with a weapon came into the cafeteria. Cause people to think about responses so that they think and plan proactively. Always preach preparation.

Method: Visibility. A successful public safety director is not locked up in an office labeled "Only open door in case of emergency!" Instead, that person is visibly accessible in the school community. Staff members occasionally approach me during my school visits and say things like, "Seeing you reminds me that I have a question about security." Relish these opportunities to address customer service questions. Use these encounters to reinforce that security is about being a presence in schools and making sure that the staff knows it. When visiting a school, make it a point to greet the principal and inquire as to whether there is anything he or she needs. Just this little effort reinforces that you are there to offer support, not to add tasks or issues.

Skill Set: Advisor and Counselor. Be available when a school principal or district administrator has a question about a public safety matter. Demonstrate an interest in receiving questions and concerns. From parental custody disputes to lockdown drill procedures, make a concerted effort to understand and address the issues. Respond with integrity. If you cannot confidently answer a specific question, be honest. No public safety director has all the answers. Offer to conduct some research, check with experts, and respond in a reasonable amount of time. Be diligent and keep your word. You never know if it is a question that could very well save a life during an incident.

Method: Take it Personally. Take ownership of your role. In education, we expect principals to take ownership of the learning of students. In the same way, we should take ownership of the safety of the students we are charged with protecting. Advocate for student safety. People with whom we work can tell if we take our jobs seriously. Display a sense of ownership. Demonstrate responsibility. Let others know that security requires a collaborative approach and that you need assistance. Permit the stress of risk management to motivate you to do your best each and every day.

Method: Love Your Job. When people ask me if I enjoy what I do, I can answer without question that I love what I do. My job is to keep kids safe. Is there a better or more important job? Public safety can be physically and emotionally taxing. However, the rewards outweigh the difficulties. I am proud to go home at night knowing that I played a part in providing an environment where students came to school and were safe to learn new things and new ideas. I cannot prevent every potential incident. Not every day is perfect. But I can surely do my best and be thankful for having the opportunity to make a difference in the lives of children. Students may never know who I am or what I do, but I can go to bed every night knowing that it is my job to be their protector. There is no better job in the world. I am thankful for the opportunity to make a difference in the lives of our students.

***

Before searching for a way to clone Brian, understand that no one person has shoulders broad enough to carry a security program alone. It takes more than one individual. It takes a culture.

Stakeholder Responses to "What Is School Security?"

We asked a broad base of stakeholders to answer the question, "What is school security?" Some representative responses follow.

"I believe that school security is a dynamic process that describes the optimal conditions for education. As school administrators, we continually work to identify areas of improvements to make our buildings and classrooms safer, so that staff and students experience a sense of safety and security when on our campus." – Linda S., Director of Communication

Linda understands the role security plays in facilitating learning. She also sees the need for a team effort. The next chapter, "How Safe is Your School?", introduces important concepts of loss prevention, or security, as they pertain to schools. It also espouses a collaborative and comprehensive approach to school security.

"School security is planning for, implementing, and evaluating all measures physically, fiscally, emotionally, and reasonably possible to create and maintain schools that provide a climate of safe and secure learning, teaching, and interacting for all students, employees, and visitors in school buildings. While is not possible to guarantee 100 percent school security, it is possible to significantly minimize risks that harm will come to anyone in a school building due to breach of security." – Tom W., Superintendent

Tom begins his answer with the planning component of school security. Implementation and evaluation rest on that foundation. Chapter 3, "Developing a Plan," emphasizes the importance of developing and documenting security practices and policies. The chapter also presents numerous helpful samples.

"School security may be defined as the process and result of providing supportive safeguards (e.g., security guards, supportive school resource officers, check-in procedures, lockdown and communication protocols, staff training, cameras and security hardware on doors, etc.) to schools that are not overly restrictive in order to ensure that teaching and learning can occur without harm coming to students or staff members. It is the very foundation of a supportive and effective learning environment. A safe and secure school gives parents peace of mind, allows teachers to focus on their core purpose, and helps students to be children who do not have to remain hyper-vigilant about their safety. An important component of school security involves social emotional learning (SEL) and anti-bullying education for all students. There should also be an identification and referral mechanism to ensure that students or staff with a known propensity for violence can receive the help that they need." – Charlene M., Director of Special Services

Charlene gives several examples of physical security measures. She is careful to assert that those measures should not be overly restrictive. Chapter 4, "Securing Your Environment," focuses on the physical security component of school security. It explores the individual elements of deterrence, detection, delay, and response. The chapter also introduces basic principles of crime prevention through environmental design (CPTED). Charlene's concern with SEL will be echoed in the next quote.

"In my mind, school security can be defined in multiple ways. There is school security as in checking in with the front desk if someone is visiting, but it could also mean how clean a school is in regards to drugs, alcohol, language, etc. School security can be physical and mental. On the physical side, there are always the 'bullies' of the school, who will physically harass others. But in today's school, the reality is that you see 10 times as much mental and psychological bullying as physical bullying. While that might not seem as impactful, physical harm may come forth from mental bullying in the form of attempted—and sometimes successful—suicide. Security is a major issue in schools today, where some environments make students feel like they are lucky to make it through the day unscathed. Just the other day, I witnessed a full-on fight break out in the hallway, which demonstrates the reality that school might not be as safe as I thought it was." – Nick K., high school student.

Nick moves quickly from the physical security component of visitor management to the need for bullying prevention efforts. Chapter 5, "Influencing Behavior," addresses violence prevention and intervention programs. At issue is the need to positively influence student behavior through bullying prevention, substance abuse prevention, and sexual harassment prevention.

"I feel a sense of sadness considering that the need for school security is our reality. Growing up, my schools were inherently safe havens, on the same level as grandparents or aunts and uncles. School was synonymous with safe, secure, unbreachable. The feeling of being secure doesn't come from metal detectors, ID badges, or kiosk check-ins. Feeling secure starts with a belief that fuels behavior that translates into action. My experience as a parent has taught me that my children are the best barometer of how safe a school is because security, for a child, is safety.

"Does the front office, the principal, vice-principals, and administrative staff believe that providing a safe environment is paramount, and—if so—do they believe they are doing it every day? From the student's perspective, this is evident in the way they are treated by the principal and staff. Do they feel welcome and part of the school family when they are in the presence of the leaders and staff? Do the teachers offer the same level of inclusiveness? Is there a sense of pride that includes everyone, a sense of ownership from bus drivers, janitorial/maintenance, and teachers to the principal that states loudly and clearly: these are our children and they belong here?

"Belief fuels behavior. Belief-driven behavior is exercised every day by everyone. I have witnessed this first hand, both positively and negatively. As an example, I observed a few students who were outside the classroom walking the halls when a teacher passed by. He didn't slow his pace, engage, or even acknowledge the three students. That behavior is counter to security efforts and fostering the feeling of being safe. In the same way, if he had confronted the students with a blanket interrogation, such as, "What are you doing out here?", it would not have felt inclusive. A confrontational tone says, "You don't belong here." On the other hand, if the teacher would have asked, "What are you three Big Reds (language reflecting the school mascot) doing out here?" it would have felt inclusive. A positive tone affirms the students as belonging to the school family, but also makes them state a reason for being there.

"Behavior fuels action. Creating a safe and secure culture takes action—not posters or banners or parent newsletters. Its starts in the main office and grows into the class-rooms. It is either fed or starved in the teachers' lounge and in the PTA meetings. We are ultimately, all of us, school security. I want school to be a safe haven again, unbreachable and impenetrable to outside forces that seek to erode or steal the inner peace children feel when they know they are safe." – Jennifer B., mom.

Jennifer reflects a mother's heart in expressing concern for the way administrators, teachers, and staff behave toward students. She draws attention to the fact that behavior, and school culture in general, is determined by the value individuals place on providing a safe learning environment. Chapter 6, "Preparing Your People," addresses the school secu-rity element of teacher and staff training. It presents ideas and strategies for positively affecting school culture through intentional awareness and instructional initiatives.

"What do we need to keep the schools safe? Of course, school security. One way schools do this is by making sure all students get into the building and teachers doing attendance to make sure all the kids are in class. We also have lockdown drills to make sure that every-one knows what to do if there is a stranger in the building. Our doors are always locked so everyone must go through the office and some schools even have cameras. This is impor-tant because it keeps all the people safe. This makes us feel comfortable because we know that there is school security." – Shoshana, fifth grade student.

Shoshana demonstrates that effective school security is not scary. Along with putting her finger on physical security measures, she clearly states the purpose of practicing lock-down drills. Shoshana has not been traumatized by these drills—she has been prepared. Chapter 7, "Managing Emergencies," tackles emergency response planning and crisis management. It addresses the collaborative development and testing of an emergency operations plan.

"As an Internet safety specialist, I believe people need to look at school safety from a technology perspective along with the typical physical security measures. Issues such as cyberbullying, careless sharing of personal information, and communicating with indi-viduals not known in real life tend to affect all aspects of one's life and can be brought into school. Educating students, parents, and staff about Internet etiquette and appropriate technology use is a very important piece of the school safety puzzle." – Karina H., Training and Education Coordinator, Bureau of Criminal Apprehension

Karina stands on the front lines in confronting the newest security risk. She intro-duces the complicated connection between cyber issues at home and at school. Chapter 8, "Tackling Social Media Risks," addresses the growing risk that social media issues and related technology present in the school environment. It identifies specific threats and provides ways to reduce risk.

Conclusion

Make no mistake—school security is not CSI. Be on guard against misconceptions, agendas, and pressures to make knee-jerk decisions.

School security is loss prevention. Administrators must undertake a comprehensive and collaborative approach to protecting students, staff and visitors.

Today's school setting is unique. Students face new challenges. Security is often considered a necessary evil. Today's school security programs must adapt. So much is at stake. Now is the time to commit to providing a safer learning environment.

References

1. Charles A. Sennewald and John H. Christman, *Retail Crime, Security, and Loss Prevention* (Oxford: Butterworth/Heinemann, 2008), 302.

2. Robert A. Leahy, "Anxiety Files," *Psychology Today* (April 30, 2008), accessed December 8, 2013, http://www.psychologytoday.com/blog/anxiety-files/200804/how-big-problem-is-anxiety/.

3. Mary Madden et al., *Teens and Technology 2013.* (Washington, DC: Pew Research Center, 2013), 2, http://www.pewinternet.org/files/old-media/Files/Reports/2013/PIP_TeensandTechnology2013.pdf.

4. Victoria J. Rideout, Ulla G. Foehr, and Donald F. Roberts, *Generation M²: Media in the Lives of 8- to 18-Year-Olds* (Menlo Park, CA: Kaiser Family Foundation, 2010), 2, http://files.eric.ed.gov/fulltext/ED 527859.pdf.

How Safe Is Your School?

Introduction: How May I Help You?

Not long ago, Bethany's father drove to her elementary school to pick her up from an extracurricular activity. He was looking forward to hearing his daughter shout, "Daddy, daddy!" as she ran to greet him. At the front entrance, he pressed the buzzer, and in a few seconds, the front office buzzed him in.

Not quite certain where to go, he moved down a corridor. He glanced in the main office as he passed by, noticing an administrative assistant talking on a cellular phone. Continuing down the corridor, he nodded to the custodian coming out of a classroom with a trash bag.

He heard people talking and walked toward the voices. They came from the cafeteria where an after-school reading group was meeting. He tried to spot his daughter among the children, but was surprised to find that Bethany was not there. The instructor suggested that he check the group that had gone outside to enjoy the afternoon.

Bethany's father moved through the door out to the playground and approached a group of students with a teacher. Once again, his daughter was not among them. "Pardon me. Where is Bethany?" he asked. The instructor shrugged his shoulders.

By chance, Bethany's father glanced across the street at a park, and there in a sandbox sat Bethany. Bethany's father grinned, started waving, and shouted, "Hi Bethany." Bethany stood up beaming at her father. Then she ran toward him screaming, "Daddy, daddy!"

The school administrators had been made well aware of a restraining order issued by the court demanding that Bethany's father stay away from Bethany. Bethany's mother had been fearful that he would try to take her, and now she was right.

This fictitious story has come true too many times. School personnel had five opportunities to stop Bethany's father before he found her playing in the sandbox—off school grounds.

The first opportunity was at the front door, which was locked as it should have been. The lock proved ineffective, though, because the administrative assistant monitoring the front door had lost her concentration thanks to a phone call and simply buzzed in Bethany's father.

She should have used the intercom connected to the front door to say, "How may I help you?" Chances are, Bethany's father would have walked away. What else could he have done? If he said he was Bethany's father here to pick up Bethany, the administrative assistant would have a list with Bethany's father's name noting the restraining order. If he tried to give someone else's name, he could not have proven a connection with the photo ID the administrative assistant would have requested when he was admitted and met by her at the door. But the administrative assistant made a mistake, and

Bethany's father got into the school. People make mistakes, and in school security it is everyone's job to make sure that mistakenly letting someone into the school building does not enable a crime.

The second opportunity to stop Bethany's father came when the administrative assistant failed to correct her error by finding the person she had granted access to the building. She continued on the phone call.

Consider the third opportunity. The custodian emptying trash in the classrooms let Bethany's father pass without challenge. Encountering an adult stranger walking the hallways after school, he should have smiled broadly and said, "How may I help you, sir?" Bethany's father may have said, "I am here to pick up my daughter." The custodian could have replied, "I can help you with that. Let's go to the office and get you a visitor's pass. Whoever is watching the office will know where she is." Unless he planned to become violent, Bethany's father would have probably decided to turn around and walk away.

The fourth and fifth opportunities to stop Bethany's father passed when neither of the two instructors followed the procedure the custodian should have followed: "How may I help you? Oh, you're looking for your daughter? I can help you. Let's go to the office and get a visitor's pass for you. Whoever is watching the office will know where your daughter is."

Now think about this scenario differently. Suppose there was no restraining order and that Bethany's father was a normal dad picking up his daughter. What would he think about the "How may I help you?" approach? Most likely, he would think his daughter's school was taking good care of his daughter. The scrutiny would not be offensive.

Bureaucracies have no faces. They mindlessly buzz people through the front door, ignore them as they walk by, and shrug and expect someone else will help. By contrast, security has a smile on its face and always asks to help. In all but a small number of cases, people will appreciate the help, which will promote community relations. In the few instances where help is unwanted, the smiling security demeanor serves as a legitimate layer of protection. The exception, of course, would be an individual planning a violent attack, but that is a subject for another chapter.

The point here is that people provide security. Everything else—cameras, access control systems, metal detectors, x-ray machines, and the security centers that monitor all of these devices—exist to support the people that provide security. In schools, they are security personnel, administrators, staff, teachers, and students.

Loss Prevention: Proactive Security

"Effective loss prevention is always preceded by extensive losses."[1]

Why do people install burglar alarm systems after being burglarized? Why would a building administrator wait until after a car comes crashing through an entryway to install vehicle barriers? Why have the great majority of safe school grant programs been introduced after the occurrence of tragic incidents? Saul Astor, who is quoted above, refers to this pattern of after-the-fact implementation as "the first law of loss prevention." Break this law! Do not wait for an improbable and costly incident before addressing security. Be proactive. The following chapters will provide a roadmap for measurably improving your ability to prevent loss.

In order to avoid confusion, the term "loss prevention" will be referred to as "security." Security can be simply defined as protection. Protection involves keeping assets safe. Assets, like nouns, can be defined as people, places and things. In the school environment, "people" consists of students, staff, and visitors. "Places" can be broken down into the school buildings, parking lots, athletic fields, and off-premises locations, such as field trip sites. "Things" refers to items such as athletic equipment, technology equipment, and student records.

Protection also implies the presence of threats, those things that put our assets at risk. Threats can be separated into two categories: 1) general societal threats, and 2) school-specific threats. General societal threats (threats that every school may face) include the following:

- Disgruntled persons: individuals who engage in vindictive, violent, or malicious acts at or directed against the place of enrollment.
- Gangs: three or more persons committed to a common purpose that have definitive rituals, symbols, vocabulary, dress, and organizational structures. They often have common ethnic and socio-economic backgrounds with territorial interests, and deal in crime, drug trafficking, and violence.
- Criminals: persons who conspire to perpetrate criminal acts for profit or economic gain.
- Psychotic persons: individuals suffering from mental disorders who experience periodic or prolonged loss of contact with reality.
- Domestic terrorists: individuals or groups who commit violent acts out of opposition to government programs for ecological, political, economic, or other reasons.
- Sexual predators: individuals who were convicted of a serious sexual crime against a minor or an adult, who have been declared to be sexual predators by the court, and have been convicted of certain enumerated felony sex offenses (within the last ten years).

School-specific threats—such as student discipline issues, acts of vandalism, and bullying incidents—must be identified in-house. These threat lists can be compiled through the use of incident records (see Figure 2.1 for an example) and local law enforcement information. Regardless of the category or type of threat, the adversary has a limited number of tactics at his or her disposal. Tactics include force, deceit, and stealth. Force involves exerting physical power against a person or thing. For example, someone might use force to break a window in order to access a building or room. Deceit is representing as true what is known to be false. The person making use of deceit might identify himself or herself as a parent when, in fact, that person is not. Stealth can be defined as artfully sly action. An individual who employs stealth might wait in a concealed area, such as overgrown foliage, for a staff member to prop open an exterior door. When the door is no longer monitored, that individual sneaks into the building.

SCHOOL: _____

Incident Records

It is important to note that this activity is designed to create a confidential, working document to be modified as appropriate, both to accommodate the needs of this school and to meet state requisites.

Indicate the number of incidents reported this past school year for the categories below.

INCIDENT TYPE	NO.	INCIDENT TYPE	NO.
Arson		Hate Crime	
Assaults (verbal)		Hostage Situations	
Assaults and Battery (physical)		Insubordination	
Bombs/Bomb Threats		Intrusion/Trespass	
Bullying		Kidnapping	
Bus/Transportation-related		Molesting	
Deaths: Accidental		Property Damage	
Suicide		Riots	
Homicides		Robberies	
Demonstrations		Shootings	
Drug/Narcotic/Alcohol		Theft	
Emergency Building Evacuations		Vandalism	
Fights		Weapons at School	
Gang related		Other:	
Graffiti/Tagging			
Harassment: Physical			
Verbal			
Ethnic			
Sexual			

What have been the most common sources and times of recurring incidents at this school?

Incident Type	Source/Place	Time-Dates

Indicate the numbers for each of the following for this time period.

Suspensions	
Expulsions	
Transfers to other schools/agencies	

FIGURE 2.1 Use a Form Like the One in this Example to Record the Number of Incidents Reported within a Given Time Period.

Making Security a Priority

All school administrators will say that security is important to them. How can a genuine commitment be demonstrated? What elements can institutionalize a commitment to providing a safe learning environment? Schools demonstrate priority when they make the commitment public and hold people responsible.

Mission Statements

Schools are beginning to publicly express commitments to providing a secure learning environment through mission statements. Effective mission statements inform the outside world about who you are and what you do. They should be easy to remember and do not necessarily have to be unique to the organization. In crafting a mission statement, do not mince words or offer qualifying sentences. Make it concise and unforgettable. For example, one district's mission statement states, "To maintain a safe and secure learning environment that provides all students with the necessary knowledge and skills to successfully complete college, other post high school education or training."[2] Mission statements like this guide the actions and decision making of the district.

A professor at an educational institution posed the following question to his class: "Who can call someone right now and demonstrate that the person is actually familiar with an organization's mission statement?" A student raised his hand and called his sibling, who immediately supplied the answer. The sibling did not perform an incredible feat of memory recall. He knew the mission statement because it was only nine words and it actually described what the institution did. The entire class listened to the sibling's voice over speakerphone as he stated, "To promote student achievement in a safe learning environment."

Simple, straightforward mission statements make sense. Transparent entities clearly state mission statements in a way that people can remember. Clear mission statements require administrators to meet specific standards. Ambiguous and verbose mission statements may not require administrators to meet standards. After all, if the entity's mission statement is vague, how can administrators be held accountable?

The late owner of the Oakland Raiders NFL franchise, Al Davis, was known to share the mission statement for his football team to anyone who would listen. In his distinctive style, he would declare, "A commitment to excellence." While the statement sounded impressive, it lacked specificity. Was the goal of the organization to be the best they could be? Or was the goal to be professional? What exactly was Al Davis promising would be excellent? Not surprisingly, the ubiquitous owner also had another motto that was much more concise: "Just win, baby." That statement demonstrates clear priority!

Make the exercise of developing the mission statement the easiest part of the process. Resolve to develop a mission statement that is congruous with your school's practices and behaviors. A restroom in a popular sporting goods store posted an interesting sign. In big bold letters it proclaimed, "We Are Committed to Keeping Clean Restrooms." One might wonder why the sign is necessary. Is it subtly asking for cooperation? Why would you need a sign to state that you keep restrooms clean when you can simply demonstrate the commitment? How should an organization communicate priorities? Imagine if the store had not posted that sign and, instead, just kept the restrooms immaculate. The sign would not be necessary because guests would naturally experience the commitment and want to play a part in preserving cleanliness.

The most effective leaders reverse engineer a problem and let their priorities speak for themselves. Develop a mission statement that communicates your priority. As mentioned, that statement has benefits. Your actions behind that priority, however, will lead all that come through your school's doors to develop their own interpretation of your mission statement. They might initially resist wearing a visitor badge and following some unfamiliar procedures. They might even feel leery about adopting any unfamiliar practices. But in the end, if your priority is safety, visitors will experience that commitment. They will not need to hear administrators and staff members explicitly state, "Nothing is more important to us than protecting the well-being of our students." They will be thinking it when they walk out to the parking lot, and they will want to be part of it.

Of course, mission statements alone do not ensure security program success. How do you head down the path toward effectiveness? What accountability pieces ensure progress?

Security Director

Who is responsible for security in your district? Did that program get delegated to someone with a separate focus, such as the director of facilities? Facility administrators often feel overwhelmed—if not unqualified—with this responsibility. Wearing too many hats can diminish the likelihood of being successful. Make security a singular focus.

If possible, appoint someone who will be dedicated to overseeing the security program. Look for someone who has security expertise and a proven track record of success. If possible, ensure that this individual has an executable plan in mind. Give this person adequate resources, such as a reasonable budget and proper human resources.

Whether or not you have a dedicated director of security, commit to a collaborative approach.

A Collaborative Approach

Effective protection cannot be devised in a vacuum. A security program developed through individual efforts or the work of a handful of participants will be woefully inadequate. A real security program depends upon a collaborative effort that solicits input from a broad base of school stakeholders.

Security Planning Team Members

Figure 2.2 illustrates a model Security Planning Team.

The chairperson box at the top signifies that person—typically an administrator—who has responsibility for oversight of the planning team. The four boxes in the center of the

FIGURE 2.2 Model Security Planning Team.

diagram depict those stakeholders that regularly function inside the building. Beginning in the administrative section and moving clockwise, the following list describes the contribution of the internal stakeholders:

- Secretaries: Also known as administrative assistants, they are positioned on the front line of the security program. Secretaries stationed in the main office tend to be most familiar with the effectiveness of security practices, such as access control. They are first to encounter visitors, most likely to receive a bomb threat phone call, and often assigned to handle postal materials.
- Outside organizations, such as Boy/Girl Scouts and community agencies: Outside organizations rent school facilities, often experience after-school operations, and bring a unique perspective. Include at least one representative in this process (see the "Outside Organization Addendum" in chapter 3).
- Principals/administrators: These individuals are most familiar with school operations, practices, and policies.
- Teachers: Teachers know the functionality of communication systems, such as intercom systems, and whether or not adequate security training has been provided.
- Counselors or social workers: These staff members oversee violence prevention/intervention programs and related issues.
- Students: Students are probably the most important and most excluded stakeholder group. They are often ahead of adults in knowledge of technology and have the best read on the safety pulse of the school (see the "Student Safety Audit" in chapter 9).
- Facility director: This person supervises the school's maintenance, grounds, and cleaning staff.
- Custodians: They are most familiar with door hardware (such as locks and exit devices), lighting maintenance, and vandalism issues.
- Nurses: Nurses maintain first aid supplies, control medication, and possess vital medical expertise.
- Security director: This individual is responsible for establishing, developing, and enforcing security measures and practices.

- Security personnel: Security personnel assist in maintaining a secure and orderly environment in the nonclassroom areas of the school, parking lot, and grounds.
- Transportation director: This person oversees routing of school buses, scheduling of special trips, and supervision of drivers and mechanical repair.
- Technology director: The director of technology ensures that staff and students have access to the technological tools and information necessary to participate effectively in the educational process.

The four boxes on the outside of the diagram depict those stakeholders that regularly function outside the building. The following list describes the contribution of these external stakeholders:

- Police: Local law enforcement officials provide loss prevention and emergency response services.
- Community-based entities, such as government agencies and religious institutions: These entities may be located in close proximity to the school or provide important, local services. Sometimes schools share facilities with local entities, such as park districts.
- Parents: Parents should be aware of and have input in security initiatives, practices, and procedures. It is important to include this stakeholder group as the alternative can lead to a negative undercurrent.
- Fire and medical: These officials also provide loss prevention and emergency response services.

Even though it may not be possible to garner each representative listed, every attempt should be made to enlist comprehensive participation.

Feel free to add a stakeholder group not mentioned above, if that particular individual or group of individuals provides a worthwhile contribution. We have seen schools successfully incorporate the assistance of influential community members, trusted vendors, and school board members. Be wary, however, of putting together a group that becomes too large.

Meeting Guidelines

In terms of meeting length, ensure that no real comparisons can be drawn between the Security Planning Team meeting and a school board meeting. While the latter may have a flexible, if not open-ended, timeframe, the former should be more strictly time-bounded. Keep the meeting to 60 or 90 minutes. Plan to hold one meeting each semester. A time near the beginning of the semester, but after the chaos of the first few weeks, is usually best in terms of setting a proactive tone.

Develop a clear and prioritized agenda. Send the agenda to stakeholders in advance of the meeting. Appoint a chairperson that can effectively facilitate a meeting and navigate through distractions. Review the effectiveness of new initiatives begun since the last meeting, problems that have been identified and submitted for consideration, and other issues important to the future safety and security of students, faculty, staff, and administrators across the district. Sufficiently address each topic and assign follow-up responsibilities before moving to the next item. Achieve consensus.

The Security Planning Team does not solve problems. It is not suited to do so. The membership is too broad. Instead, it monitors progress, identifies problems and delegates assignments to research and solve those problems to appropriate departments, other committees, or individuals who will report back on findings, actions taken, and results during future meetings.

A Comprehensive Approach

Once the Security Planning Team has been formed, you are ready to undertake a comprehensive approach to school security. There is no single-source solution. In the aftermath of the tragic Sandy Hook incident, where the perpetrator forced his way into the building, some individuals began to call for bullet-proof glass at school main entries. Unfortunately, there is no such thing as bullet-proof glass. There will always be something big enough and bad enough, such as a Scud missile, to break through reinforced glass. Of course, there are appropriate uses for bullet-resistant glass, but reinforced glass alone will not stop school violence. In the same way, other proposed single-source solutions, such as arming teachers, installing portal magnetometers (walk-through metal detectors), and the most sophisticated video surveillance systems, will not prevent shootings. Risk can only be reduced significantly with a comprehensive approach. This kind of approach involves the following five areas:

1. Developing a plan: documented security practices and policies.
2. Securing your environment: appropriate physical security measures, products, and systems.
3. Influencing behavior: violence prevention and intervention programs that address issues such as bullying, sexual harassment, and substance abuse.
4. Preparing your people: routine training and instruction provided to teachers and staff.
5. Managing emergencies: emergency preparedness initiatives.

Each of these areas will be covered in detail over the next chapters.

Threat Assessment Team

Do not confuse the Security Planning Team with a Threat Assessment Team. An increasing number of public and private organizations see the need to form Threat Assessment Teams to prevent and manage incidents of violence. A school Threat Assessment Team tackles internal threats of violence and assesses related conditions, policies, and procedures. If at all possible, internal threats should be the single focus for the team, which should not wander off into areas better left to professionals with expertise. Confidentiality is a must for a Threat Assessment Team. Team members possess knowledge about numerous employees and perhaps students within their respective departments. Meetings must never involve gossip. Instead, team members bring forward concerns for individuals in crisis in an attempt to provide protection for everyone in the school.

The Threat Assessment Team will meet once or twice a year, depending upon the speed with which a school risk profile changes. Considerations include incidents that have occurred since the last meeting and crime reports for the neighborhoods around the schools. Those crime reports should include descriptions of the kinds of crime characteristic of the area. Vandalism and assault, for instance, would indicate two different risk profiles.

Members of the Threat Assessment Team include professionals most familiar with risks faced by individual schools. Prospective members to consider are the facility director, the security director, a social worker, an administrator, and emergency responders. The team should be kept as small as possible, but include as much of a broad base of knowledge as possible. To acquire additional knowledge, consider utilizing a tip line, a text option, or some other method by which school stakeholders can share concerns. All information shared should be considered time-sensitive and flow immediately to Threat Assessment Team members. Interim meetings of the Threat Assessment Team might occur following reception of a concern. In the same way, a meeting would be convened after a major incident to determine the potential of a new, continuing threat and to investigate security lapses that may have allowed the incident to overcome existing security measures.

The Threat Assessment Team also brings valued prevention methods to the school. For example, if a staff member experiences a significant crisis at home, he/she will naturally bring that stress to the workplace. Could that increase in stress level present a potential threat? Are there actions that can be taken to address that stress in a healthy manner? Perhaps a student who is experiencing difficult family issues at home begins to exhibit substandard performance with coursework. Key school personnel should be aware of that situation. The Threat Assessment Team can make use of knowledge of risk factors or marked changes in behavior to affect situations positively.

Most schools already have documented policies that require disclosure of legal matters, such as orders of protection and law suits. Threat assessment team members collaborate on how to assist involved individuals, meet various needs that might arise, and prepare for potential risk levels. The team should engage in routine tabletop exercises. Best practice evaluations of these scenarios determine if policy or procedural adjustments should be implemented.

The Threat Assessment Team reports its findings to the Security Planning Team along with recommendations. For instance, the Threat Assessment Team might find that incidents of bullying have increased in the corridors of a particular high school. The team might recommend that the Security Planning Team assign the security director to revisit the Threat Assessment Team's investigation, confirm it, and work out security measures designed to drive bullying incidents back down. The security director would implement certain measures and report to the Security Planning Team. This does not have to be a long process. As soon as the Threat Assessment Team forms an opinion and recommendation, it can submit a written report to the Security Planning Team, which could pass an assignment along to the security director. Of course, these kinds of processes can become bogged down with bureaucratic delays. It is important to keep that thought in mind and speed up the process whenever it seems necessary.

Security incidents of this kind will ebb and flow over time, with the security director implementing plans to reduce bullying, perhaps by mounting video cameras in the school's corridors to deter bullies from being observed in the hallways and to capture video of those who remain undeterred. After a while, that problem will ease and another more serious problem requiring video may appear, and the security director may move the cameras. This is normal. The consistent and effective interaction of the Security Planning Team with the Threat Assessment Team can manage these kinds of safety and security challenges as they arise.

Finally, the Threat Assessment Team should assess the vulnerability of schools within the district to a major security event: an active shooter, a hostage situation, or some other kind of attack. It is difficult to assess the risks of such an attack. As we have learned over the years, such attacks can occur anywhere at any time, driven by a loner who has been bullied to the limit or a team that has planned out a coordinated attack for some reason. The only way to assess the risk of an attack is to assume that it exists, and make plans to overcome it when it occurs. That is the job of the Threat Assessment Team.

Emergency Planning Team

Once again, do not confuse the Security Planning Team with a crisis team. The Crisis Team, often known as the Emergency Planning Team, prepares a school's emergency response to a crisis: an attack as described above, a major fire, an extreme weather event, or another kind of emergency.

There are several kinds of emergency responses, each requiring treatment in an emergency response plan. Fire and certain kinds of attacks require evacuation plans led by evacuation teams with leaders, searchers, stairwell and elevator monitors, and aides for persons with disabilities. Severe weather and other kinds of attacks may require a response called sheltering-in-place. Again, a team with specific responsibilities is taught to manage the process. Certain attacks may combine sheltering-in-place with a lockdown to prevent outsiders from getting into the school.

Appendix A contains a form for developing an emergency response plan provided by the federal government's emergency planning website (http://www.ready.gov/). The form lists a series of steps—including the appointment of the response team members—leading to the completion of an emergency response plan.

The Emergency Planning Team will use the threat assessment developed by the Threat Assessment Team to develop an appropriate response to the various emergency threats that have been identified. Equally important, the Emergency Planning Team will develop training and drills for team members and, perhaps once a year, organize a school-wide emergency drill to give students, faculty, staff, and administrators an idea of what to expect should a crisis occur.

Financial Considerations

Before the Columbine tragedy, most schools did not have a budget line item for security. They attempted to draw from general operating funds to pay for security measures. Not surprisingly, the approval process required complicated steps and very rarely included options for sustaining the funding. As a result, the school tended to lack a commitment to maintenance, upgrades, and expansion of security systems.

Schools must consider the sustainability—the capacity to endure—of physical security systems. Security measures such as video surveillance systems are not one-time expenditures. A video surveillance system will experience growth (such as additional cameras), need updating, and require maintenance. Sometimes products fail. Sometimes they become antiquated. The system may require annual licensing fees. Funds must be set aside to ensure systems are operational and functioning optimally.

Because people generally wait for losses to occur before addressing security needs, state and federal grants tend to appear after school tragedies. In other words, schools cannot always count on the availability of grant funds. Difficult economic times can cause the diversion of grant program funds.

The US Department of Justice's Office of Community Oriented Policing Services (COPS) offers one notable, albeit dwindling, exception. COPS has consistently provided grant funding to schools through local law enforcement agencies. This annual grant, however, is no longer a security equipment grant. Instead, it helps to fund school resource officers' salaries.

Occasionally, technology grants and energy-efficiency grants permit the inclusion of security-related items, such as software. Schools may also be able to include door hardware upgrades, such as classroom security locks, when accessing title funds or block grants for facility improvement.

School security programs may also benefit from private funding sources. For example, US Cellular's "Calling All Communities" campaign annually awards $25,000 to twenty public or private schools. Winning schools may spend prize money in any way they wish. Three major private funding sources include corporate foundations, family foundations, and community foundations. Many of these foundations focus on community safety. Corporate foundations, such as the Allstate Foundation, provide grants that seek to end youth violence. Family foundations, such as the Wood Family Foundation, look for opportunities to support student safety initiatives. Community foundations, like the Greater Milwaukee Foundation, support violence prevention efforts in specific geographical locations.

In addition to public and private funding entities, schools may receive assistance from internal stakeholders. Extracurricular programs and parent organizations can assist in raising funds for security projects. Sometimes, even individual parents and local businesses will donate because of their investment in the community's well-being.

Schools can also access websites dedicated to grant-funding opportunities (see chapter 9, "School Security Resources"). Those that employ full-time grant writers often find that the individual's salary is more than covered by what is received in grants.

Do not give up on security initiatives due to a lack of funding. Money is not the only way to improve school security. The following chapters will demonstrate low-cost and no-cost ways to reduce risk.

Keys to School Security

Certain factors significantly improve the effectiveness of your security program. If the following factors are currently in place or can be implemented, capitalize on them.

Commitment from the Top

There is no substitute for administrator commitment to security. Superintendents set the tone for the district. Principals determine the culture of the school. If you garner the support of the administration, other stakeholders will join the cause.

Like CEOs in private business, school superintendents should express priorities and goals for the school district, usually in a few sentences. To keep people focused on that message, superintendents should repeat those priorities again and again, both orally and in writing. In this way, administrators help to shape the culture of the school. They literally lead faculty, staff, students, and other stakeholders to join the cause. A deep and serious commitment from the top of a school district is essential to keeping people focused on and informed about safety and security concerns in a reasonable way.

Demonstration of commitment begins with visibility. Administrators should publicly express their commitment. Articulate that commitment at board meetings, on in-service days, and in personal conversations. Participate in security trainings and emergency drills. Become certified in the basic National Incident Management System (NIMS) courses, such as the Incident Command System (ICS) for Schools: IS-100.SCa (http://training.fema.gov/EMIWeb/IS/courseOverview.aspx?code=is-100.sca).

Closely tied to visibility, administrators should also demonstrate commitment by example. Always wear your identification badge. Secure your office when leaving it. Follow visitor management procedures. As an example, a security officer once remarked that the only real resistance he had encountered with the new visitor management process was from district administrators. Avoid this kind of reputation. Set a positive example.

Administrators who have made a significant impact in the school district often get rewarded. Sometimes schools name learning centers after beloved administrators. Sometimes an administrator's legacy is captured through a portrait hung in a prominent place. Significant accomplishments deserve recognition. It may not result in traditional accolades, but place a real priority on security. When administrators demonstrate a commitment to providing a safe learning environment, students and staff benefit greatly.

Performance Accountability

Make security a responsibility upon which administrators are evaluated and recognized. Without this kind of accountability, school security will always run the risk of being relegated to second-tier priority, if not an outright afterthought. Improvement in performance is a natural outcome of responsibilities being measured. Measure the protection effectiveness of your learning environment.

Good Relationship with Emergency Responders

Local police officers and fire fighters should know their way around the K–12 campuses within their jurisdiction. That requires effort from school administrators and security. Someone on the team should take on the responsibility of forming a strong working relationship with these emergency responders.

Find out the names of the ranking police officer and fire official responsible for your school. Call each and make an appointment to visit. Say that you want to get to know them and to help them get to know what they need to know about the school or schools you are representing. Ask the police officer about the state of crime in your neighborhoods. What are the incidents of petty crime? What are the incidents of serious crime? What does he or she think that means to the security needs of your school? Invite the officer or someone he or she appoints for a visit to the school to solicit advice. Do the same thing with the fire department. The most important step comes next. Offer your school as a site for fire and police drills. First responders will appreciate the opportunity to gain familiarity with your site. The drills will also enable school faculty, administrators, staff, and students to learn what might happen in the event of an attack or a serious fire. Alternate with fire and police drills. Do it often enough that significant numbers of staff and students in the school have had the experience, so they can help those who have not.

Practices with Security Consequences

Some practices and situations immediately put your efforts to provide a safe learning environment at a disadvantage. Look for ways to avoid the potentially dangerous consequences of these practices.

Open Classroom Design

Popularized in the 1970s, the open learning environment prevents students, staff, and visitors from finding safe refuge in a locked classroom. In an open classroom school, learning takes place in pods, between dividers, and in other open areas. While this open educational concept has earned high praise, the design has evolved in a way that makes it impossible to hide from an attacker. It is important to raise this issue with architects. Ask them to give thought to renovations and new school designs that make use of this effective educational concept without sacrificing security.

If pursuing architectural adjustments is not possible, ensure that any existing rooms that can provide safe refuge, such as offices and closets, have locking mechanisms. Practice moving students and staff to those rooms as part of routine lockdown drills. If the facility does not have rooms, pursue collaborative solutions to address the matter. Get started now.

Portable Classrooms

Schools install portable classrooms, sometimes referred to as mobiles or modulars, on the property as a temporary solution to provide additional classroom space when facing capacity issues. This temporary solution often becomes a permanent problem. Portable classrooms present challenges to both access control and communications. Effective access control faces challenges when there is routine movement of students and personnel between the building and the portable classroom. Maintaining effective communications becomes difficult when standard systems in the main building do not exist in the portable classroom.

While no administrator wants portable classrooms, crowded classrooms sometimes make them unavoidable. Talk to designers about the problem of students walking outside without supervision to move from buildings to portable classrooms and back. Is there an affordable way to construct enclosed walkways?

Two-way radios can solve the communications problem. Every school should keep a supply of two-way radios on hand for teachers supervising classes outside. If something happens, a two-way radio can provide instant communications with the security office or the principal. Give teachers in portable classrooms the same capability.

Propped Exterior Doors

When someone props an exterior door open, security evaporates, and anyone can walk into the building. Even if the door is closed and locked most of the time, visible door props advertise the possibility of access.

Put an access control reader on exterior doors used routinely by teachers taking students outside. That eliminates the need for the teacher to prop the door or to carry a key that can be lost. Of course, students are often the real culprits when it comes to propping doors open. They may want to run to a nearby fast-food restaurant for a snack or just have a smoke outside and out-of-sight.

There is only one answer to this problem, and that is an alert administration, faculty, and staff. They should check the exterior doors near their offices or classrooms whenever convenient, throughout the day. Upon finding a propped door, check outside for the students who may have done it, escort them back inside, and close the door. Schools should organize regular patrols that look for exterior doors that are not secured, whether the result of propping devices or mechanical problems. For more detail, see the "Access Control" section of chapter 4, "Secure Your Environment."

Poor Relationship with Emergency Responders

Occasionally, politics prevent school administrators and emergency responders from maintaining good relations. Poor relationships present the potential for devastating consequences. If facing this kind of disadvantage, do not permit school security to suffer. Act immediately.

Strained or adversarial relations can usually be attributed to strong personalities and clashing agendas. The only real remedy involves putting egos aside for the common good. If individuals are not willing to take that step, third party mediation may become necessary. District administrators in one school found themselves at philosophical odds with local law enforcement officials regarding active shooter response procedures. As the result of a past altercation, the superintendent and the police chief did not hold one another in high esteem. Both individuals refused to compromise their respective positions. Strained relations accounted for a lack of cooperation between school and police that lasted for years. The School Board approved a security project that involved a consultant who had participated in a task force at the state level. The consultant quickly identified the impasse and invited a state official to mediate. In a short amount of time, the school and the police found common ground and achieved consensus.

State Requirements

For those that need motivation to improve school security, state governments encourage that kind of compliance-oriented mentality with several mandates. For example, most states require schools to have a basic crisis plan and a bullying policy. Numerous states require far more stringent safety measures. In Illinois, for example, all schools public and private must comply with the "School Safety Drill Act." This act calls for schools to practice at least three fire drills each year, one of which must be monitored and approved by the local fire department. Additionally, schools must conduct a lockdown drill, a shelter-in-place drill, and a bus evacuation drill.

Since 2009, the state of Illinois has required school districts to "incorporate into the school curriculum a component on Internet safety to be taught at least once each school year to students in grade 3 or above."[3] Implementation difficulty with such requirements does not release schools of obligation. Ignorance does not exonerate schools from liability.

As a final example, the Illinois Compiled Statutes mandate that data involving "attacks on school personnel, firearms in schools, and drug-related incidents in schools" be reported to the state immediately and throughout the year.[4] Since school crime statistics are notoriously underreported, this kind of mandate may not be popular with administrators and school boards. Nonetheless, schools must comply with the requirement.

Schools that do not have stringent state requirements would do well to consider the aforementioned examples to be best practices. Be proactive. Make every effort to meet standards and, in doing so, effectively address vulnerabilities. You may not be able to eliminate your risk, but you can reduce it significantly.

Conclusion

How safe is your school? This chapter has attempted to give you a way to begin evaluating school security.

The first and most important consideration involves making a commitment to provide a safe learning environment. Document that commitment. Make it part of your mission statement and ensure that it permeates your culture. Get administrators, faculty, and staff on board as friendly, helpful security providers. It should be a condition of employment, and you should give them the knowledge, tools, and clearly expressed policies to carry out that part of their responsibilities. Involve the students as well.

Take these and other steps to strengthen your security capabilities before Saul Astor's first law of loss prevention takes effect. Try to break the rule that says "effective loss prevention is always preceded by extensive losses."

Assess the general societal threats and school specific threats that your school must prepare to meet. Disgruntled persons are always a threat. Do you have a gang problem in your school? No? Are you sure? Many schools have gang problems—even suburban schools. Administrators often wrongly assume that there are no gang problems. If one student joins a gang, others will follow. Provide on-going instructional programs and maintain a culture of awareness.

The police can help you determine the threats to your school from criminals, domestic terrorists, and sexual predators. An emotionally disturbed, psychotic student with a weapon can, as we have all learned in recent years, cause great harm. Some schools have set up programs that teach students, faculty, staff, and administrators to recognize depression, consistently odd behavior, and other characteristics of emotional problems. Early intervention can help a person who might be drifting toward tragedy.

These and other issues are agenda items for your school's safety committee to consider in planning security and developing violence prevention, anti-bullying, sexual harassment, and substance abuse programs as well as emergency plans. Remember, people provide security.

References

1. Saul D. Astor, *Loss Prevention: Controls and Concepts* (Boston: Butterworth-Heinemann Ltd., 1978), n.p.

2. "Mission Statement," *Bristol Public Schools*, accessed May 8, 2014, http://www.bristol.k12.ct.us/page.cfm?p=9246.

3. "Be Internet Safe," *Illinois State Board of Education*, accessed May 8, 2014, http://www.isbe.net/edtechnology/html/internet_safety.htm.

4. "Data Analysis and Accountability: School Incident Reporting System," *Illinois State Board of Education*, accessed May 8, 2014, http://www.isbe.state.il.us/research/htmls/sch_incident.htm.

Appendix A: Emergency Response Plan

This emergency response plan form was developed by *Ready*, a national public service advertising campaign of the Department of Homeland Security and the Federal Emergency Management Agency. It can be accessed at http://www.ready.gov/sites/default/files/documents/files/EmergencyResponsePlan_0.pdf.

Emergency Response Plan

Company Name

Address

Telephone

Contact Name   Title

Last Revision Date

Policy and Organizational Statements

Identify the goals and objectives for the emergency response plan.

Define what your emergency response team is expected to do during an emergency (e.g., evacuate employees and visitors, provide first aid, etc.)

Identify any regulations covered by your plan (e.g., OSHA, fire code, etc.)

ready.gov/business

FIGURE A.1

Emergency Response Plan

Evacuation Plan

Evacuation may be required if there is a fire in the building or other hazard. The evacuation team will direct the evacuation of the building and account for all employees outside at a safe location.

Employees will be warned to evacuate the building using the following system:	
Employees should assemble at the following location for accounting by the evacuation team:	

(Post a map showing the location(s) in a conspicuous location for all employees to see.)

Person who will bring the employee roster and visitor log to the evacuation assembly area to account for all evacuees. The evacuation team leader will be informed if anyone is missing or injured.	

Evacuation Team	Name / Location
Evacuation Team Leader	
Floor Wardens (one for each floor)	
Searchers (one per floor)	
Stairwell and Elevator Monitors	
Aides for Persons with Disabilities	
Assembly Area Monitors (account for evacuees at the assembly area and inform incident commander if anyone is missing or injured)	

ready.gov/business

FIGURE A.1   Cont'd

Severe Weather/Tornado Sheltering Plan

If a tornado warning is issued, broadcast a warning throughout all buildings instructing everyone to move to shelter.

Shelter-In-Place Team Assignments	Name / Location
Team Leader	
Person to monitor weather sources for updated emergency instructions and broadcast warning if issued by weather services	
Persons to direct personnel outside to enter the building	
Persons to direct employees to designated tornado shelter(s)	

Tornado Warning System & Tornado Shelter Locations	
Location of tornado warning system controls	
Location of tornado shelters	

Shelter-In-Place Plan

If warned to "shelter-in-place" from an outside airborne hazard, a warning shoudl be broadcast and all employees should move to shelter.

Shelter-In-Place Team Assignments	Name / Location
Team Leader	
Direct personnel outside to enter the building; then close exterior doors	
Shutdown ventilation system and close air intakes	
Move employees to interior spaces above the first floor (if possible)	
Person to monitor news sources for updated emergency instructions	
Assembly Area Monitors (to account for evacuees at the assembly area)	

Shelter-In-Place Shutdown of Ventilation System

Location of controls to shutdown ventilation system:	
Location of air handling units, fan rooms, or air intakes:	

ready.gov/business

FIGURE A.1   Cont'd

   **Emergency Response Plan**

Lockdown Plan

Persons trained to use the warning system to warn persons to "lockdown"

Name	Location

Instructions for Broadcasting Warnings

Where to Access the Warning System
(e.g., telephone, public address system, etc.)

Instructions for using the system

FIGURE A.1   Cont'd

Medical Emergency Plan

If a medical emergency is reported, dial 9-1-1 and request an ambulance. Provide the following information:

- Number and location of victim(s)
- Nature of injury or illness
- Hazards involved
- Nearest entrance (emergency access point)

Alert trained employees (members of the medical response team) to respond to the victim's location and bring a first aid kit or AED.

Personnel Trained to Administer First Aid, CPR, or use Automated External Defibrillator (AED)

Name	Location / Telephone

Locations of First Aid Kits and Automated External Defibrillator(s)

Locations of First Aid Kits and "Universal Precautions" kit (used to prevent exposure to body fluids)	
Locations of Automated External Defibrillator(s) (AEDs)	

Procedures

- Only trained responders should provide first aid assistance.
- Do not move the victim unless the victim's location is unsafe.
- Control access to the scene.
- Take "universal precautions" to prevent contact with body fluids and exposure to bloodborne pathogens.
- Meet the ambulance at the nearest entrance or emergency access point; direct them to victim(s).

ready.gov/business

FIGURE A.1   Cont'd

Emergency Response Plan

Fire Emergency Plan

If a fire is reported, pull the fire alarm, (if available and not already activated) to warn occupants to evacuate. Then Dial 911 to alert Fire Department. Provide the following information:

- Business name and street address
- Nature of fire
- Fire location (building and floor or)
- Type of fire alarm (detector, pull station, sprinkler waterflow)
- Location of fire alarm (building and floor)
- Name of person reporting fire
- Telephone number for return call

Evacuation team to direct evacuation of employees and visitors.

Procedures

- Evacuate building occupants along evacuation routes to primary assembly areas outside.
- Redirect building occupants to stairs and exits away from the fire.
- Prohibit use of elevators.
- Evacuation team to account for all employees and visitors at the assembly area.
- Meet Fire Department Incident Commander (IC). Inform the IC if everyone has been accounted for and if there are any injuries. Provide an update on the nature of the emergency and actions taken. Provide building floor plans, keys and other assistance as requested.
- Assign personnel to verify that fire protection systems are operating normally and to operate building utility and protection systems as directed by the fire department.

Property Conservation

Identify preparations before a forecast event such as severe weather.

Identify how you will assess damage; salvage undamaged goods; and cleanup the building following an incident.

Identify the contractors, equipment, and materials that would be needed. Update the resource table at the end of this plan.

ready.gov/business

FIGURE A.1   Cont'd

Annexes

Hazard or Threat-specific

Instructions: Review the following list of hazards and identify those hazards that are foreseeable. Review the links to information provided within the Ready Business website to develop specific emergency procedures.

Natural hazards (geological, meteorological, and biological)

Geological hazards

- Earthquake
- Tsunami
- Volcano
- Landslide, mudslide, subsidence

Meteorological Hazards

- Flood, flash flood, tidal surge
- Water control structure/dam/levee failure
- Drought
- Snow, ice, hail, sleet, arctic freeze
- Windstorm, tropical cyclone, hurricane, tornado, dust storm
- Extreme temperatures (heat, cold)
- Lightning strikes (Wildland fire following)

Biological hazards

- Foodborne Illnesses
- Pandemic/Infectious/communicable disease (Avian flu, H1N1, etc.)

Technology caused event

- Utility interruption or failure (telecommunications, electrical power, water, gas, steam, HVAC, pollution control system, sewerage system, other critical infrastructure)

Human-caused events (accidental and intentional)

Accidental

- Hazardous material spill or release
- Nuclear Power Plant Incident (if located in proximity to a Nuclear power plan)
- Explosion/Fire
- Transportation accident
- Building/structure collapse
- Entrapment and or rescue (machinery, confined space, high angle, water)
- Transportation Incidents (Motor Vehicle, Railroad, Watercraft, Aircraft, Pipeline)

Intentional

- Robbery
- Lost Person, Child Abduction, Kidnap, Extortion, Hostage Incident, Workplace violence
- Demonstrations, Civil disturbance
- Bomb threat, Suspicious package
- Terrorism

ready.gov/business

FIGURE A.1 Cont'd

 **Ready** Business. **Emergency Response Plan**

Appendices

Emergency Response Teams

Identify the members of emergency response teams not identified elsewhere.

- Facilities or building management staff familiar with building utility and protection systems and those who may assist with property conservation activities.
- Security
- Others trained to use fire extinguishers, clean up small spills of hazardous materials.

Team	Member Name	Location	Work Telephone	Home/Cell Telephone

ready.gov/business

FIGURE A.1 Cont'd

Public Emergency Services & Contractors

Emergency Service	Name	Emergency Telephone	Business Telephone
Fire Department			
Emergency Medical Services			
Police Department			
Emergency Management Agency			
Hospital			
Public Health Department			
State Environmental Authority			
National Response Center (EPA)			
Electrician			
Plumber			
Fire Protection Contractor			
Elevator Service			
Hazardous Materials Cleanup			
Cleanup / Disaster Restoration			

Warning, Notification & Communications Systems

The following systems are used to warn employees to take protective action (e.g., evacuate, move to tornado shelter, shelter-in-place, or lockdown) and provide them with information. The Communications capabilities enable members of our emergency team to communicate with each other and others.

Warning System	Fire Alarm	
	Public Address	
	Other (describe)	
Notification System	Electronic	
	Telephone call tree	
Communications Capabilities	Telephone	
	Two-way radio	

ready.gov/business

FIGURE A.1   Cont'd

   **Emergency Response Plan**

Fire Protection Systems

Document the fire protection systems including the types of systems, location, area, or hazard protected, and instructions.

System Type	Location	Access Point / Instructions
Sprinkler System	Control Valve	
	Control Valve	
	Control Valve	
Fire Pump		
Special Extinguishing Systems	Computer Room	
	Kitchen	
	Manufacturing Area	

Revision History

Revision No.	Date	Description of Changes	Authorization

Plan Distribution & Access

The Plan will be distributed to members of the emergency response team and department heads. A master copy of the document should be maintained by the emergency response team leader. The plan will be available for review by all employees.

Provide print copies of this plan within the room designated as the emergency operations center (EOC). Multiple copies should be stored within the facility EOC to ensure that team members can quickly review roles, responsibilities, tasks, and reference information when the team is activated.

An electronic copy of this Plan should be stored on a secure and accessible website that would allow team member access if company servers are down.

Electronic copies should also be stored on a secured USB flash drive for printing on demand.

ready.gov/business

FIGURE A.1   Cont'd

Developing a Plan

Introduction

The superintendent felt angry with himself. He read the e-mail from the district security director again. It made two recommendations. First, buy a supply of "away" smartphones from each of the major wireless providers: Verizon, AT&T, T-Mobile, Sprint, and perhaps others. Second, implement a crisis communications policy.

"Much of our district and surrounding districts are in rural areas served well by only one or two wireless service providers," said the e-mail. "We should develop a policy that ensures communications with coaches, club advisors, and teachers when they take students to athletic activities or other events in remote areas."

The security director would develop a list of wireless services available in small towns and schools regularly visited by groups from district schools. The adult supervisor would refer to the list before the trip and check out a phone from the wireless company or companies serving that area.

Second, institute a policy requiring adult supervisors to call their home schools upon arrival at a destination and before leaving. That way, if something does happen to the wireless service, the calls can be made on a landline.

There it was in writing, thought the superintendent, a good idea he had left in his inbox for a month with a flag on it.

Now a member of the choir had been hospitalized. When the tornado warning told everyone in the area to take cover, a call to the school where the competition was held just missed the departure of the bus. The group was on the road more than an hour away and out of communication—the local wireless service was different than the choir director's service. The freak storm had run the bus off the road and turned it over. The superintendent felt responsible. The unhappy school board agreed.

What Keeps You up at Night?

Borrowed from a real school experience, this story may pale in comparison to more serious incidents that some administrators have had to face. There is, nonetheless, a number of issue-raising questions that should be asked. If the suggested policy had been in place, which outcomes would have changed? If student safety is such an important issue, why are administrators slow to develop related preparedness practices? Which stakeholders should be involved in policy development? In terms of safety and security concerns, what keeps you up at night?

Keeping the First Law of Loss Prevention (see chapter 2, "How Safe is Your School") in mind, it is worth remembering that unpleasant experiences should not be the driver of security policies and practices. Instead, proactive collaboration to prevent incidents and prepare for emergencies is the place to begin. Ask your stakeholders to focus on their own areas of expertise in identifying potential risk exposures or vulnerabilities. Develop corresponding practices and policies. Document and disseminate those practices and policies. Train and drill staff and students, based on those policies. Provide related instruction to other relevant stakeholders.

Commitment and Accountability

Begin with a commitment. There is no price tag that can be placed on the importance of providing a safe learning environment. The protection of students, staff, and visitors must be a priority. Those tasked with overseeing this important responsibility should be treated with "R-E-S-P-E-C-T." Starting at the superintendent's level, administrators must set the tone for how the security program is perceived. Get on board by following security practices and supporting related initiatives. Others, including neighboring districts, will follow your example and adopt your attitude.

One important change that schools should consider, sooner rather than later, is to make security a responsibility upon which administrators are evaluated and recognized. Without this kind of accountability, school security will always run the risk of being relegated to second-tier priority, if not a complete afterthought. Improvement in performance is a natural outcome of responsibilities being measured. Develop a way to effectively measure security goals (see Figure 3.1).

Documenting Practices

Policy development is a continuous improvement process. Keep in mind that policy development in the school arena differs significantly from most disciplines or fields. Policies relating to safety, and involving students, must 1) be driven by proven best practices; 2) be designed for a district's particular needs (e.g., a nuclear site near the town, a high rate of poverty, etc.); and 3) evolve both from experiential learning gained by going through an unfortunate incident (e.g., tornado sheltering changes) and when new and better information is obtained. The remainder of this chapter contains several sample policies. The list should not be considered exhaustive. Information contained in these sample policies is presented for general educational purposes and to increase overall security awareness. It is not intended to be legal advice or services, and should not be used in place of consultation with appropriate professionals. The headings that follow designate other chapters in the book to which the policy relates. So, for example, in the following section, the visitor management policy relates to chapter 4, "Securing Your Environment."

Visitor Management (Chapter 4)

Good access control relies on effective visitor management. Traditional procedures permit visitors to sign a registry with little to no oversight before being issued a sticker. The following practice greatly improves upon those procedures.

STRATEGIC PLAN

YEAR ___ CONTENT AREA 1	GOALS TO ACCOMPLISH	GOALS ACCOMPLISHED	TASK COMPLETION	X
Strategic Plan Goal: *We will provide a safe learning environment.* *Example: Complete emergency preparedness plans and train staff and students in procedures.*				
	Objective: Emergency preparedness training to be completed for all staff commencing with Student Services support staff, e.g. counselors, social workers, etc.	Training sessions offered at all school staff meetings	First month of school	X
	Student Services will continue to offer support to Social Workers/SpEd, in terms of: ▪ Emergency preparedness ▪ Mental health concerns ▪ Chemical health concerns		Ongoing	X
CONTENT AREA 2	**GOALS TO ACCOMPLISH**	**GOALS ACCOMPLISHED**	**TASK COMPLETION**	**X**
	Emergency Management: ▪ Continued development of services/training for Emergency Response Team ▪ Develop another staff training on grief recovery ▪ Post grief recovery resources for parents and staff on web ▪ Update Mandatory Reporting policy	Grief Recovery Plan completed Not completed; plan for _____ In process Both the policy and a pamphlet were completed and distributed. Presented to social workers in fall.	October 15 – draft February 28 – final December 1 September 5	X X

FIGURE 3.1

District X's visitor management practice requires all visitors to enter the facility through the main entrance. Designated main office personnel will engage each visitor in the secured vestibule via the visitor intercom system. Every visitor will be asked to state a purpose for visiting. Once a legitimate purpose has been stated, designated personnel will electronically grant access to the main office. Upon approaching the main desk, all visitors will follow the credential exchange procedure. The credential exchange procedure requires all visitors to produce a photograph ID, be signed in (using a visitor log form like the one shown in Figure 3.2), and be authorized by designated personnel before access to the rest of the facility is permitted. Designated personnel will give the visitor a badge that hangs on a colored, break-away lanyard around the neck while holding the photograph ID in a designated lockbox until another exchange can be made upon signing out at the conclusion of the visit. Visitor lanyards and staff lanyards must be separate and distinct colors.

Electronic Access Agreement (Chapter 4)

Electronic access systems involve significant financial investment. The value of these systems is determined by card holders. Require all employees and designated personnel to complete the following agreement.

Visitor Log   Date: _____

Name (Print)	Representing (Organization, Firm)	Time IN	Time OUT	Purpose of Visit	Person Visiting	Picture ID Yes No	Vehicle Type License #

FIGURE 3.2

I have received a keyless access card for (*insert school name*). I understand that I am not to transfer, duplicate, or allow anyone else access to this card without written consent or authorization from the school administrator. In the event I lose or misplace my card, I will report it to the administrator immediately. At the end of the each school year, I will return the card assigned to me to the principal's office.

Card # _____

Access level _____

Print name: _____

Card assigned by: _____

Signature of staff: _____

Date received: _____

School-Sanctioned Off-Site Event (Chapter 4)

The following practice addresses the critical need for a life-line of communications between the school and individual staff members that are engaged in school sanctioned off-site activities, such as field trips and professional development events.

School Sanctioned Off-Site Event

Every staff member engaged in a school sanctioned off-site event must have a school-approved, on-site staff member as an accountability partner. Upon arrival in the room where the majority of the time will be spent, the off-site staff member must call that accountability partner to report a safe arrival. This will also serve to establish the primary line of communications. If a connection cannot be established due to poor cellular service, the off-site staffer should attempt to utilize another means of communication (e.g., a landline telephone) until a reliable line of communications can be established.

Outside Organization Addendum (Chapter 4)

Most schools permit outside organizations to rent their facilities. Whether that organization is utilizing your gymnasium, auditorium, or classrooms, they should be required to abide by the security practices specified in the following form. Include it as part of your standard rental agreement.

Outside Organization Addendum
If you or one of your associates witness suspicious activity, please call (*Insert Name*) at (*Insert Phone Number*) immediately.

All outside organizations must provide a list of potential attendees at least 24 hours in advance of the activity.

Organizations utilizing the (*Insert Room/Area Being Rented*) must park in the (*Insert Name of Parking Lot*) lot and enter the facility through door # (*Insert Exterior Door Number*). Once inside the designated area, access to the rest of the facility is strictly prohibited.

In case of a fire emergency, please consult posted evacuation maps and follow directions designating approved evacuation routes and rally areas.

Note: Failure to comply with the practices and requirements above may result in penalties and/or potential forfeiture of facility rental rights.

Employee Separation Procedure[1] (Chapter 4)

Develop procedures to address separation, such as employee terminations and student expulsions. In addition to the following sample procedure, document practices that stipulate when to utilize a two-person rule, notification of staff and law enforcement, mandatory cool-off period (period of time during which the employee/student is not permitted to return), etc.

1. Notice (resignation/separation): The employee shall notify his/her immediate supervisor regarding termination of employment with the district. This notice must be in writing, state the last day of work, and be signed by the employee.

    The supervisor will notify the human resources department by submitting the employee's letter of resignation and by submitting a completed separation form. In the case of paraeducators, once the letter of resignation and separation form have been received, the human resources department will notify the assistant director of student services.

2. Separation Form: The employee's immediate supervisor will provide the separating employee with a copy of a separation form to be completed prior to the employee leaving district employment. The employee and the employee's immediate supervisor shall complete their respective sections and return the form to the human resources department prior to the employee's last day of work. The employee shall return all district property (ID badge, keys, computer, etc.) to the immediate supervisor on or before the last day of work.

3. Separation Meeting: There is a great deal of important information to discuss and several decisions to be made at the time of separation. The employee will contact the human resources department to arrange a meeting to review the following:
   * Retirement
   * ERISA – Health insurance continuation
   * Last pay period
   * Update mailing information

   At this meeting, the employee may also wish to participate in an exit interview as described below.

4. Exit Interview: Upon separation from district employment, an employee is encouraged to contact the human resources department to schedule an exit interview. The purpose of the exit interview is to share any ideas, concerns, or thoughts about working for the district. No records of the interview will be filed in the employee's personnel file.

5. Exit Interview Questionnaire: If the employee does not wish to participate in an exit interview, the employee will be given an exit interview questionnaire with a postage paid envelope and asked to complete and return the questionnaire.

Employee Resignation Form

Name:

Position:

Date written:

School or department:

My final date of employment will be:

My reason for resigning is:

I certify that this resignation is executed by me voluntarily and of my own free will.

Employee signature_____

Date_____

Supervisor acknowledges receipt:

Supervisor signature_____

Date _____

Submit this form to the human resource department on the date signed.

Employee Separation Checklist – Supervisor Portion

Employee name:

Employee ID number:

School or department:

Position title:

Supervisor:

Separation date:

Supervisor is responsible for completing:

Supervisor must submit an online request to have employee's secured access to the building disabled by notifying _____ in the _____ Department.

Cancel specific software/server/shared files access (e.g., user accounts, e-mail, SMS/WinSchool, scheduling software, list serves, websites). Human resources will notify the IT department once the letter of resignation has been received.

Remind the employee to remove district licensed software if they have it installed on a personally owned system. Licensing is only valid during employment.

Transfer of ownership of all active and archived files or libraries.

Voice mail account deleted.

Supervisor is responsible for collecting the following applicable items and/or address the following issues:

Obtain letter of resignation or retirement from the employee.

Keys (office, building, cabinet, desk, vehicles, other).

Card keys (office, building, other).

Master keys.

Badge/ID (office, building, other).

Keyless entry account changed.

Equipment at home returned (computers, laptops, printers, modems, etc.).

Documentation/manuals (software manuals, procedure manuals, etc.).

Tools/equipment/safety equipment.

Fuel card.

Parking permit.

Phone credit card.

Cell phone and accessories.

Pager(s) and/or radio(s).

Electronic devices (e.g., camera, laptop, tablet).

If authorized purchaser, contact suppliers and vendors to cancel employee as authorized purchaser.

Cancel any signature authority.

Department specific property.

Submit all final travel reimbursements.

Submit all final timesheets and leave requests.

Department issued uniforms.

Supervisor's signature _____

Date _____

Instruction – Employee Separation, Supervisor Portion

For employees that are departing the district, the supervisor is to provide the employee separation information sheet to the departing employee immediately upon notification of resignation or retirement.

The supervisor should complete the following employee separation checklist for terminating employees. The purpose of the checklist is to document procedures to revoke secured access privileges and secure all equipment. The supervisor needs to follow the checklist to ensure a smooth transition and to provide for the continuation of any benefits/services the employee may need. The supervisor should initiate this form and start completing it as soon as the departure notice is received from the employee.

Employee Separation Checklist

Employee Separation Information

All outstanding fees or balances (course advances, insurance premium payments, travel advances, library fees, etc.) have been settled. Outstanding balance may be deducted from last paycheck.

Cancel any meetings or out-of-district activities that are scheduled prior to the last day of employment to work with your supervisor to achieve a smooth transfer of duties.

Update your home mailing address so you can receive future correspondence (final paycheck, W2, benefit information, etc.).

Benefits: I have been advised to meet with a representative from the HR Department to discuss benefit and payroll options.

Your coverage of benefits will terminate unless you are a benefit eligible retiree. You may be eligible to continue to purchase certain benefits after you leave. Upon loss of coverage for you and/or your eligible dependent(s), a COBRA notification packet will be mailed to you and/or your eligible dependent(s) within 14 days of the date the human resources department receives official confirmation of an employee's separation from employment. The law requires that this packet be sent by mail to the last known address of the employee and/or the employee's eligible dependent(s).

I have removed all personal files from district servers and computers.

I have informed my supervisor of the location of job related files and made those files accessible to my supervisor.

I have been provided an opportunity for an exit interview.

Employee signature: _____

Date: _____

Exit Interview Questionnaire

Please take some time to complete this questionnaire. The purpose of the questionnaire is to provide you the opportunity to share your ideas, thoughts, and concerns in relation to your work with the district upon your separation from employment. The results of this questionnaire are for informational purposes and will be used to inform decisions related to employment practices. This questionnaire will not be placed in your personnel file. Your participation in this process is voluntary and information that you provide will help us to grow as an organization. Please complete the questionnaire and return it in the envelope that has been provided.

Employee name:
Position:
School or department:
Date:

1. What are you going to do next?
2. If other employment:
    *   What attracted you to your new job?
    *   How does the new job differ from your current one in terms of job expectations?
    *   Benefits?
    *   Compensation?
3. Could you explain what led you to your decision to leave your position?
4. Under what conditions would you have stayed?
5. What did you like most about your position?
6. What did you like least about your position?
7. Were the expectations for the position made clear to you during the hiring process?
8. Does the job description accurately describe job expectations?
9. Did you receive adequate training and orientation for the position? If not, please describe areas where additional orientation and or training would have been helpful.
10. Are there any changes to our employment practices that you would recommend?
11. Do you have suggestions for how we might improve working conditions within the district?
12. Is there anything else you would like to share?
13. If you have concerns, have you shared them with your supervisor?

Thank you for your participation in the process. Your comments and suggestions are appreciated.

Date warned:
Date adopted:
Legal reference(s):
Cross reference:

Bullying Prevention (Chapter 5)

Most states require school districts to create and maintain a policy on bullying prevention. The following is a sample policy.

Bullying Prohibition
I. PURPOSE

A safe and civil environment is needed for students to learn and attain high academic standards and to promote healthy human relationships. Bullying, like other violent or disruptive behavior, is conduct that interferes with students' ability to learn and teachers' ability to educate students in a safe environment.

District X is committed to fostering and maintaining a safe and civil educational environment in which all members of the school community are treated with dignity and respect. The school district prohibits bullying, harassment, and any other attempts to victimize others.

The school district cannot monitor the activities of students at all times and eliminate all incidents of bullying, particularly when students are not under the direct supervision of school personnel. However, to the extent such conduct affects the educational environment of the school district and the rights and welfare of its students and is within the control of District X in its normal operations, District X intends to prevent bullying and to take action to investigate, respond, remediate, and discipline those acts of bullying that have not been successfully prevented.

The purpose of this policy is to assist District X in its goal of preventing and responding to acts of bullying, intimidation, violence, retaliation, and other similar behaviors.

II. DEFINITION

A. "Bullying" means written or verbal expression, physical acts or gestures, and pattern thereof by a student that is intended to cause or is perceived as causing distress to a student or a group of students and which substantially interferes with another student's or students' educational benefits, opportunities, or performance.

Bullying includes, but is not limited to, conduct by a student against another student that a reasonable person under the circumstances knows or should know has the effect of:

1. harming a student or a group of students;
2. damaging a student's or a group of students' property;
3. placing a student or a group of students in reasonable fear of harm to his or her person or property;
4. creating a hostile educational environment for a student or a group of students; or
5. intimidating a student or a group of students.

B. "Immediately" means as soon as reasonably possible.

C. "On school district property or at school-related functions" means all school district buildings, school grounds, school property, school bus stops, school buses, school vehicles, school contracted vehicles, or any other vehicles approved for school district purposes, the area of entrance or departure from school grounds, premises, or events, and all school-related functions, school-sponsored activities, events, or trips. While prohibiting bullying at these locations and events, the school district does not represent that it will provide supervision or assume liability at these locations and events.

III. GENERAL STATEMENT OF POLICY

A. An act of bullying, by either an individual student or a group of students, is expressly prohibited on school property or at school-related functions. This policy applies not only to students who directly engage in an act of bullying but also to students who condone or support another student's act of bullying. This policy also applies to any student whose conduct constitutes bullying that interferes with or obstructs the mission or operations of the school or the safety or welfare of the student, other students, or employees or volunteers. The misuse of technology including but not limited to teasing, intimidating, defaming, threatening, or terrorizing another student, teacher, administrator, volunteer, contractor, or other employee of the school district by sending or posting e-mail messages, instant messages, text messages, digital pictures or images, or website postings, including blogs, also may constitute an act of bullying.

B. No teacher, administrator, volunteer, contractor, or other employee of District X shall permit, condone, or tolerate bullying.

C. Apparent permission or consent by a student being bullied does not lessen the prohibitions contained in this policy.

D. Retaliation against a victim, a good-faith reporter, or a witness of bullying is prohibited.

E. False accusations or reports of bullying against another student are prohibited.

F. A person who engages in an act of bullying, reprisal, or false reporting of bullying, or permits, condones, or tolerates bullying shall be subject to discipline for that act in accordance with school district's policies and procedures. District X may take into account the following factors:

   1. The developmental and maturity levels of the parties involved;

   2. The levels of harm, surrounding circumstances, and nature of the behavior;

   3. Past incidences or past or continuing patterns of behavior;

   4. The relationship between the parties involved; and,

   5. The context in which the alleged incidents occurred.

     Consequences for students who commit prohibited acts of bullying may range from positive behavioral interventions up to and including suspension and/or expulsion. Consequences for employees who permit, condone, or tolerate bullying or engage in an act of reprisal or intentional false reporting of bullying may result in disciplinary action up to and including termination or discharge. Consequences for other individuals engaging in prohibited acts of bullying may include but not be limited to exclusion from school district property and events and/or termination of services and/or contracts.

G. District X will act to investigate all complaints of bullying and will discipline or take appropriate action against any student, teacher, administrator, volunteer, contractor, or other employee of District X who is found to have violated this policy.

H. Reports of bullying are classified as private educational and/or personnel data and/or confidential investigative data and will not be disclosed except as permitted by law.

I. Submission of a good-faith complaint or report of bullying will not affect the complainant's or reporter's future employment, grades, or work assignments, or educational or work environment.

J. District X will respect the privacy of the complainant(s), the individual(s) against whom the complaint is filed, and the witnesses as much as possible, consistent with District X's obligation to investigate, take appropriate action, and comply with any legal disclosure obligations.

Reprisal

District X will discipline or take appropriate action against any student, teacher, administrator, volunteer, contractor, or other employee of District X who retaliates against any person who makes a good-faith report of alleged bullying or against any person who testifies, assists, or participates in an investigation, or against any person who testifies, assists, or participates in a proceeding or hearing relating to such bullying. Retaliation includes but is not limited to any form of intimidation, reprisal, harassment, or intentional disparate treatment.

Training and Education

A. District X will provide information and any applicable training to staff regarding this policy.

B. District X will annually provide education and information to students regarding bullying, including information regarding this policy prohibiting bullying.

C. The administration of District X will respond to bullying in a manner that does not stigmatize the victim, and make resources or referrals to resources available to victims of bullying.

D. District X may implement violence prevention and character development education programs to prevent and reduce policy violations. Such programs may offer instruction on character education including but not limited to character qualities such as attentiveness, truthfulness, respect for authority, diligence, gratefulness, self-discipline, patience, forgiveness, respect for others, peacemaking, and resourcefulness.

Notice

District X will give annual notice of this policy to students, parents or guardians, and staff, and this policy shall appear in the student handbook.

School Board Adoption: _____

Reporting and Response Procedure Guidelines

A. Any person who believes he or she has been the victim of bullying or any person with knowledge or belief of conduct that may constitute bullying shall report the alleged acts immediately to an appropriate school administrator designated by this policy. A person may report bullying anonymously. However, the school district's ability to take action against an alleged perpetrator based solely on an anonymous report may be limited.

B. District X encourages the reporting party or complainant to use the report form available from the administrator of each building or available from the district office, but oral reports shall be considered complaints as well.

C. The school administrator or administrator's designee (hereinafter building report taker) is the person responsible for receiving reports of bullying at the building level. Any person may also report bullying directly to the superintendent or school board. If the complaint involves the building report taker, the complaint shall be made or filed directly with the superintendent or the school district human rights officer by the reporting party or complainant.

D. A teacher, school administrator, volunteer, contractor, or other school employee should be particularly alert to possible situations, circumstances, or events that might include bullying. Any such person who receives a report of, observes, or has other knowledge or belief of conduct that may constitute bullying should inform a building report taker immediately. School district personnel who fail to inform the building report taker of conduct that may constitute bullying in a timely manner may be subject to disciplinary action.

School District Action

A. Upon receipt of a substantive complaint or report of bullying, District X should undertake or authorize an investigation by a school official or a third party designated by District X.

B. District X may take immediate steps, at its discretion, to protect the complainant, reporter, students, or others pending completion of an investigation of bullying, consistent with applicable law.

C. Upon completion of the investigation which verifies that an act of bullying has taken place, District X will take appropriate action. Such action may include but is not limited to warning, suspension, exclusion, expulsion, transfer, remediation, termination, or discharge. Disciplinary consequences will be sufficiently severe to try to deter violations and to appropriately discipline prohibited behavior. Action taken by District X for violation of this policy will be consistent with the requirements of applicable collective bargaining agreements; applicable statutory authority; school district policies; and regulations.

D. District X is not authorized to disclose to a victim private educational or personnel data regarding an alleged perpetrator who is a student or employee of District X. Upon completion of an investigation and/or subsequent disciplinary action, school officials will notify the parent(s) or guardian(s) of students involved in a bullying incident and the remedial action taken, to the extent permitted by law.

Dating Violence (Chapter 5)

The purposes of a Dating Violence policy is to prevent, respond to, and educate students, staff and school community on incidents of dating violence. Those victimized by dating violence suffer academically and face potentially higher levels of risk at school. The New Jersey Department of Education provides the following model policy.[2]

1. A statement that dating violence will not be tolerated.

The district board of education/board of trustees has determined that a safe and civil environment in school is necessary to learn. Acts or incidents of dating violence, whether they be verbal, sexual, physical or emotional, will not be tolerated and will be dealt with according to school district/charter school student code of conduct.

2. Procedures for reporting incidents of dating violence.

All acts or incidents of dating violence shall be reported to the school's principal or his or her designee (vice/assistant principal, guidance counselor, student assistance counselor, school resource officer, school nurse, etc.) in compliance with existing school district/charter school policy. This report should be made verbally as soon as possible but no later than the end of the student's school day. A written report regarding the act or incident of dating violence should be submitted to the principal or to his or her designee by the reporting staff member no later than one day after the act or incident occurs. Staff is required to report all acts or incidents of dating violence. These could include:

- Witnessed or reliable information concerning acts or incidents that are characterized by physical, emotional, verbal or sexual abuse;
- Digital or electronic acts or incidents of dating violence; and
- Patterns of behavior which are threatening or controlling.

3. Guidelines for responding to at-school incidents of dating violence.

Protocol for Staff Members.

Any school staff member who witnesses or learns of an act or incident of dating violence is required to take the following steps:

- Separate the victim from the aggressor.
- Speak with the victim and the aggressor separately.
- Speak with witnesses or bystanders separately.
- Inform the principal or his or her designee of the act or incident.
- Prepare written report of incident for principal or his or her designee.
- Monitor the interactions of the victim and the aggressor. Student safety should be the priority.

Protocol for Administrators.

Any school administrator who witnesses or learns of an act of dating violence is required to take the following steps:

- Separate the victim from the aggressor.
- Meet separately with the victim and the aggressor.
- Take written statements from the victim and alleged aggressor.
- Review the victim's and aggressor's written statements to ascertain an understanding of the act or incident. Questions may be asked of either individual for clarification.
- Further investigate the incident by speaking with bystanders/witnesses of the act or incident. All statements should be documented.
- The school administrator should make the determination to involve the school resource officer or police department.
- After an assessment by a school social worker, counselor, or psychologist, if a determination is made that the victim or aggressor's mental health has been placed at risk, appropriate referrals should be made.
- Contact should be made with the parents/guardians of both the victim and the aggressor. A recommendation of a meeting should be made to discuss the act or incident with the principal or his or her designee.
- Schools must notify both parties in writing of the outcome of the investigation into the act or incident of dating violence.

Protocol for working with the victim of an act or incident of dating violence.

Administrators shall consider adopting the following methods for dealing with victims of dating violence:

* Student safety should be the first priority. Interaction between the victim and the alleged aggressor should be avoided. The burden of any schedule changes (classroom, bus, etc.) should be taken on by the alleged aggressor.
* Schedule a conference with the victim and his or her parents/guardians.
* Identify any means or actions that should be taken to increase the victim's safety and ability to learn in a safe and civil school environment.
* Alert the victim and his or her parents/guardians of school and community based resources that may be appropriate, including their right to file charges if the act or incident violated the law.
* Monitor the victim's safety as needed. Assist the victim with any plans needed for the school day and after school hours (e.g., hallway safety, coordination with parents/guardians for transportation to and from school). An individualized safety plan may be developed if deemed necessary.
* Discuss a school approved stay-away agreement between the victim and the alleged aggressor.
* Encourage the victim to self-report any and all further acts and incidents of dating violence that occur at school in writing to the principal or his or her designee.
* Document all meetings and action plans that are discussed.

Protocol for working with the alleged aggressor of an act or incident of dating violence.

Administrators shall consider adopting the following methods for dealing with the alleged aggressor in an act or incidents of dating violence:

* Schedule a conference with the aggressor and his or her parents/guardians.
* Give the alleged aggressor the opportunity to respond in a written statement to the allegations of an act or incidents of dating violence at school.
* Alert the alleged aggressor and his or her parents/guardians of both school- and community-based support and counseling resources that are available.
* Identify and implement counseling, intervention, and disciplinary methods that are consistent with school policy for acts or incidents of this nature.
* Review the seriousness of any type of retaliation (verbal, emotional, physical, sexual, electronic/digital) toward the victim who reported the act or incidents of dating violence. Address the fact that consequences would be issued consistent with the school's student code of conduct and procedures for any type of retaliation or intimidation toward the victim.
* Document all meetings and action plans that are discussed.

Protocol for the documentation and reporting of an act or incidents of dating violence.

School districts and charter schools should establish a procedure for the documentation and reporting of acts or incidents of dating violence that occur at school.

- Dating violence statements and investigations should be kept in files separate from student academic and discipline records. This is recommended to prevent the inadvertent disclosure of confidential information.
- Every act or incident of dating violence at school that is reported should be documented in an appropriate manner. This should include statements, planning actions, and disciplinary measures, as well as counseling and other support resources that are offered and prescribed to the victim or alleged aggressor.

4. Discipline procedures specific to at-school incidents of dating violence.

The district board of education/board of trustees shall require its school administrators to implement discipline and remedial procedures to address acts or incidents of dating violence at school. These policies and procedures should be consistent with the school's student code of conduct. The policies and procedures specific to acts or incidents of dating violence at school should be used to address the act or incident as well as serve as remediation, intervention, education, and prevention for all individuals involved. The responses should be tiered with consideration given to the seriousness and the number of previous occurrences of acts or incidents in which both the victim and alleged aggressor have been involved.

The consequences and remedial measures listed below are examples and may be expanded upon. Consequences:

- Admonishment
- Temporary removal from the classroom
- Classroom or administrative detention
- In-school suspension
- Out-of-school suspension
- Reports to law enforcement
- Expulsion

The possibility of retaliation toward the victim of any act or incident of dating violence should be considered when administering consequences to the alleged aggressor based on the severity of the act or incident.

Remediation/intervention:

- Parent conferences;
- Student counseling (all students involved in the act or incident);
- Peer support group;
- Corrective instruction or other relevant learning or service experiences;
- Supportive student intervention;
- Behavioral management plan; and/or
- Alternative placements.

5. Warning Signs of Dating Violence.

A pattern of behaviors may be an important sign that a student is involved in an unhealthy or abusive dating relationship. Warning signs shall be included in the school district's/charter school's dating violence policy to educate the school community on the characteristics that a student in an unhealthy or abusive relationship might exhibit.

Warning signs may include but not be limited to the following:

- Name-calling and put downs. Does one student in the relationship use name-calling or put downs to belittle or intimidate the other student?
- Extreme jealousy. Does one student in the relationship appear jealous when the other talks with peers?
- Making excuses. Does one student in the relationship make excuses for the other?
- Canceling or changing plans. Does one student cancel plans often, and at the last minute? Do the reasons make sense or sound untrue?
- Monitoring. Does one student call, text, or check up on the other student constantly. Does one student demand to know the other's whereabouts or plans?
- Uncontrolled anger. Have you seen one of the students in the relationship lose his or her temper or throw and break things in anger?
- Isolation. Has one student in the relationship given up spending time with family and friends? Has the student stopped participating in activities that were once very important?
- Dramatic changes. Has the student's appearance changed since starting the relationship? Has he or she lost or gained weight? Does the student seem depressed?
- Injuries. Does the student in the relationship have unexplained injuries? Does the student give explanations that seem untrue?
- Quick progression. Did the student's relationship get serious very quickly?

Statistics:

- Victims of alleged aggressors of teen dating violence are more likely to bring a weapon to school.
- Victims of teen dating violence have lower academic achievement and grades of D and F.
- 5 percent of girls reported missing at least one day of school a month due to safety concerns.
- 43 percent of teen dating violence victims report that the dating violence experience occurred in a school building or on school grounds.
- 83 percent of the acts or incidents of dating violence that occurred at school involved physical abuse.

Many of these warning signs make a connection to one student in the relationship asserting control and power over the other. Recognizing one or more signs of teen dating violence plays an important role in shaping a policy to prevent, educate, and intervene in acts or incidents of dating violence.

Reporting (Chapter 6)

Routinely remind staff members to report suspicious activity. Incidents such as the Boston Marathon bombing remind us about the potential for domestic terrorism. The United States Air Force developed a list of seven signs of terrorism. These signs include:

Surveillance
Inquiries
Tests of Security
Acquiring Supplies
Suspicious or Out-of-Place Behavior
Trial Runs
Getting into Position

Schools are most likely to encounter surveillance and inquiries. Surveillance involves drawing of maps or diagrams of potential targets, annotation of information on maps or diagrams, the use of vision-enhancing devices (e.g., binoculars, cameras, videotape, or night vision) near potential targets, and the possession of blueprints of important facilities. Inquiries involve solicitation of information pertaining to critical US infrastructure and can be detected by taking note of any unusual inquiries into military or first responder operations. It is important for law enforcement officials to remember that while a small innocuous piece of information may seem harmless in and of itself, these bits of so-called "harmless" information gathered over time by terrorists could allow them to piece together information which would be considered sensitive knowledge.

Terrorism is the use of force or violence against persons or property in violation of the criminal laws of the United States for purposes of intimidation, coercion, or ransom. Terrorists typically plan their attacks in a way that generates the greatest publicity for their causes and creates massive fear among the public. Acts of terrorism include threats of terrorism; assassinations; kidnappings; hijackings; bomb scares and bombings; cyberattacks (computer-based); and the use of chemical, biological, nuclear, and radiological weapons.

Suspicious activity can be reported anonymously at 866-SPEAKUP.

Bomb Threat (Chapter 7)

In the unlikely event that you receive a bomb threat phone call, the form in Figure 3.3 equips the person answering the telephone to gather information from the caller. This information is critical for emergency responders. To ensure immediate access, the form should be kept within arm's reach of the telephone.

BOMB THREAT CHECKLIST

Description Detail Report

Questions to Ask:

1) When is the bomb going to explode?

2) Where is it right now?

3) What does it look like?

4) What kind of bomb is it?

5) What will cause it to explode?

6) Did you place the bomb?

7) Why?

8) What is your address?

9) What is your name?

Exact wording of the threat: _____

_____
_____
_____
_____
_____

Sex of caller: _____   Race: _____

Length of call: _____   Age: _____

Date: _____   Time: _____

Number at which call was received:

_____

Notes:

Callers Voice - Circle as Applicable:

- Calm
- Angry
- Excited
- Slow
- Rapid
- Soft
- Loud
- Laughter
- Crying
- Normal
- Distinct
- Slurred
- Nasal
- Stutter
- Lisp
- Raspy
- Deep
- Ragged
- Clearing throat
- Deep breathing
- Cracked voice
- Disguised
- Accent
- Familiar

If voice is familiar, whom did it sound like?

_____

Background Sounds:

- Street noises
- Animal noises
- Clear
- Static
- Music
- House noises
- Motor
- Factory machinery
- Voices
- PA system
- Local call
- Long distance call
- Phone booth
- Office machinery

- Other   _____
_____

Threat Language:

- Well-spoken (educated)
- Incoherent
- Foul
- Irrational by threat maker
- Taped
- Message read

Remarks: _____
_____
_____

FIGURE 3.3

Media Coordination (Chapter 7)

Many schools have been negatively affected by inadvertent and deliberate comments made by unauthorized staff members to media outlets. The following policy proactively addresses that issue.

In keeping with District X's "One Voice–Once Message" policy, all media inquiries must be referred to District X's designated media coordinator (*insert name*) at (*insert number*). This is Code of Conduct issue.

I agree to abide by the above media coordination policy.

Employee Signature_____

Date_____

Continuity of Operations (Chapter 7)

Continuity of operations describes efforts to ensure that essential functions continue to be performed during a wide range of emergencies, including environmental, violence and technology related incidents.

- A continuity of operations plan should contain a table of contents to ease the burden of end users in locating key information, especially during an incident. An executive summary should briefly outline the organization and content of the plan and describe what the plan is to be used for, whom it affects, and the circumstances under which it should be executed/implemented. Further, it should discuss the key elements of planning and explain the organization's implementation strategies.
- The introduction should explain the importance of continuity of operations planning to the district. It may also discuss the background for planning, referencing recent events that have led to the increased emphasis on the importance of this capability for the district. The purpose section should explain why the organization is developing a plan. It should briefly discuss applicable district, local, county, state, and federal guidance and explain the overall purpose of planning, which is to ensure the continuity of mission-essential functions. Because of today's changing threat environment, this section should state that the plan is designed to address the all-hazard threat.
- The applicability and scope section describes the applicability of the plan to the organization as a whole—district offices as well as individual schools, co-located and geographically dispersed—and to specific personnel groups. It should also include the scope of the plan. Ideally, plans should address the full spectrum of potential threats, crises, and emergencies (both natural and those instigated by people).
- A delegations of authority section should identify, by position, the authorities for making policy determinations and decisions to act on behalf of the school or district administrative head, district leadership, school board members, and other key individuals. Delegations should specify at least two alternate authorities and any limitations based on this delegation. Legal counsel should review these delegations along with state law limitations to such actions.
- The orders of succession should identify those that will assume key positions within the school/district during an emergency when the incumbents are unable or unavailable to execute their duties. Orders should be of sufficient depth to ensure the organization's ability to manage and direct its essential functions and operations.
- The decision process section should explain the logical steps associated with implementing a continuity of operations plan, describe the circumstances under which a plan may be activated (both with and without warning), and identify who has the authority to activate the plan. This process can be described in this section or depicted in a graphical representation.
- The alert, notification, and implementation process section should explain the events following a decision to activate the plan. This includes employee alerts and notification procedures and the continuity of operations plan implementation process.

The essential functions section should include a list of the district's prioritized essential functions. Essential functions are those organizational functions and activities that must be continued under any and all circumstances. Districts should:

- Identify all functions and determine which must be continued under all circumstances and those that are considered nonessential, allowing for recognition of those services that will cease in emergency situations.
- Prioritize these essential functions.
- Establish staffing and resource requirements.
- Integrate supporting activities.
- Develop a plan to perform additional functions as the situation permits.
- Examples of essential functions:
- Transportation (of students or evacuees).
- Communications (internal and external audiences).
- Instructional services (distance learning).
- Facility use (accessible main buildings or alternative locations).

The alternative facilities section should explain the significance of identifying an alternate facility, the requirements for determining an alternate facility, and the advantages and disadvantages of each location. Performance of a risk assessment is vital in determining which alternate location will best satisfy an organization's requirements.

- Determine if relocation within the district is feasible or if arrangements must be made with other school districts, agencies, or partners.
- Provide for reliable logistical support, services, and infrastructure systems.
- Consider prepositioning assets and resources at alternate facility (e.g., computers, servers, etc.), if feasible.
- Determine which essential functions and services can be conducted from a remote location (e.g., home) and those that need to be performed at a predesignated alternate facility.

Alternate facilities should provide:

- Sufficient space and equipment.
- Capability to perform essential functions within 12 hours for up to 30 days.
- Reliable logistical support, services, transportation, and infrastructure systems.
- Consideration for health, safety, and emotional well-being of personnel.
- Interoperable communications.
- Computer equipment and software.

The mission critical systems section should address the district's mission-critical systems necessary to perform essential functions and activities. Organizations must define these systems and address the method of transferring/replicating them at an alternate site (i.e., any items without which a school cannot function that may need to be evacuated with staff/students or that need to be purchased for the alternate facility.

Examples of mission critical systems:

- Computers/server.
- Medications.
- Medical devices.
- Generators.

The interoperable communications section should identify available and redundant critical communication systems that are located at the alternate facility. These communication systems should provide the ability to:

- Communicate externally with teachers, staff, students, parents, staff, other agencies, and organizations.
- Communicate internally with leadership, staff, and students.
- Ensure connectivity between internal and external parties in the event that primary means of communication fail.
- Ability to operate at the alternate facility within 12 hours for up to 30 days.

Consider viable methods of communication in the event cellular towers and landlines are inoperable. Also consider access to county/state radio frequencies, satellite phones and National Oceanic and Atmospheric Administration (NOAA) radios.

The vital resources section should identify what records are vital to each organization and how they will be handled. Vital records are electronic and hard copy documents including references and records needed to support essential functions during a continuity of operations situation and to reconstitute normal operations after the emergency ceases. Two types of vital records:

- Emergency operating records (i.e., emergency operations plans and directives, orders of succession, delegations of authority, references indicating who performs which essential functions).
- Legal and financial records (i.e., personnel records, Social Security records, payroll records, retirement records, insurance records, contract records, student records, and medical records).

Human capital management is the sum of talent, energy, knowledge, and enthusiasm that people invest in their work. This section might include diagrams or charts that enhance all personnel's understanding of their position and duties during a continuity of operations situation. A plan for keeping employees informed of their status can be part of this section.

- Place the most qualified people in the positions necessary to perform essential functions.
- Consider reassignment of personnel from nonessential functions.
- Management is responsible for accounting for all staff during a continuity of operations situation.

Most employees will:

- Fulfill their predesignated emergency support function.
- Go home.
- Remain available.
- Wait for further directions.

The devolution section should address how an organization will transfer statutory authority and responsibility for essential functions in the aftermath of a worst-case scenario, one in which the leadership is unable or unavailable for an extended amount of time. Steps used in this process:

- Identify likely triggers and authorities for devolution implementation.
- Describe how and when devolution will occur.
- Identify the resources that will be required to continue essential functions under a devolution scenario.

This reconstitution section should cover the process by which teachers, staff, and ultimately students resume normal operations at the original (or replacement) primary operating facility. For example:

- Notification procedures for all staff and students returning to school must also be addressed.
- Conducting after-action reviews to determine the effectiveness of continuity of operations plans and procedures.

The planning responsibilities section should include additional delineation of continuity of operations responsibilities of each key staff position in the planning team (i.e., who creates the plan, who maintains the plan, and when they must accomplish these tasks). It should also address how the district plans to ensure that the plan contains the most current information. Federal guidance states that organizations should review the entire plan at least annually. Key evacuation routes, roster and telephone information, as well as maps and room/building designations of alternate locations should be updated as changes occur.

The tests, training, and exercises section of the plan ensures that the plan is capable of supporting operations of essential functions, all equipment and systems work as required, all employees are able to deploy to the alternate facility within the required time frame, supply chain and infrastructure capabilities are addressed, and any deficiencies are identified. This section should also include a schedule of planned test, trainings and exercises and after-action reports.

The appendix should cite a list of authorities and references that mandate the development of this continuity of operations plan and provide guidance toward acquiring the requisite information contained in the plan. This appendix should contain operational checklists for use during a continuity of operations event. Checklists may be designed to list the responsibilities of a specific position or the steps required to complete a specific task. For example:

- Emergency calling directory.
- Key personnel roster.
- Essential functions checklist.
- Alternate site acquisition checklist.
- Emergency operating records and IT checklist.
- Emergency equipment checklist.

The alternate locations appendix should include general information about the alternate location/facility, including the address, points of contact, and available resources at the alternate location.

The maps and evacuation routes appendix should provide maps, driving directions, and available modes of transportation from the primary facility to the alternate location. Evacuation routes from the primary facility should also be included.

The definitions and acronyms appendix should contain a list of key words, phrases, and acronyms used throughout the plan and within the continuity of operations community. Each key word, phrase, and acronym should be clearly defined.

Social Media Policy (Chapter 8)

(http://newhampton.wikispaces.com/Social+Media+Policy)

The following policy addresses the use of electronic technologies.

Social media are a powerful set of communication tools. These tools are also new and emerging technologies changing the ways we teach, learn, work, and live. As adults who work with young people, we should constantly challenge ourselves with new teaching, learning, and communication tools, while also remembering our responsibilities as mentors, guides, and role models. The purpose of this policy is to guide faculty and staff in the appropriate use of social media tools at the workplace.

Social media tools include but are not limited to:

- Blogs
- Wikis
- Facebook and other social utilities
- Twitter
- Photo/video sharing sites (including our own web site)

Understand the Public Nature of Social Media. Everything you say or do with social media is largely public. Although privacy filters and settings are very good, mistakes still happen. Would you distribute pictures of yourself drinking to your students? Consider how you portray yourself and your ideas. Derogatory, slanderous, or libelous public messages made over the school network are violations of our Acceptable Use Policy (AUP).

Define a purpose for your use of a social media tool. If you connect with old friends on Facebook, is this a good tool for managing your classroom? Perhaps you will set up a Ning (online platform for creating custom social networks) for your class, but connect only with your personal friends on Facebook.

Understand Privacy Settings. Various social media tools have a varying degree of privacy controls; understand and use them. Facebook may be a useful classroom management tool if you clearly define this as your purpose for using Facebook. Set your privacy controls to limit the access your student 'friends' have to your personal content.

"Friending." Adult members of our community refrain from "friending" current or prospective students on Facebook. Adult members of our community "friend" recent graduates only after careful consideration.

Understand Your Role as an Adult. You are the adult online as well as offline. If, in careful consideration of the above guidelines, you notice photos, posts or other evidence of concerning or destructive behavior, note that you are duty bound and possibly legally bound to respond. Failure to respond to concerning behavior may in the best case result in the student assuming you tacitly approve of the behavior or in the worst case lead to a dangerous or harmful situation for the student.

If you wish to "friend" current students, you must clarify your role with the student in relation to this guideline and document your intended use of this social media tool with the academic office.

Understand that you are a professional. Gossip is a bad idea. Online it is a very bad idea. It is considered good professional practice not to gossip, talk about your colleagues behind their backs, or slander your employer. Social media can widely amplify the voice of the user and thus also the negative consequences for engaging in this type of behavior.

Photo and Video Use Policy. To prepare video for publication on the web please use only music to which the school owns the rights (like music produced by our own students and faculty) or royalty free music or CC music (like music from Jamendo or all of the clips included with iMovie). Do not use students' full names (see Student Information below).

Student Information. We frequently publish photos, videos, and text relating to students at our school, but that we do so in the context of the following guidelines:

- All students must have a signed media release on file for their image to appear in photos or videos on the site.
- We will refrain from associating a student's full name with their image. Therefore, when captioning pictures or video of students, use only their first names.
- Only publish the first initial and last name of students in rosters or student lists.
- At the request of a parent/guardian, we will remove any tags, captions, or other identifying text.
- At the request of a parent/guardian we will remove a student's image from our website.

Electronic Technologies Acceptable Use Policy[3] (Chapter 8)

The following policy further addresses the use of electronic technologies.

I. Purpose

The purpose of this policy is to set forth guidelines for access to acceptable and safe use of the district's electronic technologies. Electronic technologies include but are not limited to computers and peripherals, printers, telephones, and the applications they support and/or access. The policy complements the district's website and intranet policy.

II. Definitions

The term "users" refers to any person using the district's electronic technologies.

The term "Internet" refers to an electronic communications network that connects computer networks and organizational computer facilities around the world.

The term "intranet" refers to the district's network, which restricts access to authorized users, which may include students, staff, parents, contractors, vendors, and volunteers.

The term "electronic technologies" refers to, but is not limited to, computers and peripherals, printers, telephones, and the applications they support and/or access.

III. General Statement of Policy

The school district provides technology resources to its students, staff, parents, and community for educational, administrative, and informational purposes. The goal in providing these resources is to promote educational excellence in X District by facilitating resource sharing, innovation, and communication with the support and supervision of parents, teachers, and support staff.

Educational Purpose

Access to the technology in the school district has been established for educational purposes. The use of the district's electronic technologies is a valued resource to our community. All electronic technologies must be used in support of the educational program of the district. This access may be revoked at any time for abusive or inappropriate conduct related to the use of electronic technologies.

School computers, telecom, memory devices, networks, and related hardware and software are the property of the school district. At no time does the district relinquish its exclusive control of electronic technologies. Inappropriate use of district electronic technologies, including interfering with network functions and the standardization of technologies, may result in the limitation or revocation of access.

Depending on the nature and degree of the violation and the number of previous violations, unacceptable use of electronic technologies may result in one or more of the following consequences: suspension or cancellation of use or access privileges; payments for damages and repairs; discipline under other appropriate district policies, including suspension, expulsion, exclusion, or termination of employment; or civil or criminal liability under other applicable laws.

Use of electronic technologies during the employee duty day should be restricted exclusively to educational purposes.

Unacceptable Uses

Users are responsible for anything set on the network with their name or other individual identifier (e.g., an IP address) on it. Users shall not engage in any activity that disrupts or hinders the performance of the district's electronic technologies. Specifically, the following uses of the district's electronic technologies are considered unacceptable:

A. Users will not use the district's electronic technologies to access, review, upload, download, store, print, post, receive, transmit, or distribute:
  1. Pornographic, obscene, or sexually explicit material or other visual depictions that are harmful to minors;
  2. Obscene, abusive, profane, lewd, vulgar, rude, inflammatory, libelous, threatening, disrespectful, or sexually explicit language;
  3. Materials that use language or images that are inappropriate in the educational setting or disruptive to the educational process;
  4. Information or materials that could cause damage or danger of disruption to the educational process;
  5. Materials that use language or images that advocate violence or discrimination toward other people (hate literature) or that may constitute harassment or discrimination, or any other material that would violate any law;
  6. Orders made by shopping online during time designated as off-limits by the district; or
  7. Personal photos, files, or music not related to educational purposes for any extended length of time.
B. Users will not use the district's electronic technologies to knowingly or recklessly post, transmit, or distribute false or defamatory information about a person or organization, to harass another person, or to engage in personal attacks, including prejudicial or discriminatory attacks.
C. Users will not use the district's electronic technologies to engage in any illegal act or violate any local, state, or federal statute or law.
D. Users will not use the district's electronic technologies for political campaigning.
E. Users will not physically or electronically vandalize district technologies nor use the district's electronic technologies to vandalize, damage, or disable the property of another person or organization.
  1. Users will not make deliberate attempts to degrade or disrupt equipment, software, or system performance by spreading computer viruses or by any other means.
  2. Users will not tamper with, modify, or change the district's electronic technologies software, hardware, or wiring or take any action to violate the district's security system.

3. Users will not use the district's electronic technologies in such a way as to disrupt the use of the system by other users.

4. Users may not add or remove any software nor modify the equipment, software configuration, or environment. All electronic technology requests must go through the district's technology department processes.

F. Users will not use the district's electronic technologies to gain unauthorized access to information resources or to access another person's materials, information, or files without the implied or direct permission of that person.

G. Users will not use the district's electronic technologies to post information in public access areas regarding private information about another person. Private information includes personal contact information about themselves or other persons, or other personally identifiable information including but not limited to addresses, telephone numbers, identification numbers, account numbers, access codes or passwords, labeled photographs, or other information that would make the individual's identity easily traceable, and will not repost a message that was sent to the user privately without permission of the person who sent the message.

H. Users will not attempt to gain unauthorized access to the district's electronic technologies or any other system through the district's electronic technologies. Users will not attempt to logon through another person's account, or use computer accounts, access codes, or network identification other than those assigned to the user. Access through any means other than an individual's user logon and password is not permitted.

I. Messages, files, and records on the district's electronic technologies may not be encrypted without the permission of appropriate administrative school authorities. Users must keep all account information and passwords private.

J. Users will not use the district's electronic technologies in any way that may violate trademark copyright laws or usage licensing agreements:
1. Users will not use another person's property without the person's prior approval or proper citation.
2. Users will not load, download, or exchange pirated software or copy software to or from any school computer including freeware and shareware.
3. Users will not plagiarize works they find on the Internet or other information resources.

K. Users will not use the district's electronic technologies for unauthorized commercial purposes or for financial gain unrelated to the mission of the district. Users will not use the district's electronic technologies to offer or provide goods or services or for product advertisement, except as authorized by the district administration.

L. The district does not support personal equipment. Users will not install any personal equipment or software on any district-owned systems.

Filter

A. With respect to any of its computers with Internet access, the school district will monitor the online activities of minors and employ technology protection measures during any use of such computers by minors and adults. The technology protection measures utilized will use best efforts and industry standard approaches to block or filter Internet access to any visual depictions that are obscene, violent, child pornography, or harmful to minors:

B. The term "harmful to minors" means any picture, image, graphic image file, or other visual depiction that:

    1. Taken as a whole and with respect to minors, appeals to a prurient interest in nudity, violence, sex, or excretion; or

    2. Depicts, describes, or represents, in a patently offensive way with respect to what is suitable for minors, an actual or simulated sexual act or sexual contact, actual or simulated normal or perverted sexual acts, or a lewd exhibition of the genitals; and

    3. Taken as a whole, lacks serious literary, artistic, political, or scientific value as to minors.

C. Access to chat rooms, discussion boards, school-issued e-mail and other forms of direct electronic communications are limited to applications approved by the district and/or hosted within the district domain for the safety and security of minors.

D. An administrator, supervisor, or other person authorized by the superintendent may disable the technology protection measure during use by an adult to enable access for bona fide research or other lawful purposes.

E. The district is obligated to monitor and/or review filtering activities.

F. The school district will educate students about appropriate online behavior, including interacting with other individuals on social networking websites and in chat rooms and cyberbullying awareness and response.

Limited Expectation of Privacy

By authorizing use of the school district's electronic technologies, the school district does not relinquish control over content or data transmitted or stored on the network or contained in files. Users should expect only limited privacy in the contents of personal files on the district's electronic technologies.

A. Routine maintenance and monitoring of the district's electronic technologies may lead to a discovery that a user has violated this policy, another school district policy, or the law.

B. An individual investigation or search will be conducted if school authorities have a reasonable suspicion that the search will uncover a violation of law or school district policy.

C. Parents have the right at any time to investigate or review the contents of their child's files and e-mail files. Parents have the right to request the termination of their child's individual account at any time.

D. District staff are advised that the school district retains the right at any time to investigate or review the contents of their files and e-mail files based upon legal complaints or specific allegations regarded as misuse of technologies. In addition, district staff are advised that data and other materials in files maintained on or transmitted through the district's electronic technologies may be subject to review, disclosure, or discovery.

E. The district will cooperate fully with local, state and federal authorities in any investigation concerning or related to any illegal activities or activities not in compliance with school district policies conducted through the district's electronic technologies.

Electronic Technologies Acceptable Use Agreement

A. The proper use of the Internet and the educational value to be gained from proper Internet use are the joint responsibility of students, parents, and staff of the district.

B. This policy requires the permission of and supervision by the school's designated professional staff before a student may use a school account or resource to access the Internet.

C. The electronic technologies acceptable use agreement for students must be read and signed by the user and parents or guardians. The Internet use agreement for employees must be signed by the employee. The form must then be filed with the district.

D. All users shall be responsible for the protection and security of their passwords. Users shall have the ability to change passwords to maintain the confidentiality of logon codes.

Limitation on School District Liability

Use of the district's educational technologies is at the user's own risk and is provided on an "as is, as available" basis. The district will not be responsible for any damage users may suffer, including but not limited to loss, damage, or unavailability of data stored on the district's systems, delays or changes in or interruptions of service, or misdeliveries or nondeliveries of information or materials, regardless of the cause. The district is not responsible for the accuracy or quality of any advice or information obtained through or stored on the district's electronic technologies. The district will not be responsible for financial obligations arising through unauthorized use of the district's educational technologies or the Internet.

Consistency with Other School Policies

Use of the district's electronic technologies must not violate other policies and regulations of the district, including but not limited to Policy X Gifts and Donations, Policies X/X Nondiscrimination, Policies X/X Harassment and Violence, Policy X Website and Intranet, Policy X Instructional Materials Selection and Review, and Policy X Curriculum Goals.

User Notification

A. All users shall be notified of the district policies relating to electronic technology acceptable use.

B. This notification shall include the following:
   1. Notification of unacceptable use of district electronic technologies;
   2. Notification that Internet use is subject to compliance with district policies.

3. Disclaimers limiting the district's liability relative to:
    a. Information stored on district systems including diskettes, hard drives, servers, CDs, DVDs, memory sticks or similar devices, or any other storage device:
    b. Information retrieved through the district's computers, networks, or online resources;
    c. Personal property used to access the district's computers, networks, or online resources; and
    d. Unauthorized financial obligations resulting from use of district resources/accounts to access the Internet.
4. A description of the privacy rights and limitations of school sponsored/managed Internet accounts.
5. Notification of password ownership and password protection procedures.
6. Notification that, even though the district may use technical means to limit student Internet access, these limits are not impenetrable and are not the sole means of enforcing the provisions of this policy.
7. Notification that goods and services can be purchased over the Internet that could potentially result in unwanted financial obligations and that any financial obligation incurred by a student through the Internet is the sole responsibility of the student and/or the student's parents.
8. Notification that student e-mail addresses may be provided to district-approved third- party providers for access to educational tools and content.
9. Notification that the collection, creation, reception, maintenance, and dissemination of data via the Internet, including electronic communications, is governed by School Board Policy X Public and Private Personnel Data and School Board Policy X Protection and Privacy of Pupil Records.
10. Notification that, should the user violate the district's acceptable use policy, the user's access privileges may be revoked, school disciplinary action may be taken, and/or appropriate legal action may be taken.
11. Notification that all provisions of the electronic technologies acceptable use policy are subordinate to local, state and federal laws.

Parents' Responsibility—Notification of Student Internet use

A. Outside of school, parents bear responsibility for the same guidance of Internet use as they exercise with information sources such as television, telephones, radio, movies, and other possibly offensive media. Parents are responsible for monitoring their student's use of the district's educational technologies, including school-issued e-mail accounts, and of the Internet if the student is accessing the district's electronic technologies from home or through other remote location(s).
B. Parents will be notified that their students will be using district resources/accounts/school-issued e-mail to access the Internet and that the district will provide parents

the option to request alternative activities not requiring Internet access. This notification should include:

1. A copy of the electronic technologies acceptable use agreement provided to the student user;
2. A description of parent/guardian responsibilities;
3. A notification that the parents have the option to request alternative educational activities not requiring Internet access and the material to exercise this option;
4. A statement that the electronic technologies acceptable use agreement must be signed by the user, parent or guardian, and the supervising teacher prior to use by the student; and
5. A statement that the district's electronic technologies acceptable use policy is available for parental review.

Implementation and Policy Review

A. The superintendent or designee is directed to develop the necessary guidelines for the implementation of this policy. The superintendent or designee may develop appropriate user notification forms, guidelines, and procedures necessary to implement this policy for submission to the school board for approval.
B. The superintendent or designee shall revise the user notifications, including student and parent notifications, if necessary, to reflect the adoption of these guidelines and procedures.
C. The district's Internet policies and procedures are available for review by all parents, guardians, staff, and members of the community.

Student Use of Social Media (Chapter 8)

The following policy addresses student use of social media.

1. Students accessing or using weblogs, wikis, and podcasts per student assignment are required to keep personal information out of their postings. Students will not post or give out photographs of themselves without signed parental permission. Students will not post their family name, password, user name, e-mail address, home address, school name, city, country, or other information that could help someone locate or contact them in person.
2. Students using a Learning Management System, such as Moodle, will not share their user name or password with anyone other than their teachers and parents.
3. Students will not login as another individual.
4. Students using weblogs, wikis, podcasts, or Moodle will treat these tools as a classroom space. Speech that is inappropriate for class is not appropriate on weblogs, wikis, podcasts, or Moodle. Students are expected to treat others and their ideas online with respect.

5. Assignments on weblogs, wikis, podcasts, or Moodle are like any other assignment in school. Students, in the course of completing the assignment, are expected to abide by policies and procedures in the student/parent handbook, including those policies regarding plagiarism and acceptable use of technology.
6. Student blogs are to be a forum for student expression. However, they are first and foremost a tool for learning.
7. Students shall not use the Internet to harass, discriminate, or threaten the safety of others. If students receive a comment on a blog or other tools used in school that makes them feel uncomfortable or is not respectful, they must report this to a teacher and must not respond to the comment.
8. Students accessing blogs, wikis, or podcasts from school using school equipment shall not download or install any software without permission and shall not click on ads or contests.
9. Students should be honest, fair and, courageous in gathering, interpreting and expressing information for the benefit of others. Always identify sources and test the accuracy of information from all sources.
10. Students will treat information, sources, subjects, colleagues, and information consumers as human beings deserving of respect. Gathering and expressing information should never cause harm or threaten to be harmful to any person or group of people.
11. Students are accountable to their readers, listeners, viewers, and to each other. Admit mistakes and correct them promptly. Expose unethical information and practices of others.
12. Failure to follow this code of ethics will result in academic sanctions and/or disciplinary action per the parent/student handbook.

Student Data Privacy (Chapter 8)

Privacy concerns spike when viewed against the daunting backdrop of the Internet. The following advice involving student data privacy practices was provided by a law enforcement officer dedicated to the school arena.

Maintain awareness of relevant federal, state, tribal, or local laws, particularly the Children's Online Privacy Protection Act, which includes requirements for providing online educational services to children under 13. Be aware of which online educational services are currently being used in your district. Conducting an inventory of all such services is one specific step districts can take.

Create policies and procedures to evaluate and approve proposed online educational services, including both formal contracts and no-cost software that requires only click-through consent. When possible, use a written contract or legal agreement. Provisions should be included for security and data stewardship; the collection of data; the use, retention, disclosure, and destruction of data; the right of parents and students to access and modify their data; and more.

Conclusion

These examples of policy planning illustrate how administrators and security directors should respond to security incidents that occur in district schools or incidents in other schools reported in the news. Ask yourself if your district has a policy designed to prevent such incidents and to mitigate injuries if a problem arises anyway. If not, develop a written policy.

Do not attempt to do it by yourself. Collaborate with the frontline people. Ask the choir director of the opening narrative what she would recommend to deal with a weather emergency when on the road with the choir. Talk to the football coach, too, and the security director. Gather views and develop a policy. When a security incident erupts, there is no time to plan. You must simply put an existing plan into effect.

Likewise, when a teacher makes a mistake on a social media site, there is no way to un-ring the bell. Most of these kinds of mistakes will be innocent, yet potentially damaging to a good teacher, the school, and the district. Prevent those mistakes with a clear written policy.

What might happen? Figure it out ahead of time, and then formulate a policy to prevent it.

References

1. "Employee Resignation and Separation Procedure," *Milton Town School District*, accessed May 8, 2014, http://www.mtsd-vt.org/MTSD/Documents/Policies/D9P%20-%20Employee%20Resignation%20 and%20Separation%20Procedure.pdf.

2. "Model Policy and Guidance for Incidents Involving Dating Violence," *New Jersey Department of Education*, accessed May 8, 2014, http://www.nj.gov/education/aps/cccs/chpe/dating/policy.pdf.

3. "Policy 428: Employee Use of Social Media," *Independent School District 719, Prior Lake – Savage Area Schools, Minnesota*, August 6, 2012, http://meghanpotter.efoliomn.com/Uploads/ 428_Employee_Use_of_Social_Media.pdf.

4

Securing Your Environment

Introduction: Coming Full Circle

No one believes it will happen here, but every school day offers up dozens of ways that it could happen here.

Imagine the beginning of a school day. As students file in, no one notices an intruder. Who would notice? He looks a little more mature than other students but dresses like a student. No one sees the gun in his pocket. A walk-through metal detector would have caught it, but no one wants to make the school look like a prison.

If you ignore it, it really can happen here. If you think about security in the right way and give yourself the right tools, you can prevent it from happening here—maybe not always, but most of the time.

For many years, pre-K–12 schools paid too little attention to physical security. The events of the last few years have persuaded most administrators and school security professionals that school security must adapt to the modern realities. Those realities include protecting students—as well as faculty and staff—from neighborhood crime when on school grounds, whether inside or outside; protecting everyone from the rare but almost always lethal active shooter; and protecting students from parents, other relatives, or any adults not specifically authorized to pick students up from school. Realities we have always known include protecting the school community from fire, severe weather, and other natural or human-made disasters.

These are a few of today's concerns. Some have responded by turning their schools into fortresses locked down tightly with today's highly effective physical security technology. Others have tried but then given in to the pressure of daily educational responsibilities.

What is an adequate level of physical security? What is too little? What is more than necessary? How do security professionals and administrators make those judgments? Experience helps, of course, but experience alone is not enough. It also takes a reasoned examination and analysis of the specific risks and vulnerabilities faced by particular schools—followed by plans to mitigate those risks and overcome those vulnerabilities.

For the time being, please assume that a security assessment has been carried out, and decisions have been and are being made in light of its findings.

Physical security as it relates to pre-K–12 schools breaks down into five components:

- Deterrence
- Detection
- Communications
- Delay
- Response

Deterrence

Deterrence is the act of discouraging someone from engaging in criminal behavior. In a 2012 hostage incident in Pittsburgh, the presence of security officers in the lobbies of some buildings deterred or discouraged the hostage-taker from entering. The building he did enter had no security officer. Other forms of deterrence include exterior signs, bright exterior lighting, and fencing. Video cameras can also deter criminals. No one has figured out how to measure deterrence. All we know is that it is sometimes effective and sometimes ineffective.

Detection

Detection is the ability to discover undeterred activities and incidents as they occur. Unlike deterrence, detection systems can be measured. For instance, over the course of a year, a security officer may detect 95 percent of the attempted break-ins at a facility. Similarly, video surveillance systems and electronic access control systems will detect some attempted break-ins while they are underway. Sometimes detection deters criminals. Thieves may run away when an alarm goes off. Sometimes alarms do not deter thieves, and they continue their criminal behavior.

Communications

Communications systems enable physical security programs to function effectively. When an access control system detects a nighttime break-in attempt, for instance, an alarm communicates with a security officer monitoring systems in the security center. In turn, that officer may radio patrolling officers and direct them to the site of the break-in. During the day, another kind of emergency might cause an administrative assistant to use the PA system to notify faculty and staff to activate an emergency response plan designed to protect students. A mass notification system could advise parents through e-mail and voice and text messaging systems. Telephones, intercoms, two-way radios, and other communications equipment might be relied on during emergencies, as well.

Delay

Delay slows the movements of an adversary. Locked doors, windows, and other possible barriers delayed the attempted criminal break-in described above long enough for the communication system to summon a security response. In the case of a break-in detected after the fact, interior gates could continue to delay the progress of perpetrators. Other delaying tools include fences, vehicle barriers, and speed reducing features.

Response

Security programs succeed or fail based on the quality of the response. Think about everything that comes before the response to a nighttime break-in: deterrence has discouraged a number of criminal activities; detection has discovered an actual break-in; communications has alerted everyone; and an emergency response is under-way. School resource officers, security personnel, administration, and any faculty and staff that happen to be in the building have taken up positions that have been drilled, positions that enable them to protect others and themselves, if necessary. At least one responder is communicating with local law enforcement.

When an event ends, a second response phase begins—the recovery. An effective emergency response plan has assigned school resource officers, security personnel, administrators, faculty, and staff to recovery jobs. Specific recovery activities depend upon the scope of the incident. Every recovery plan would communicate with students and parents over the PA and mass notification systems. Another group trained in first aid would care for the injured until emergency medical technicians arrive. Still others would deal with property damage. The goal is to return to normal as efficiently as possible.

Selecting Products, Systems, and Measures

What is the most effective way to provide a safe learning environment? Which measures have the most value? What combination of systems and practices will result in the most risk reduction? While these questions cannot possibly be answered with a specific formula or magic wand, it is important to remember the guiding principle of asset prioritization. In chapter one, we mentioned that assets are like nouns: people, places, and things. Where schools are concerned, what is the most important asset? The obvious answer is people! As simple as that concept may seem, it is not always the same answer in other arenas. For example, I spent many of my childhood days at Argonne National Laboratories. Argonne is a US Department of Energy facility in Chicago's southwest suburbs. The most important asset at Argonne in those days was definitely not people. Of course, it would have been tragic if harm would have come to people, and Argonne did an excellent job of protecting them, but the most important asset on the campus was things. Included in the category of "things" at Argonne National Laboratories was nuclear materials—uranium and plutonium supplies. Whereas harm to individuals would have been tragic, loss of nuclear materials would have been catastrophic from a societal standpoint. As a result, Argonne's first expenditure of planning time and funding was spent on protecting things. The public, however, did not look at the campus' security measures with the concept of asset prioritization in mind. Instead, people simply began to assume that high fences, razor wire, guard booths, and layers of intrusion detection systems must be the most effective kind of security for all applications. That assumption is incorrect.

Shifting the focus back to schools now, we must ask how much value an intrusion detection (burglar alarm) system has in protecting people? The answer is very little! This is not to suggest that schools should abandon installing burglar alarm systems. On the contrary, these systems should ideally be part of every school building. They are not, however, where the first expenditure of planning time and funding should be spent. In fact, if people are the number one asset in schools, the first hour of planning and the first dollar of spending should be spent on addressing two areas: communications and access control. Nothing protects people better than effective communications and access control. Without excellent communications, Murphy's Law is bound to find you in a situation where you need help but cannot contact someone or in circumstances where an emergency announcement was made but you could not receive it. Where access control is concerned, too many schools operate with ineffective visitor management procedures and, at any given time, have no way of accounting for those that are in the facility or have left the facility. The point of this discussion can be summed up with a challenge: invest in improving communications and access control! In the interest of taking a comprehensive approach, we will also discuss physical security measures such as video surveillance and intrusion detection.

Communications

An effective approach to assessing communications capabilities and needs involves taking inventory of existing systems and devices, such as landline telephones, PA systems, intercom systems, two-way radios, and cellular phones. To which methods of communication do staff members have access throughout the school building? What is their primary means of emergency communication? Once identified, the following options should be optimized as described.

Landline Telephones

If not available in every classroom, almost every school has landline telephones in offices and related areas such as conference rooms. Audit telephones to ensure that every one is functional. If your school has recently upgraded from traditional telephones to Voice Over Internet Protocol (VOIP), be sure to remove the old units.

Label every telephone with emergency dialing instructions. For example, specify how someone would dial 911. Can that emergency number be dialed directly or does your system require another digit, such as an 8, to be dialed first in order to obtain an outside line? Whatever the sequence, spell it out on the telephone. Next, what is the quickest way to reach the main office? Can someone simply dial 0 or is there a three- or four-digit extension? Post the quickest sequence on the telephone. When someone in the building dials the main office extension, is it possible that the phone call would go to voicemail? If so, attempt to avoid that possibility by forwarding calls into a "hunt group" or enabling phone features such as "no answer/busy transfer" (a feature that forwards calls that would ordinarily go to voicemail to another extension). Finally, is there an after-hours number that someone in the building could dial when the main office is not staffed? If so, post that number on the telephone.

Public Address

Most schools have PA systems that permit one-way communication, such as announcements made from the main office to all areas of the building. Effective PA systems provide

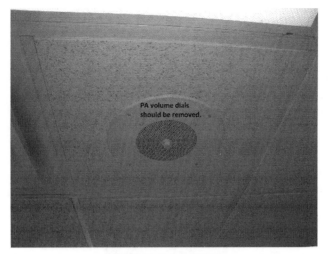

FIGURE 4.1 Volume Dial 1.

an excellent method of on-site mass notification. To ensure that your system is effective, consider the following questions. Does your PA system reach all areas of the building with clarity and appropriate volume? Some areas that are often forgotten include restrooms, boiler rooms, gymnasiums, cafeterias, and auditoriums.

Occasionally, schools have volume dials (see Figures 4.1 and 4.2) on walls or speakers in areas such as offices, conference rooms, and the nurse's office. To ensure that emergency announcements are always received, volume dials should be removed.

Does your PA system have exterior capabilities? If not, consider adding exterior speakers. Please remember that without exterior PA, emergency announcements should be made in two steps: 1) over the PA system, and 2) through a system such as two-way radios that can reach those outside the building.

Intercom Systems

Traditional intercom systems are really just PA systems that have a two-way capability. In other words, announcements can be made from the main office to all areas, but rooms that have call buttons can also contact the main office. Examples of intercom system brands include Telecor, Rauland, DuKane, and Bogan. To ensure that your intercom system is effective, consider the following questions.

Are call buttons visible and accessible in all rooms? Too often, we find call buttons that are obstructed or difficult to locate (see Figure 4.3). Schools can increase visibility by marking call buttons with red borders.

Is your intercom system programmed correctly? Test this important aspect by pushing a button from classrooms, offices, gymnasiums, and conference rooms. Can the main office correctly identify that room? If not, consider creating a conversion chart that can

FIGURE 4.2 Volume Dial 2.

be placed by the main unit. Contact your sound vendor to schedule an appointment to accurately program the system.

Does your intercom system have a duress (panic) feature? Approximately 50 percent of the systems we test have a panic feature that activates when the call button is hit and held. In rare occasions, the panic feature is activated when the button is pushed three times. For the sake of simplicity, the hit and hold option is preferable. When this feature is activated, the main office receives a different signal, such as a quicker sequence of tones. If the panic feature is activated, main office staff should recognize that an emergency incident is occurring and refrain from attempting to have a conversation with the originating room. Instead, main office staff should immediately dispatch designated response personnel to the location. In this situation, accurate programming becomes an absolute necessity.

Two-Way Radios

Two-way radios are one of the most effective means of on-site communications. They provide one-button, instant communications with an entire group of individuals across a campus. To ensure that your two-way radio system is effective, consider the following questions.

Do you have walkie-talkies or two-way radios? Making a distinction may sound petty, but can be critical. Walkie-talkies can be purchased at a department store, are made of

FIGURE 4.3 Intercom Call Button (Below Poster and Behind Books).

inexpensive materials, and generally run on basic batteries. In addition, the frequencies they utilize are common band. In other words, the local construction workers or taxi company may also use common band frequencies. Imagine hearing one of those individuals hurl an expletive that is received on the walkie-talkies your recess monitors are carrying near young students. Even worse, imagine attempting to communicate internally during an emergency only to experience interruption due to external cross-talk. Two-way radios, on the other hand, tend to be far more durable, run on lithium ion batteries, and require a frequency license that provides private, in-house communication.

Are your two-way radios Federal Communication Council (FCC) compliant? In January 2013, the FCC required school two-way radios to move to a digital, narrow-banding frequency.

Who is required to carry a two-way radio? All administrators, facilities personnel, and staff members that monitor student movement should be required to carry two-way radios. This practice should be documented, disseminated, and tested. Due to wardrobe limitations, female staff members generally have a more difficult time complying with this practice. The two most common objections include: 1) "I don't wear a belt so it is difficult to keep my two-way radio with me," and 2) "Two-way radios are too big and bulky to carry around." The first objection can be overcome with accessories such as strap holsters (see Figure 4.4). The second objection can be overcome with a little perspective. Challenge the objector to watch a movie that was made in the 1970s. That person will be reminded that just one generation ago two-way radios used to be the size of small suitcases and had antennas that scraped ceilings.

Cellular Phones

Despite society's penchant to be emotionally tied to personal cellular telephones, these devices should never be viewed as the primary means of emergency communications. Consider the physical education (PE) teacher who is monitoring a class on an athletic field. If one of the students has a medical incident, the PE teacher that is relying primarily on a cellular phone must wake up the phone, unlock the phone, press the icon that brings up a dial pad, dial the school's 10-digit number, and hope that the call does not go to a menu

FIGURE 4.4 Radio Strap Holster.

or voicemail. If it does, the PE teacher must send a runner to the building to get help while precious seconds tick away. If emergency responders arrive a heart beat too late, lives will never be the same. And, the next day, the PE teacher will carry a two-way radio.

Now consider a staff member in the main office who has just notified staff inside the building of a lockdown situation. Remembering that there are also people on the athletic field, that person must now look for the PE teacher's cellular phone number, dial 10 digits, and hope that the call does not result in voicemail. Cellular phones are an outstanding secondary means of emergency communication, but should never be the primary option. Take steps to have your staff members identify and get used to utilizing a more reliable means of emergency communication.

The wild card aspects of cellular phones can be addressed to some extent. For example, all personnel should be encouraged to program ICE information into personal cellular phones. ICE stands for "In Case of Emergency." For those that have smartphones, ICE applications can be downloaded from your app store at little or no cost. This application will permit users to store primary and secondary contact numbers, as well as personal information that could significantly aid emergency responders. Significant information may involve medical conditions, allergies, or a decision to be an organ and tissue donor. Most handset providers have developed programmable workarounds so that ICE can be accessed even if the phone is locked. For those that do not have smartphones, simply access your contact list and add a listing for ICE. In fact, many handsets have a slot pre-programmed for ICE.

More and more cellular phone applications are being offered and will be introduced to make your smartphone a safety tool. Many of these applications make use of the Global Positioning System (GPS) component of the cellular phone. Some provide users with capabilities such as having a personal panic button and accessing local databases for registered sex offenders.

Access Control

An effective approach to assessing an access control program involves taking inventory of existing practices and capabilities. From exterior doors to electrical cabinets, the challenge to restrict external and internal stakeholder access can seem daunting. How can access control be improved without greatly affecting the culture of the school and community? What access control practices are currently documented? Which practices need the most improvement? As you survey the following areas, remember to determine changes through collaboration and consensus. Communicate significant changes to internal and external stakeholders before implementation.

Closed Campus

A closed campus can be defined as one where exterior doors are closed and secured. Access to the facility is restricted to a monitored entrance or entrances. For schools in warm climates, such as Florida and Southern California, architectural designs can make attaining a closed campus difficult, if not impossible. For schools that cannot implement a closed campus practice, it is important to move toward a "close" campus. In other words, begin reducing the number of open exterior doors to as few as possible. For example, a school that currently operates with four points of unmonitored entry should strive for the ultimate goal of one monitored point of entry. If that scenario is presently unrealistic, the school should attempt to move from four points of entry to three, keeping the long-term goal of one in mind.

Door-propping poses the greatest challenge to closed campus practices. Too often, school administrators tolerate door propping due to the overwhelming number of exterior doors. Here is a typical conversation that I have with administrators:

> Admin: "We can't run a closed campus because we have 40 exterior doors. You can't stop them all from being propped open."
> Me: "Really? Are all 40 doors being propped open?"
> Admin: "Well, not all 40 …"
> Me: "How many are being propped open? Could it be that we could count on one hand how many are being propped open? Could it be that we already know which ones, that we already know why they are being propped open, and that, in most cases, we already know by whom?"

Please do not give this obstacle to school security more credit than it deserves. Applying the three Rs of school security is an effective method for stopping door propping. The three Rs are report, record, and remove. Twice a day (at a minimum), someone in the facility should be tasked with walking the perimeter of the building. When and if that person finds a door that is propped open, he/she should follow the first R and report the discovery. Whoever receives the report must follow the second R and record it. The benefit and purpose of recording is that it produces documented patterns. The final and most important R involves removing it. As simple as this sounds, we repeatedly find door props in schools that have been utilized for years and never removed. Failure to remove door props can often be the result of a bystander approach to the problem. In this phenomenon, people adopt the belief that removing door props is worthless because those who are propping doors will always find another way to prop them. This is completely illogical. Imagine if you were standing with a law enforcement officer and witnessed a criminal act. You would expect the police officer to respond. It would not make sense if the officer considered the situation, shrugged, and stated, "Well, I could stop this incident, but there will always be crime in America." Willingness to do nothing might be the greater crime. The three Rs of school security also apply when addressing graffiti and tagging.

For those schools that cannot practice a closed campus for one reason or another, we recommend keeping the campus as closed as possible. Strive to restrict access to the fewest entry points and make efforts to monitor those entry points. Above all, place a focus on accounting for students. If the school permits students to leave for lunch, require those students who have that privilege to register a cellular telephone number. Group those student numbers in a mass notification segment that can alert students who have left the campus. Then, should a situation arise where it would be unsafe to return to the property, the school can notify students with detailed response instructions.

Electronic Access Control

Electronic access control systems offer a number of advantages over conventional locks and keys. Cards, fobs, keypads, and sometimes biometric sensors unlock doors in such systems. Cards seem generally to be the key of choice in pre-K–12 schools. Administrators, faculty, staff, and a few students with responsibilities requiring access after-hours might have card access to the building.

A cardholder can swipe a card with a magnetic strip through a reader or present a proximity card to a reader. Information coded onto the magnetic strip or an integrated circuit inside the proximity card identifies the cardholder to the system, which looks for the name in a database. If that name has permission to enter that door, the system unlocks the door. This rendering of the process assumes that the individual identified by the card is the person using the card. Facilities that need a higher level of security might provide a keypad for the individual to enter a code by hand after swiping or presenting the card.

Electronic access control systems offer three advantages: easy re-keying, monitoring who visits after-hours, and limiting where those in the building can go after-hours. When someone loses a key or keys to a school building, facilities personnel must re-key all of the affected locks and make new keys for everyone that needs a key to those doors. It can be very expensive and time consuming. Furthermore, key control, a term that describes the methods utilized to ensure that specific keys are given to authorized individuals, is notoriously difficult. It is not uncommon for a school to find that several generations of family have keys to the building. When an electronic access control card goes missing, the system administrator simply disables the card and issues a new one. It is, by contrast, inexpensive and fast.

Electronic systems record who enters along with the time and date. The system administrator can monitor that log and look for anomalies. If a staff member with access privileges related to a weekly after-school activity returns to school every evening, the administrator might ask for an explanation. It is also possible to control where in the building those with access cards can go. Electronic systems can enable cardholders to enter any door or just one door. Senior administrators, maintenance, and a limited number of others could receive access to all doors. Faculty members might be limited to doors leading into their departments. Complementary access control measures, such as hallway gates, could prevent access to other areas of the school as well. An administrator might set access card codes to limit after-hours student access to the gymnasium, cafeteria, or another room where a student activity is scheduled. The administrator could also limit access to a particular day of the week between certain hours.

Finally, electronic access control systems can secure interior rooms such as those with administrative computers housing confidential information or science laboratories with dangerous chemicals or equipment. The system will monitor access attempts and can be set to report the name of anyone trying to enter without authorization, something an administrator should investigate.

Credentials such as cards and fobs may soon be replaced with cellular smartphones that rely on near field communications (NFC). This technology is based on radio frequency identification standards. Compared to cards and fobs, personal smartphones are less likely to be lost and less likely to be borrowed.

Locked/Secured Vestibule

Many pre-K–12 schools have changed their main entrances to enhance access control capabilities. They have added locked vestibules inside the main entry. At the beginning of the school day when students arrive, the vestibule doors can be opened to allow free access while designated staff members monitor the arrival of students. Once the day begins, however, a custodian would lock the doors to the vestibule. When visitors arrive, they would pass through the outer entrance doors, which allows them to get out of the weather. To continue through the vestibule doors, visitors would have to discuss their business with security personnel or someone trained in visitor management practices in the main office.

If possible, the vestibule might contain a counter with a pass-through window into the main office. If not, office and visitor could communicate with a video camera and an intercom. Security personnel or a designated staff member from the office would escort visitors cleared for admittance to the main office where they would be recorded in the visitor management system and receive a visitor badge attached to a colored, break-away lanyard.

At the end of the school day, the vestibule doors would once again open, this time to allow students an unencumbered exit while designated staff members monitor the dismissal of students.

Visitor Management Procedures

Visitor management has traditionally been one of the weak spots in the school's access control program. Visitor registries were completed by the visitor on the honor system and seldom checked by office staff. There was no way to verify if the visitor wrote his or her actual name and, often times, the visitor's handwriting was not legible.

To make matters worse, schools asked visitors to wear stickers. Numerous clothing fabrics, however, can be damaged by stickers (see Figures 4.5 and 4.6) or do not support the adhesion necessary to keep the sticker in place. Why attempt to utilize something that has such low security value? In most instances, stickers have been chosen in an effort to reduce the cost of replacing visitor badges that were issued to visitors but rarely returned by visitors.

Today's visitor management software systems automate the process of vetting visitors and printing visitor badges. When a visitor arrives in the office, office personnel ask for a driver's license or another government-issued identification credential. The visitor management system hardware can scan the ID and screen the visitor's identity by searching databases of registered sex offenders, restraining orders, and other problems. The system

FIGURE 4.5 Visitor Sign.

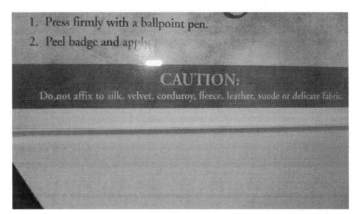

FIGURE 4.6 Visitor Sticker.

administrator can also manually enter information denying admission to certain visitors. A parent with sole custody, for instance, might ask the system administrator not to allow a noncustodial parent to visit or pick a child up from school. The administrator would, in turn, enter that information into the system. If a noncustodial parent attempted to visit the child, the system would flag the restriction. Ideally, the system would simultaneously notify designated personnel authorized to address such instances.

Once the system has cleared the visitor, as noted above, he or she would receive a visitor badge attached to a colored, break-away lanyard to wear at all times while at school. If the system produces a sticker, we recommend leaving the backing on the sticker and placing it into a clear badge holder attached to a colored, break-away lanyard.

To verify that a visitor has left, many districts require the return of the badge and lanyard to the office at the end of the visit. This verification can be particularly important to first responders as they attempt to account for persons in the school. To ensure that the return takes place, the system administrator can keep the visitor's driver's license or other ID credential until the visitor's credential is returned.

Faculty, Administrator, Staff and Student IDs

For a visitor management system to work optimally, everyone in the school building, with the exception of elementary-aged students, must wear an ID on a colored, break-away lanyard. The goal of the system is to identify everyone in the school by name and function. The badges might say: "Hi, my name is Mike Smith. I'm a teacher." Teachers might wear badges attached to red, break-away lanyards. Administrators might wear badges attached to blue, break-away lanyards. Students might wear badges attached to green, break-away lanyards. And visitors might wear badges attached to fluorescent green, break-away lanyards.

If everyone wears badges and lanyards, anyone without a badge and lanyard would stand out. Administrators, faculty and staff would approach anyone without a badge, explain the policy and escort the individual to the office. Training (see chapter 6, "Preparing Your People") can be provided to enable people to carry out the policy without giving offense.

To make it seem less onerous to those who do not want to wear the badge, the friendly messages on the badge would make it easier for everyone within the school community to get to know each other. Who can object to that?

Classroom Door Locks

Classroom doors play a significant role in slowing adversarial movement. All classroom doors should have locking mechanisms and, for the sake of consistency, they should all have the same kind of locking mechanisms.

The majority of schools have classroom doors that lock from the outside. Almost all classroom doors swing open into the hallway. This combination of features presents risk to the teacher that has to step into the hallway to secure the classroom during an event that necessitates a lockdown. If the teacher cannot immediately locate the key to lock the door, the entire situation becomes even more complicated.

Consider the following potential solutions to reduce this risk. To avoid expenditures, some schools have dealt with this issue by keeping classroom doors both locked and open. A manufacturer-designed hold open feature in the door closer is the best way to keep the door open. In the event of a lockdown, the teacher simply reaches for the door handle and pulls the door closed. Other schools have decided to keep doors closed and locked at all times. Obviously, this option can be disruptive to a teacher from an operational standpoint if students are frequently leaving and returning to the classroom.

Schools that have some funding sometimes pursue an option that involves replacing locking mechanisms that lock from the outside with locking mechanisms that lock from the inside with a push button or a thumb turn. This replacement option aids in timeliness because it does not require a key to operate. This solution, however, presents an additional risk in that an unauthorized person can enter an unsecured room and lock out staff members. Schools that have an ample supply of funding are beginning to pursue options that permit all classroom doors to be locked electronically with the push of a button.

The best option, taking into account both budget and operations, involves replacing locking mechanisms that lock from the outside with locking mechanisms that lock from the inside with a key. In this scenario, teachers are required to keep that key on the staff ID lanyard so that it can be accessed and utilized as efficiently as possible.

The riskiest options employed today rely on relatively inexpensive aftermarket products that cover strike plates, prop open locked doors, or prevent ingress from the hallway. The products that cover strike plates, such as magnets or moveable plastic pieces, must be removed in order for the door to freely lock. The products that prop doors open must be kicked out of the way before the door can be secured. The products that prevent ingress from the hallway often require prior knowledge to utilize. Beware of these kinds of quick-fix solutions. These products can get jammed in the door frame or wedged underneath the door, and actually prevent doors from securing. They can be used by adversaries to keep authorized individuals from entering. They may violate fire egress codes or ADA codes. Consult fire marshals and door hardware manufacturers to review legitimate solutions.

Secured Interior Rooms

Effective interior access control depends on securing every vacant room in the facility. In addition, unassigned lockers, electrical cabinets, technology device carts, and cabinets and desk drawers that have locking mechanisms should be secured.

Personal convenience motivates staff members to leave empty classrooms and offices unlocked and accessible. We often find that staff members leave personal items, such as purses and handheld electronic devices, on desks in unattended rooms. Locked doors prevent theft and unmonitored activities.

Custodial closets and utility rooms should never be accessible without a key. Restricting access to these areas keeps unauthorized persons from entering rooms that present various dangers.

The advent of technology devices, such as laptops and tablets, supplied by the school for educational purposes presents an attractive target for thieves. These devices should be stored in secured interior rooms. Technology device carts and other expensive items, such as shared printers, should never be stationed in common areas, such as hallways.

Vehicle Barriers

Vehicle barriers can protect students, staff, and visitors on athletic fields, in playground areas, near building entries, and at other pedestrian areas. Do not wait for an accident to occur before addressing this area of access control. How can schools proactively address this vulnerability?

Bollards, short vertical posts that are sunk into the ground, generally provide the best kind of vehicle barriers (see Figure 4.7). Alternative barrier types vary in effectiveness. For example, while cement planters provide sturdy obstruction, they also can send projectiles flying if targeted with improvised explosive devices (IEDs). Other options, such as traffic barricades, offer more value in visually deterring vehicle access than in actually stopping vehicles. Schools located in cold weather climates often avoid use of bollards due to the frequent need for snowplows to push snow from parking areas and walkways onto athletic fields. As a result, some vendors are now carrying various kinds of removable bollards.

Perimeter fencing provides good border definition and can deter unauthorized persons from accessing the property, but rarely supplies the kind of protection required to prevent vehicle access.

Discouraging Roof Access

Single story school buildings are especially vulnerable to unauthorized roof access. Building features such as decorative stone construction, trees planted near the facility, and utility piping often exacerbate the situation. In addition to eyewitness accounts, often from concerned

FIGURE 4.7 Bollards.

neighbors, alcohol paraphernalia and vandalism provide evidence that unauthorized persons have accessed the roof. What remedies can be employed to discourage roof access?

The best plan of action involves collaboration and consensus. Decisions made in a vacuum can be dangerous. For example, one school that experienced a high frequency of unauthorized roof access delegated decision making authority to the facilities personnel. One staff member suggested putting grease on the piping so that trespassers would slip. While there may be some merit to the suggestion, the potential safety risks far outweigh the benefits. Instead of acting on one person's opinion, administrators decided to convene the Security Planning Team. In short order, the group determined to make use of sheet metal bolted tightly to the brick wall (see Figures 4.8 and 4.9). The school has not had unauthorized roof access since moving forward with this collaborative solution.

Sometimes solutions simply involve the use of common sense. Obvious solutions include removing tree branches that overhang the building, storing ladders in secured areas, and installing slats in chain link fences that are close to the building. In other cases, solutions may require expert assistance or even trial-and-error initiatives. No matter what the situation, remember the safety net provided by collaboration and consensus.

Occasionally, a security assessment will discover that interior roof access points present an area of vulnerability. One school had several, accessible roof hatches that were not secured and, in investigating the matter, found that a vendor had accidentally left the hatches in that condition. The school has now implemented security practices that hold both internal and external stakeholders accountable.

Video Surveillance

The security industry lacks codes and standards that apply to the design and use of physical security devices and systems, such as video surveillance. Even industry experts and

FIGURE 4.8 Roof Access Before.

FIGURE 4.9 Roof Access After.

vendors in the school arena seem to have a hard time agreeing on best practices. As a result, schools tend to approach the use of video surveillance systems in very different ways. Security assessments uncover everything from the use of fake cameras to state-of-the-art systems that are almost too advanced for those that manage them.

For liability reasons, fake cameras should never be used. Someone that experiences victimization in the field of view of a fake camera may come to the school with the hope of ultimately receiving justice based on accessing recorded video. When the victimized person discovers that the system is not functional, a law suit may potentially be filed against the school because the fake camera conveyed an expectation of security. For the same reason, functional cameras must also have recording capabilities. The need to review recorded video for evidentiary purposes depends on it. Schools that utilize a single camera at the main entry but lack recording capabilities should add a recording device immediately. Consider nothing less than a digital video recorder (DVR).

Video surveillance systems provide value in several areas: deterrence, surveillance, assessment, and forensics. As mentioned earlier, the deterrence element is difficult to measure. We do know, however, that those who engage in criminal behavior sometimes escape being identified by vandalizing cameras or concealing their identity by wearing things such as masks or hoodies.

The surveillance aspect of video surveillance occurs when a security officer or designated staff member watches a monitor in the hopes of detecting an event happening in real time. Unfortunately, tests have shown that the likelihood of being successful in this endeavor is very low. It is worth noting that success rates increase as monitoring time spans decrease. In other words, the person tasked with monitoring during a five-minute passing period will be more successful than the person monitoring a three-hour, after-school event.

The assessment aspect of video surveillance takes place when a security officer or designated staff member receives notification about a potential incident. For example, a lunch monitor may see suspicious activity across the cafeteria and communicate that information to someone that has access to the monitor. That person can, in turn, look at a specific camera view to more accurately assess the situation before deciding how to respond. The advent of video analytics has significantly improved the value of the assessment aspect. Video analytics employ software and algorithms that automatically detect certain kinds of motion occurring in a fixed-background scene. When those predetermined movements take place, the system sends notification to security personnel or a designated staff member.

The forensics aspect of video surveillance accounts for all of the recorded information. This aspect also represents the chief value of a school's video surveillance system. School administrators, security personnel, and local first responders all depend heavily on recorded information. High profile incidents such as the Boston Marathon bombings in April 2013 illustrate how vital forensics can be to investigators.

Since people are the highest priority asset category, video surveillance systems should be designed from the inside out. The school that installs exterior cameras first has inadvertently determined that the things category of asset prioritization is more important than the people category. A basic video surveillance system should begin with the installation of cameras at main entries. These cameras ensure that all persons entering and leaving the building will be recorded with a time and date stamp. Next, install cameras in interior areas that are difficult to monitor or have experienced discipline incidents. After addressing the important interior areas, pursue strategic placement of exterior cameras. All cameras should be added based on need and collaborative input. Standard recording systems range from DVRs to network video recorders (NVRs). NVRs generally get paired with centralized Internet protocol cameras.

Finally, ensure that your video surveillance system has remote monitoring capabilities. The ability to monitor cameras remotely can be granted to individuals, such as authorized staff members and local law enforcement officers. Images can be accessed with devices ranging from desktop computers to smartphones.

Intrusion Detection

An intrusion detection or security alarm system seeks to detect unauthorized entry into a school building or designated interior area. Standard systems consist of door contacts and motion sensors. Systems should be monitored at a central station. In instances where staff members have the ability to arm and disarm the system, schools should issue individual codes for audit trail purposes. Maintain a level of accountability by reviewing audit reports on a routine basis to look for anomalies.

Intrusion detection systems can be optimized by installing panic buttons in key areas such as the main office. Ensure that staff members stationed in those areas test panic buttons at least once each semester.

Key Concept–Testing Physical Security Devices

20th-century loss prevention expert Saul Astor coined several laws of loss prevention. We have adapted one of those laws to focus specifically on schools. It states, "School security programs and systems tend to fail only upon being tested."[1] In other words, schools assume that because they have visitor sign-in procedures, all visitors must be following them. Unfortunately, a casual glance at the typical visitor registry will find that names are difficult to read and that many visitors never signed-out of the building. Where security equipment is concerned, a simple audit of the video surveillance system often finds cameras that are not functional and fields of view that are not optimal. The way to break this law of loss prevention is by resolving never to let the bad guy or the victim be first to test your security.

Consider system testing similar to preventative maintenance in ensuring the reliability of your investment in security. Good planning is the unshakeable foundation of effective testing. Your security plan should specify both the scope and the frequency for testing programs and systems. In an environment given to academic testing and governed by safety code compliance, security program testing should feel natural. From regularly scheduled tests to periodic spot checks, most testing can be conducted by school personnel. For situations that are more complicated or where greater objectivity is required, schools can call on the services of vendors and consultants. In either case, make sure to document methods of testing and actual test results. If testing is not documented, the argument can be made in a court of law that testing never occurred.

Planning may be testing's foundation, but implementation is the key. Movement from checklists to action requires training and—occasionally—cultural change. Neither training nor cultural change will be realized to any measureable degree without stakeholder support. It is never enough to simply announce a new practice. Success will be determined by whether or not that practice is actually adopted. Before we conducted an assessment of a middle school, we were told that administration had recently adopted new visitor management procedures. Upon arriving at the school, we were surprised to find that the administrative assistant at the main desk did not ask us to follow the new process. She had no idea that the purpose of our visit was to review security measures. When we mentioned that we had heard talk of a new visitor management process, she explained that she found it to be unnecessarily cumbersome. She then waved us through with a smile. School administrators had laid a solid foundation, but lack of stakeholder support had rendered the procedures ineffective.

Five methods—visual inspection, walk test, performance test, personnel interviews, and staff/student questionnaires—can contribute to a successful testing program.

Visual Inspection

Visual inspection involves simple examination of the specific systems and measures that make up your security program. Visit the campus at night and rate exterior lighting at building entries and in parking areas. Look at foliage and shrubbery in those same areas and decide whether or not trimming would help promote better natural surveillance. Push open exterior doors to determine if they close and latch properly. While conducting an assessment, we visually inspected a classroom to ensure that the intercom call button was visible and accessible. When we could not locate the call button, we asked the teacher to point us in the right direction. The teacher turned out to be a substitute and had no idea where the button was located. After some searching, we found it behind a poster! Document your results so that everything from investigating potential solutions to issuing work orders can begin sooner than later.

Walk Test

Closely aligned to the visual inspection, schools should also conduct routine walk tests. The walk test seeks to determine whether or not systems and measures are really functioning. Can someone at a video surveillance monitor track individuals as they move throughout the facility? What things are safety monitors looking for when moving through assigned patrol routes? Determine the items that should be tested, make a checklist that addresses those items, and get in motion. Once again, document all of the findings and take corrective actions.

Performance Test

Whereas the preceding tests are friendly in nature, the performance test can be labeled as adversarial. In other words, the performance test adopts a black-hatting technique (adversarial approach) and attempts to defeat existing security measures. For example, some schools ask us to try to gain access to buildings without following visitor management procedures. We arrive on campus in casual attire with the intention of gaining access through doors that should be closed and locked. When we gain entry—and we always do—we attempt to access key internal areas, such as boiler rooms and administration offices, without being challenged. The results of this kind of limited scope performance testing should be documented as well.

Personnel Interviews

School staff, students, and third-party entities that utilize your facilities outside of normal operations possess critical information about the merits of your security measures. Do not be afraid to ask these stakeholders about the effectiveness of your program. You may not want to hear the truth, but you need to hear it. A high school teacher once shared an experience where she requested access to a restricted area. A facilities person was dispatched to unlock the door for her. Without knowing the facilities person on a first name basis or even asking for a key, she was surprised to be handed one for future use. That teacher expressed to us her amazement at the school's lack of key control practices. Please remember, substantive information from these interviews should be documented.

Staff/Student Questionnaires

In cases where it makes more sense to cast a wider net than conducting individual interviews, distributing student/staff questionnaires may be the course to pursue. Periodically surveying stakeholder groups raises security awareness, encourages compliance with existing security practices, and uncovers weaknesses in security measures. On one occasion, a student clearly described the parking area where drugs were being sold as the place on campus he felt least safe. In another instance, a student commented on the ease with which students could avoid the morning arrival process of going through a portal magnetometer (walk-through metal detector). After reviewing completed questionnaires, actionable items and areas of concern should be documented and addressed collaboratively.

Crime Prevention Through Environmental Design

Effective school building security also makes use of a design discipline called Crime Prevention Through Environment Design or CPTED (pronounced SEP-ted). Pioneered by Oscar Newman in his 1973 book, *Defensible Space*, CPTED applies proven principles to site and building design.[2] The key CPTED principle is that criminals want to work in private, without being seen; they feel uncomfortable when people are able to see them. Conversely, people typically enjoy being around other people. They feel safe in the company of others.

The Centers for Disease Control recommends CPTED, describing it as a focus on "reducing crime opportunities and on promoting positive social behavior. It does not change the motivation of individual perpetrators."[3]

CPTED school sites and buildings play to these goals by facilitating natural access control and natural surveillance, while clearly identifying gathering areas in locations that provide sightlines across the property and making those areas easily accessible. Natural access control and natural surveillance fit together to reduce criminal behavior.

Natural access control begins at the perimeter of the property with a design element, sometimes referred to as border definition, which signals the change of ownership from public grounds to school grounds. The element could be an attractive fence—wrought iron, perhaps—or landscaping. The choice would depend upon the risk and vulnerability assessment. A school located near or in a high crime area might choose the fence. A school in a relatively crime-free area might choose landscaping—a shrubbery hedge or a line of trees. Experts caution that shrubbery should be no more than three feet high so as not to provide a hiding place. That is an especially important rule for shrubbery placed against the exterior of the school building, near windows and entries. Tall bushes conceal. Short ones do not. In the same way, tree limbs should be cleared to a minimum height of eight feet. Clear lines of sight, especially at entries, in parking lots, and along walkways, contribute to the principle of natural surveillance.

The orientation of the school building on the site should allow clear sightlines to the edges of the property from windows in the main office, faculty lounge, guidance counselor offices, the library, and classrooms—all around the building. Again, the idea is to use the site and the buildings on the site to signal anyone who comes onto the property that he or she is clearly visible to people in the school building and on the grounds. This adds natural surveillance to natural access control.

The CDC suggests windows that allow views out from the inside and in from the outside. Students will feel safer knowing that teachers and administrators in lounges, offices, and meeting rooms throughout the school can see out onto and across the parking areas and grounds. Criminals and vandals likewise will feel ill at ease being so easily seen.

The CDC recommends signage and well-marked entrances and exits to direct people easily and efficiently from place to place. Clearly marked directional signs and clearly defined spaces may also include décor, perhaps created by students, that shows school pride. School buildings that host community voters when school is in session can post signs, hang banners, and make clear distinctions between public and restricted areas in an attempt to control access.

Further, maintenance is important to CPTED's access control concepts. Experience with CPTED shows that well-maintained grounds where graffiti is removed immediately and buildings, light fixtures, and corridors are kept in constant repair send a message to criminals and vandals. The message: "We take pride in these spaces. All of us are constantly watching to make sure they remain in good repair. If you are contemplating a crime or an act of vandalism, any number of people will likely see you and send someone in authority to stop you."

Two more natural surveillance ideas round out these concepts: place safe activities in unsafe places and place unsafe activities in safe places. That sounds counter-intuitive. Why would anyone put a safe activity in an unsafe place? Suppose a small grassy area near the parking lot just outside the school's cafeteria has grown a little rundown. Some students go outside at lunch to smoke. Fights occasionally break out in this area. Bullying incidents are being reported there in growing numbers. Most students avoid the area out of a little bit of fear. Now give the area a makeover. Install attractive outdoor seating. Put in some attractive new landscaping, along with stands that can hold student artwork. Invite teachers to hold classes and study halls there on nice days. Ask teachers and security to stroll through the area regularly. Schedule club meetings in that place. Groups going on field trips can meet there before getting on the bus. Make sure that something is always going on with a number of people. These safe activities will drive out the unsafe activities.

What about the converse? Place unsafe activities in safe areas. Many schools have had problems with students smoking, bullying and some other forms of violence in restrooms over the years. Some have gained control by removing the doors and orienting the interior walls to block views of the urinals and stalls. Such a design allows smoke and loud threatening talk to move into the hallway outside the restroom where there are a lot of people. Passing teachers, administrators, and staff will smell the smoke and hear any loud talk. Offenders will realize that there will not be time to conceal wrong behaviors when someone approaches.

People—both students and adults—inside and outside of the building help to maintain order by their presence and ability to see and understand what is going on. Add to that a regular—though not heavy handed—patrolling security monitor, and natural surveillance and natural access control really can make students, faculty, administrators, and staff feel safer while giving criminals and vandals reasons to look for an easier target.

Conclusion

Maybe the worst that can happen will not happen to a school in your district. But any number of bad things will happen in some, if not all, of the schools for which you are responsible over the course of your career as a school security professional. The right physical security measures in the right place at the right time will mitigate the injuries or property damage that bad events might otherwise cause. Mastering the physical security continuum of deterrence, detection, communications, delay, and response is the key to preparing a defense against vandals, thieves, bullies, arsonists, and other kinds of criminals that eventually make their way to every school.

Think about deterrence, for instance. Access controlled doors, visible security cameras, signs informing people security cameras are protecting the school, patrolling security officers, and a CPTED-based design that fosters natural surveillance will deter some criminals.

Every now and then, however, a criminal will decide to take on the school's physical security defenses. That is where detection comes into play. Access controlled doors with alarms, regularly monitored cameras, an effective visitor management system with color coded badges, and patrolling security officers will all help detect a person who does not belong.

When that happens, the communications system informs administrators, security personnel, and—if necessary—the police, to carry out various responses. Locked doors and barriers, both during the day and at night, will delay an intruder while the security team mounts the response.

In short, deterrence, detection, communications, delay, and response provide a road-map for analyzing and preparing a defense against virtually any kind of security threat. Now is the time to proactively and collaboratively secure your environment.

References

1. Saul D. Astor, *Loss Prevention: Controls and Concepts* (Boston: Butterworth-Heinemann Ltd., 1978).

2. Newman, Oscar, Defensible Space; Crime Prevention Through Urban Design, Macmillan Publishing Co (October 1973).

3. http://www.cdc.gov/violenceprevention/youthviolence/cpted.html.

Influencing Behavior

This chapter includes contributions from Robin Hattersley Gray, editor of Campus Safety magazine, and Sheri Jacobs, school safety consultant, school administrator, and former assistant director of the Minnesota School Safety Center.

Introduction

Mrs. Hetrick has a heart for the underdog. At least once each year she asks her children if they know of anyone in their grade that has been mistreated or left out by the other students. She then encourages her children to be especially kind to that classmate. The Hetrick family recently moved to a new city and school district and one evening, somewhere between the meatloaf and chocolate pudding, Mrs. Hetrick decided to enquire about this year's students. The oldest child, Joshua, was reluctant to respond to the question. Fifth grade in a new school was hard enough, but the move several weeks earlier to the middle school for sixth grade was even more difficult. He missed his old friends and was not being very successful in making new ones. Slight of stature, trying to get used to wearing glasses, and regularly lugging around a trumpet case, Joshua was finding himself the target of teasers. When Mrs. Hetrick pressed the question with him, Joshua broke down in tears. "It's me. It's me," he said.

The Hetricks were stunned. Joshua has always been a friendly and likeable child. His conduct at home gave no indication that he was having problems. Later that evening, Mr. Hetrick sat down with Joshua to get the details about what was happening. Joshua described teasing about his name, his athletic ability, and his class participation. Mr. Hetrick asked if any of the teasing involved physical contact. Joshua hung his head in shame and related the details of how a boy in his gym class slapped him on the back of the head and called him an expletive almost every day in an unsupervised area of the locker room. Mr. Hetrick's face turned red. His son was being bullied and something had to be done immediately.

This family was lucky to hear about bullying. Most families will not. Not from victims. The bullying victim and the sexual abuse victim are ashamed to talk about it. The bully and the sexual abuser know that his or her behavior is wrong and will not talk about it. The drug user knows his behavior is wrong and will not come forward either.

That is not the whole picture. An unacceptable percentage of K–12 students across your district has the same problems but will not ask for help. At the same time, percentages of bystanders are living in fear that they may be victimized. You have to figure out how to find both the victims and the victimizers—and help them.

Losing our children academically, emotionally, and physically, as a result of unprecedented, unknown bullying behavior is a tragedy of staggering proportions. Yet schools are both funded and focused on student success as measured by test scores and whether or not schools make their annual yearly progress. What would happen, one may wonder, if the reverse were true: if schools were funded and focused on making and keeping our learning environments bully-free zones?

It is estimated that 160,000 children miss school every day for fear of an attack or act of intimidation while at school. Today, American schools harbor approximately 2.1 million bullies and 2.7 million of their victims.[1] Criminologist Stuart Henry states:

Our nation's schools should be safe havens for teaching and learning, free of crime and violence. Any instance of crime or violence at school not only affects the individuals involved but also may disrupt the educational process and affect bystanders, the school itself, and the surrounding community.

Students are more likely to experience success and growth in all areas of their life if they feel safe to learn. For many students, the safest place for them to be is at school.[2] So, as a nation, shouldn't we provide our students with a safe school environment? Researcher Karen M Hawkins states:

The goal of any school is to be a place of learning and for students to learn, they must feel emotionally and physically secure. In an arena where lethal shootings can share headlines with teasing and bullying, safety for school children is a critical challenge of educators.[3]

This chapter will focus on providing insight into the nature of bullying, practical suggestions for your consideration and potential implementation, and resources for building a safe school community. It will also attempt to provide foundational information on dating violence. Even though the topic of substance abuse is closely related, it is too vast to consider in this publication.

Defining Bullying

Best practices in bullying prevention require school district leaders to place a priority on mitigating incidents of acts of aggression, sexual harassment, and physical or emotional harm to another student. In *Schools Where Everyone Belongs*, Stan and Julia Davis offer a succinct, yet comprehensive definition of bullying.

Bullying is a form of social interaction—not necessarily long-standing—in which a more dominant individual (the bully) exhibits aggressive behavior that is intended to, and does, in fact, cause distress to a less dominant individual (the victim). The aggressive behavior may take the form of a direct physical and/or verbal attack or may be indirect. More than one bully and more than one victim may participate in the interaction.[4]

The bully may also be referred to as a "bully-victim" or a "bully *as* victim." Both the bully and the bully-victim may not be that different from each other or may be one and the same.[5] This much discussed relationship between bully and victim is well defined as follows:[6]

- Peskin et al (2006)[a] identify bully-victims as those who are both bullied by others and who bully others. Peskin further suggests that children may also be a victim at home and a bully at school.
- Taking this a step further than childhood bullying behavior, a child could have been a victim throughout childhood and suddenly act out aggressively as s/he moves into adolescence or adulthood. Perren (2005)[b] states that research has found that children who bully others but are also bullied themselves form a sub-group that is called "aggressive victims," "proactive victims," or "bully-victims."
- However, sub-groups may also overlap in terms of bullying characteristics. In other words, Rigby (1993)[c] proposes that, "the tendency to bully others and the tendency to be victimized by others are not polar opposites. It is important to realize that although bullies and victims are on the opposite ends of the spectrum, they really are not all that different."

The Bystander

In addition to the bully and the bullied (bully-victim), there is often the bystander. Bullying interaction occurs once every seven minutes, with teachers rarely intervening in what they witness. In addition, in 88 percent of bullying incidents, peers are present (Morrison 2011)[6] . These powerful statistics reveal that a quick change in staff behavior can have a monumental impact. Interestingly, Morrison also states that in the majority of bullying episodes where peers are present and witness the behavior, the more likely it is that the bullying episode will be extended. However, in the majority of episodes (57 percent), peer intervention stops bullying within ten seconds, regardless of strategy.

For a better understanding of the bystander effect and its pervasiveness amongst both staff and students, consider the following two enlightening, research-based texts: 1) Barbara Coloroso's *The Bully, the Bullied, and the Bystander*, and 2) *Prior Knowledge of Potential School-Based Violence: Information Students Learn May Prevent a Targeted Attack*, US Secret Service and the US Department of Education (free online on at http://www.secretservice.gov/ntac/bystander_study.pdf). Also known as "The Bystander Study," this latter resource represents the third and final release from the collaborative research of the above stated agencies. The initial study, *The Safe School Initiative*, revealed ten key findings applicable to the bullying discussion:[7]

[a]Peskin, M., Tortolero, S., & Markham, C. (2006). Bullying and victimization among black and Hispanic adolescents. *Adolescence 41*(163), 467–484. Retrieved October, 2007.

[b]Perren, S. (2005). Bullying and delinquency in adolescence: victims' and perpetrators' family and peer relations. *Swiss Journal of Psychology, 64* (1), Retrieved September, 2006.

[c]Rigby, K. (1993). Dimensions of interpersonal relation among Australian children and implications for psychological well-being. *Journal of Social Psychology 133* (1), Retrieved October 2006.

Incidents of targeted violence at schools rarely were sudden impulsive acts.
Prior to most incidents, other people knew about the attacker's idea and/or plan to attack.
Most attackers did not threaten their targets directly prior to advancing the attack.
There was no useful or accurate "profile" of students who engaged in targeted school violence.
Most attackers engaged in some behavior prior to the incident that caused others concerns or indicated a need for help.
Most attackers had difficulty coping with significant losses or personal failures.
Moreover, many attackers had considered or attempted suicide.
Many attackers felt bullied, persecuted, or injured by others prior to the attack.
Most attackers had access to and had used weapons prior to the attack.
Despite prompt law enforcement responses, most shooting incidents were stopped by means other than law enforcement interventions.

Bullycide

The three studies conducted by the US Secret Service and the US Department of Education demonstrate that bullying is an integral contributing factor to school violence. In fact, if left to fester in relationships between students, or between students and staff, bullying often serves as the precursor to targeted violence.

In *Bullycide: Death at Playtime*, Neil Marr and Tim Field coined the term *bullycide*.[8] Bullycide is the suicidal act a student commits because, in his/her mind, it is less painful than going to school and being teased, taunted, and humiliated.

> These are the last words written in thirteen-year-old Vijay Singh's diary before he hung himself:
> I shall remember forever and will never forget:
> Monday: my money was taken.
> Tuesday: names called.
> Wednesday: my uniform torn.
> Thursday: my body pouring with blood.
> Friday: it's ended.
> Saturday: freedom.[9]

In 1999, one out of every thirteen US high school students reported making a suicide attempt in the last twelve months; in 2000, approximately 2,000 students succeeded (it is not known what percentage of these suicides were bullycides).[10] New bullying statistics from 2010 are reporting that there is a strong connection between bullying, being bullied, and suicide, according to a new study from the Yale School of Medicine. Some victims have even turned to public and viral arenas, such as YouTube, to tell their stories before committing suicide. Suicide rates are continuing to grow among adolescents, especially among middle school students. In fact, suicide rates among adolescents have grown by more than 50 percent in the past thirty years.[11]

Bullying vs. Harassment

Be careful in defining various forms of bullying behavior. People often make the mistake of using the terms sexual harassment and bullying interchangeably. These two behaviors are not necessarily the same. For example, bullying is not based on a student's gender—sexual harassment is. Additionally, bullying is not a violation of federal and state civil rights laws—sexual harassment is.[12] Bullying in itself is not illegal, but when it leads to an illegal activity, it is then punishable by law.

> *Per the US Department of Education's Office for Civil Rights (OCR), school districts are required to employ a Title IX Coordinator to handle potential violations of students' rights. This coordinator should be trained specifically in how to discern the difference between bullying behavior and harassment (sexual or otherwise). Additionally, both students and staff must receive sexual harassment training.[13]*

Street Law is a student-based training program for youth offenders on bullying and harassment, which is under the auspices of the Office of Juvenile Justice and Delinquency Prevention, US Department of Justice.[14] The program makes a plethora of resources available in reproducible format. It even includes a guide that teaches students to draft a student-designed bullying policy. Include students on the planning teams when drafting or updating district prevention policies. Incorporate resource materials, such as Street Law, into student training on harassment and bullying. The following instructional piece from *"What Does the Law say About Bullying?"* requires students to define bullying as it pertains to the law.[15]

Fact 1: Bullying is Often a form of Assault and, Therefore, Punishable by the Law

> *Assault is an intentional physical act or a threat of attack with a clear or obvious ability to carry out that threat, so that the victim feels danger of physical attack or harm. It is not necessary for actual injury to occur before a person can be charged with assault. The only requirement is that the person intended to do harm. People who are assaulted can bring criminal charges against their assailant or they can sue their wrongdoers in a civil court.*

Fact 2: Bullying is Often a Form of Sexual Harassment, and Therefore, Punishable by Law

> *Sexual harassment is unwelcome sexual advances, requests for sexual favors, and other verbal or physical conduct that is of a sexual nature that occurs in a workplace or a school. According to recent a Supreme Court case, school boards and school officials can be held responsible (sued) if the school leadership showed deliberate indifference to "student-on-student" harassment that was severe enough to prevent victims from enjoying educational opportunities. In a separate case, the Supreme Court ruled that students who were harassed by teachers could sue for damages (money in a lawsuit) from the school.*

Fact 3: Bullying also Breaks the Law when it Becomes
  Extortion (using threats to obtain the property of another);
  Hate acts or crimes;
  Weapons possession;
  Murder;
  Arson (the deliberate and malicious burning of another person's property);
  Hazing;
  Rape or sexual assault;
  A violation of civil rights (may include bullying based on racial or ethnic prejudice or sexual harassment); and/or
  Slander (spoken expression about a person that is false and damages that person's reputation).
  Victims of sexual harassment can also sue their harassers directly
  Protect your school community by increasing understanding of both bullying and sexual harassment. Inform all school stakeholders on the stipulations of the law and on school district policies. Make a commitment to pursue this essential component of safe school operations.

Addressing the Bullying Problem

Brenda Morrison is one of the leading voices and international experts on bullying and restorative justice measures. Dr. Morrison defines bullying as a relationship problem in which an individual or group uses power aggressively to cause distress to another.[6] In other words, the child is trapped in an abusive situation and, like all abusive situations, the maltreatment will continue until intervention occurs.

  Dr. Morrison posits the following key points about understanding bullying:
  Bullying is a relationship problem that requires relationship solutions.
  Promoting a positive school climate reduces bullying and antisocial behavior.
  Whole school communities can teach relationship skills and educate hearts and minds.
  Three Rs to remember: respect, responsibility, reparation/restoration.
  In Dr. Morrison's webinar "Safe and Supportive Schools" (2011), she explicates the various forms of bullying and their incidence rates:

Physical Bullying	39 %
Verbal Bullying	59 %
Relational Bullying	50 %
Excluding others from the group, rolling of eyes, tossing of hair, ignoring and shunning, gossiping, spreading rumors, telling secrets, setting others up to look foolish, damaging friendships.	
Cyberbullying	17 %

Allan Beane, author of *Protect Your Child from Bullying* (also author of *The Bully Free Classroom*), writes from the perspective of fathering a son who was bullied in both middle and high school. He offers poignant suggestions for parents on how to identify and observe characteristics in their children that the child may not feel comfortable bringing up to them. The book is also applicable to school leaders, as it provides suggestions for handling various bullying behaviors.

In terms of prevalence, Dr. Beane states that incidences of bullying are quite consistent globally.[16] In the United States, it is estimated that 30 percent of teens (over 5.7 million) are involved in bullying as a bully, a target of bullying, or both.[17] A study of 15,000 US students in grades six through ten found that 17 percent of students reported having been bullied "sometimes or more often" during the school year. Approximately 19 percent said they bullied others "sometimes or more often," and 6 percent reported both bullying and being a victim of bullying. Six out of ten American students witness bullying at least once a day.[18]

Bullying Prevention Programming

Bullying prevention is an integral part of a comprehensive, effective school security program. Carefully plan, develop, and train prevention protocols. Begin by adopting key policies, such as bullying prohibition, violence prevention, sexual harassment, and discipline. Additionally, consider the implementation of a formal anti-bullying program at the elementary school level. If financial expenditure is not possible, make use of the resources suggested in this chapter.

Next, appoint a planning team to identify acts of aggression and bullying in the district. This team should include at least one social worker, a school psychologist, a special education teacher, an ESL teacher, a gifted-talented teacher, a dean or counselor, a board member, and the communications director. It is important that the team is representative of student subgroups who tend to be targeted or who target others. Once established, rotate in parents, students, and relevant community leaders.

Set clear timelines to conduct the study and report its findings. Ensure that good documentation of progress is taking place. Communicate with school stakeholders so that everyone is aware of the initiative. There are many innovative ways creative, caring staff can develop best-practice strategies that meet the needs of the school community. It is possible to make your learning environment safer and more welcoming.

Effective bullying prevention efforts are holistic. Use data to track results and concerns, then train faculty, staff, and family members on bullying and intervention strategies. Educate students in social-emotional literacy, relationships, community, and the dynamics of bullying.[19] Incorporate workshops on character development and provide staff development opportunities in social-emotional literacy. A holistic approach will pave the way for greater understanding of the whole child, and overall wellness will become an innate part of a healthier culture.

The Discipline Plan

In the same way that most school districts have an anti-bullying policy yet lack a bullying prevention program, many districts have a discipline policy but lack a real schoolwide discipline plan. When a schoolwide plan is not in place, aggressive, unruly behaviors are not addressed in a consistent, controlled, non-threatening manner. From the classroom to the superintendent's office, behavior expectations for staff, students, and even parents need to be clear, reasonable, and reinforced. For staff, this includes a code of ethics appropriate to their respective workgroup, such as faculty or administration.

Effective classroom management represents one of the more feared aspects of teaching, especially for new teachers. New teachers are rarely assigned mentors in their new job assignments and do not receive adequate training in classroom discipline in their teacher preparation programs. Place special emphasis on this arena, because what happens in the classroom is at the heart of what educators must manage well so that students feel safe to learn. Require all teachers to have a discipline policy on file in the principal's office. A model classroom discipline policy should include: 1) the teacher's expectations for a safe and positive learning environment, 2) the student's consequences for both minor and major disruptions, and 3) reinforcement of school district policies regarding sexual harassment, bullying, and other behaviors the district deems inappropriate.

Require teachers to review the classroom discipline policy with students during the first week of school. Send it home for parent review and require the student to return the signed policy as a graded assignment. Teachers should have signed agreements at fall conferences. Most parents want to see that teachers are taking their child's safety and learning seriously. This process initiates essential staff, parent, and student communication. Remember: keep the discipline policy on file in the administrative office to protect all concerned parties.

The diagram in Figure 5.1 serves as a model for developing a comprehensive district-wide discipline plan.

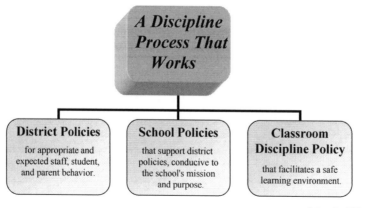

S Jacobs 2014

FIGURE 5.1

James Kaufmann writes about responding to aggressive behavior with consequences that are immediate but appropriate to the offense. He states, "If teachers, parents, and others dealing with aggression learn to use effective nonviolent consequences, the level of violence in our society will decline."[20] Stan Davis delineates a helpful discipline process that includes a suggested three-step process (reporting, investigating, and supporting time for reflection) that works well for "reducing peer-to-peer aggression."[21] Davis also includes a discussion on a rubric-based discipline system by grade level with sample formats districts can use. Kent Peterson asserts, "Schools need to have a behavior management system that has procedures that students understand and consequences that are clear and fair. Such systems make the process of dealing with rule-breaking more successful and easier to administer."[22]

Program Purpose

Bullying prevention programming is often considered a soft security issue when compared to tangible physical security measures and related emergency planning. As a result, this aspect of school security faces funding challenges. Unless a district is fortunate enough to have healthy sums of crime levy funding designated to healthy school climate, an educational foundation that has implemented an anti-bullying program, or access to a special revenue stream, bullying prevention programming will not survive. Do not accept this fate.

Convene your planning team. Brainstorm resources your district may be able to access. Solicit assistance from community stakeholders. Seek support from corporations, the faith community, action councils, and foundations. These organizations want to make a difference in the community. Share your needs and present potential solutions. Attempt to organize a collaborative effort to make the entire community safer. At minimum, you will secure a position of improved advocacy for child safety.

Taking a proactive stance to mitigate incidents of bullying will attest to your competency as a district leader who understands the nature of children and the pulse of the community. Margaret Wheatley, author of *Turning to One Another*, states, "There is no power for change greater than the community discovering what it cares about."[23] Wheatley further inspires hope for overcoming challenges in asserting, "We can't be creative if we refuse to be confused."[24] School leaders must be willing to be vulnerable in their search for answers in improving community wellness.

Building A Safe School Environment

At the district level, successful bullying prevention programming depends on creating a healthy school climate that is reflected in all district operations, such as:

- Mission statement;
- Strategic plan;

- A reasonable and viable bullying prohibition policy, as required by respective state statute, and any other relevant policies, such as sexual harassment; and
- Available funding that principals can use for staff training, student development, resources, and materials.

At the building level (school and other learning center facilities), successful bullying prevention programming depends on creating a healthy school climate that is reflected in all building operations, such as:

- Aesthetics that should be immediately apparent to a visitor:
  - A welcome desk with an attendant who cheerfully asks, "How may I help you?";
  - Welcoming signs on doors that include different languages, representative of the community;
  - Signs that detail visitor management practices and expectations;
  - Signs that reflect safe learning environment goals, such as "This is a Bully-Free Zone," placed strategically throughout the facility; and
  - Demonstrations of school pride, such as student artwork, bright lighting, and a clean environment.
- Communications, such as the school newsletter, that express a commitment to safety and wellness.
- School sponsored events that emphasize school pride and healthy relationship building.
- Staff engagement that holds staff accountable for their contributions in fostering a safe environment for colleagues, students, parents, and community.

In the aftermath of the Columbine tragedy, a group of Nashville, Tennessee students created a website, pledging their commitment to a healthy school community:[25]

As a part of my community and my school, I WILL:

- Pledge to be a part of the solution.
- Eliminate taunting from my own behavior.
- Encourage others to do the same.
- Do my part to make my community a safe place by being more sensitive to others.
- Set the example of a caring individual.
- Eliminate profanity towards others from my language.
- Not let my words or actions hurt others.
- And if others won't become a part of the solution, I WILL.

Most importantly, the quality and quantity of staff to student connectedness can have a profound effect on the culture of your schools. This concept is well articulated in an excerpt from *Schools Where Everyone Belongs* (Davis 73). Reciprocal caring, respectful, and participatory relationships are the critical determining factors in whether a student learns; whether parents become and stay involved in the school; whether a program or strategy is effective; whether an educational change is sustained; and, ultimately, whether a youth feels he or she has a place in this society. When a school redefines its culture by building a vision and commitment on the part of the whole school community that is based on these three critical factors of resilience, it has the power to serve as a "protective shield" for all students and a beacon of light for youth from troubled homes and impoverished communities.[26]

Build strong, healthy relationships, and impress upon your staff the need to take the time to build a positive rapport with a student. Consider the following exercise to test peer-staff relationships. Implement it at a staff workshop day that is well into the school year, such as the second quarter or second trimester. Place graph-sized post-it paper around the auditorium listing all students' names. Provide staff with sticker dots and have them place those dots by the students with whom they have a relationship. Restrict it to students who are not presently in their class, but with whom they have a connection. After teachers post their dots, evaluate the results. Assessments may be disappointing. Remember that school may be the only place where a student experiences a positive connection with an adult. Use the data to create an action plan for reaching out to those students who are the least connected to staff. This activity can significantly affect staff members and ultimately reap positive benefits for improving the wellness of your learning environment.

Policy Development

Carefully crafted violence prevention policies protect your staff, students, the district, and the community as a whole. It sends a message to the broader community that the district has taken the time and effort to protect its most precious stakeholders—the children—against harm. Predators and offenders tend to avoid a well-protected and reporting community. Consider the following questions regarding policy development:

Has your board implemented an anti-bullying policy?
Has district leadership provided direction and expectations for other district leaders on this policy? Is it a part of their evaluation?
Are incidents being reported, documented, and reviewed by your governing body?
Has the board funded/supported an anti-bullying program?
Have staff received training and/or attended conferences?
What other violence prevention policies have you put in place?
Appendix A includes an actual school district bullying prohibition sample policy for your reference and adaptation.

Document and Communicate

Document

Ensure that building administrators maintain appropriate documentation that meets with Family Educational Rights and Privacy Act (FERPA) stipulations, yet provides necessary directory information for the district. Invite and expect communications from building administrators on bullying prevention efforts. Implement a reporting system, supported by school district policy, wherein incidences of bullying are sent to the district office in a timely manner, depending on the severity of the incident.

Communicate

Ensure that no external communications are sent that violate confidentiality about an incident. Seek assistance and/or review by your communications director for proper handling of disseminated information. Routinely remind your staff that all media inquiries must be referred to the designated media coordinator.

Summative Key Messages

As summarized by Morrison (2011)[6], the following are the primary messages of an anti-bullying policy:

Bullying is a relationship problem that requires relationship solutions.
Promoting a positive school climate reduces bullying and antisocial behavior.
Whole school communities can teach relationship skills and educate hearts and minds.
Three Rs: respect, responsibility, reparation/restoration.

What is Cyberbullying?

As a rule, adults feel intimidated by the onslaught of new technology. Most have no personal experience with the distress that accompanies aggressive behavior in an electronic environment. Students, on the other hand, typically welcome technology advances. They are very familiar with electronic intimidation. As a result, many school administrators have encountered difficulty in conceptually moving beyond traditional bullying behaviors into the arena of cyberbullying. Social media and related technology present an enormous challenge. Some school districts have even assigned personnel, such as student services staff and school resource officers, to monitor social media sites, both as a form of threat assessment and in follow-up to reported incidences of cyberbullying.

What is Cyberbullying? Bill Belsey, president of Bullying.org, states, "Cyberbullying involves the use of information and communication technologies such as e-mail, cell phone, and pager text messages, instant messaging, defamatory personal websites, and defamatory online personal polling websites to support deliberate, repeated, and hostile behavior by an individual or group that is intended to harm others" (Beane 121). Allan Beane expounds on this by explaining that cyberbullying can be even more destructive than traditional bullying because it "intensifies the victim's feelings" once the information has been published and he/she realizes there is no way it can just be deleted forever. This is the difficult concept to grasp (Beane 122).

According to US legal definitions, "Cyber-bullying could be limited to posting rumors or gossips about a person in the Internet bringing about hatred in other's minds; or it may go to the extent of personally identifying victims and publishing materials severely defaming and humiliating them" http://definitions.uslegal.com/c/cyber-bullying/.

Definition of the Cyberbullying Problem

The cyberbullying conundrum is complicated. It weaves a web of intricate lies and convoluted perceptions about what is real and unreal. Cyberbullying is deceptive, hurtful, and devastating to its victims who feel helplessly trapped by its far-reaching tentacles. "The last thing fourteen-year-old Dawn-Marie Wesley heard before she killed herself late in 2000 was the voice of one of her tormenters. The cell phone message said, 'You're dead.'"[27]

Intensifying cyberbullying's many complexities, a cyberbully could be a cyberbully by proxy. In other words, the cyberbully manipulates someone else into conveying hurtful, dishonest, or obscene information about someone. Even adults can be unknowingly trapped by their children into this lair. In her 2011 webinar, Brenda Morrison further defined the nature of cyberbullying:

- Takes away the feeling of safety from being at home.
- Harsh and offensive; it enables the person who is bullying not to see the pain in the other person.
- Humiliating, the audience can be the entire world, forever.
- "Virtually" anonymous, it can hide the identity of the bully or allow them to impersonate someone; not knowing who is doing the bullying increases insecurity and social unease.
- Seems inescapable; the wired world allows individuals to contact others (both for positive and negative purposes) at all times and in almost all places.

In "Cyberbullying Research: 2013 Update," an article posted on the Cyberbullying Research Center website, Justin Patchin expresses the following concern: "Research about cyberbullying has not been making it into mainstream discussions in the media, even though research in this area has flourished."[28] He and his colleagues extensively reviewed all of the published research they could find in the summer of 2013 on the prevalence rate for cyberbullying and have summarized their findings in a April 2014 report, "Summary of our Research" (Patchin 1). Patchin et al, in congruence with other researched studies on cyberbullying, have found prevalence rate data on both cyberbullying victimization and cyberbullying others to be quite consistent (see charts below, Patchin 1). They concluded that "one out of every five teens experienced cyberbulling, while about one out of every five teens admitted to cyberbulling others."

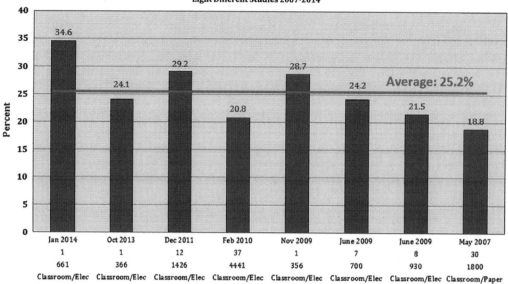

Justin W. Patchin and Sameer Hinduja
Cyberbullying Reseach Center
www.cyberbullying.us

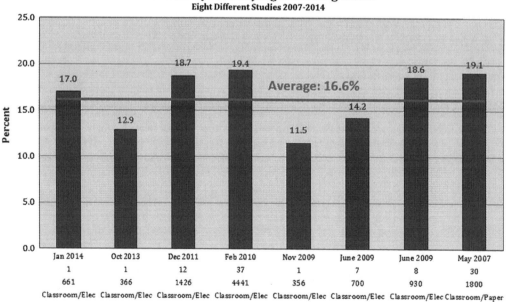

Justin W. Patchin and Sameer Hinduja
Cyberbullying Reseach Center
www.cyberbullying.us

Consider the following conclusions, which the Patchin researchers refer to as "broad generalizations based on recent research," that are most helpful to school leaders.[29]

- Adolescent girls are just as likely, if not more likely, than boys to experience cyberbullying (as a victim and offender) (Floros et al., 2013; Kowalski et al., 2008; Hinduja & Patchin, 2009; Schneider et al., 2012)[d].
- Cyberbullying is related to low self-esteem, suicidal ideation, anger, frustration, and a variety of other emotional and psychological problems (Brighi et al., 2012; Hinduja & Patchin, 2010; Kowalski & Limber, 2013; Wang, Nansel, & Iannotti, 2011)[e].
- Cyberbullying is related to other issues in the real world including school problems, antisocial behavior, substance use, and delinquency (Hinduja & Patchin, 2007; Hinduja & Patchin, 2008; Kowalski & Limber, 2013)[f].
- Traditional bullying is still more common than cyberbullying (Lenhart, 2007; Smith et al., 2008; Wang, Nansel, & Iannotti, 2011)[g].

[d]Floros, G.D., Simos, K. E., Fisoun, V., Dafouli, E., and Geroukalis, D. (2013). Adolescent online cyberbullying in Greece: The impact of parental online security practices, bonding, and online impulsiveness. *Journal of School Health, 83*(6), 445–453.

Kowalski, R. M., Limber, S. P. & Agatston, P.W. (2008). Cyber Bullying: Bullying in the Digital Age. Malden, MA: Wiley-Blackwell.

Hinduja, S. & Patchin, J. W. (2009). Bullying beyond the Schoolyard: Preventing and Responding to Cyberbullying. Thousand Oaks, CA: Sage Publications.

Schneider, S.K., O'Donnell, L, Stueve, A., and Coulter, R.W.S. (2012). Cyberbullying, school bullying, and psychological distress: A regional census of high school students. *American Journal of Public Health, 102*(1), 171–177.

[e]Brighi, A., Melotti, G., Guarini, A., Genta, M. L., Ortega, R., Mora-Merchán, J., Smith, P. K. and Thompson, F. (2012). Self-Esteem and Loneliness in Relation to Cyberbullying in Three European Countries, in Cyberbullying in the Global Playground: Research from International Perspectives. In Q. Li, D. Cross & P.K. Smith (Eds.), Wiley-Blackwell, Oxford, UK.

Hinduja, S. & Patchin, J. W. (2010). Bullying, cyberbullying, and suicide. *Archives of Suicide Research, 14*(3), 206–221.

Kowalski, R. M. & Limber, S. P. (2013). Psychological, Physical, and Academic Correlates of Cyberbullying and Traditional Bullying. *Journal of Adolescent Health, 53*(1), S13–S20.

Wang, J., Nansel, T. R., & Iannotti, R. J. (2011). Cyber Bullying and Traditional Bullying: Differential Association with Depression. *Journal of Adolescent Health, 48*(4): 415–417.

[f]Hinduja, S. & Patchin, J. W. (2007). Offline consequences of online victimization: School violence and delinquency. *Journal of School Violence, 6*(3), 89–112

Hinduja, S. & Patchin, J. W. (2008). Cyberbullying: An exploratory analysis of factors related to offending and victimization. *Deviant Behavior, 29*(2), 129–156.

Kowalski, R. M. & Limber, S. P. (2013). Psychological, Physical, and Academic Correlates of Cyberbullying and Traditional Bullying. *Journal of Adolescent Health, 53*(1), S13–S20.

[g]Lenhart, A. (2007). Cyberbullying and Online Teens. Pew Internet & American Life Project, June27. (http://www.pewinternet.org/PPF/r/216/report_display.asp).

Smith, P. K., Mahdavi, J., Carvalho, M., Fisher, S., Russell, S., and Tippett, N. (2008). Cyberbullying: its nature and impact in secondary school pupils. *Journal of Child Psychology and Psychiatry 49*(4): 376–385.

Wang, J., Nansel, T. R., & Iannotti, R. J. (2011). Cyber Bullying and Traditional Bullying: Differential Association with Depression. *Journal of Adolescent Health, 48*(4): 415–417.

- Traditional bullying and cyberbullying are closely related: those who are bullied at school are bullied online and those who bully at school bully online (Hinduja & Patchin, 2009; Kowalski & Limber, 2013; Ybarra, Diener-West, & Leaf, 2007)[h].

Observant, engaged teachers stand on the frontline of those that hear and observe student behaviors. They are often the first to detect victims of cyberbullying and/or bullying through student work that is handed in, overhearing conversations in the classroom or hall, and/or noticing students who are taking advantage of lab time on their social media sites and e-mail. This is now exacerbated by the fact that many students carry their own laptops, iPads, cell phones, and whatever comes along next. As school leaders, make sure to inform your staff of the importance of reporting anything concerning or suspicious. Make it clear that your staff will not be bystanders.

Cyberbullying Policy

Similar to the implementation of a bullying prohibition policy, districts must implement technology policies conducive to their school setting (see chapter 2, "Developing a Plan"). One school district has both a website and Internet use policy and a student use of information technology policy. These policies include a limited expectation of privacy clause wherein "the school district does not relinquish control over content or data transmitted or stored on the network or contained in files. Users should expect only limited privacy in the contents of personal files on the district's electronic technologies."

Additionally, it is advisable to have separate code of ethics cheat sheets for both students and staff utilizing social media. Some districts include this in an Internet use policy. This code of ethics should be signed by both the student and the parent and returned to the school.

Start at the Elementary Level

Determine what age is most appropriate to commence training students about cyberbullying. Keep in mind that many students at the elementary level already have cell phones and laptops. In fact, many children begin using technology in preschool, and they have had exposure to technology before that at home. While it is important to start teaching students about bullying first, they eventually need to understand that all forms of communication require appropriate and responsible behavior.

In Katherine Lee's article entitled "Cyberbullying and Grade School-Age Kids," she states,

Cyberbullying is often perceived as a problem that affects only older children and teens. But the fact is that cyberbullying can happen at anytime once a child begins using the

---

[h]Hinduja, S. & Patchin, J. W. (2009). Bullying beyond the Schoolyard: Preventing and Responding to Cyberbullying. Thousand Oaks, CA: Sage Publications.

Kowalski, R. M. & Limber, S. P. (2013). Psychological, Physical, and Academic Correlates of Cyberbullying and Traditional Bullying. *Journal of Adolescent Health, 53*(1), S13–S20.

Ybarra, M., Diener-West, M., & Leaf, P. J. (2007). Examining the Overlap in Internet Harassment and School Bullying: Implications for School Intervention. *Journal of Adolescent Health, 41*: S42–S50.

internet to e-mail, IM (instant message), or join social network sites or starts using a cell phone to text. As younger and younger children go online and have access to devices like computers, smartphones, and iPads the potential for problems like cyberbullying is also increasing among young children.[30]

Experts suggest that talking about cyberbullying at a young age is important to do, just like talking to them about smoking, drug use, or other at-risk behavioral choices. Lee states that "[children] need to understand that hurtful messages, embarrassing photos, and other aggressive or mean online or cellular behavior is bullying, just like physical or other face-to-face bullying."[31]

Training

Be prepared for cyberbullying. Mitigating incidences of students causing harm to one another through the use of technology while they are under your supervision is a formidable task that requires all staff to be knowledgeable, prepared, proactive, and accountable. Set clear expectations for staff that drive technology awareness and the need to address related student behaviors.

Provide staff instruction regarding the reporting process for incidences of cyberbullying. In his advice for parents, Dr. Allan Beane includes a list of how to report cyberbullying to service providers.[32] While Beane's list is not exhaustive, it is the kind of resource that especially equips administrative and student services staff. Additionally, the school resource officer serves a critical role in ascertaining whether cyberbullying (and bullying) incidences need to be reported to police and whether a crime has potentially been committed.

Numerous credible and helpful websites are available in helping devise strategies for keeping your school community safe.[33] Barbara Coloroso states that "[t]he characteristics of bullying—1) an imbalance of power, 2) the intent to harm, 3) the threat of further aggression, and 4) the creation of terror—are magnified with the use of electronic technologies."[34]

Nancy Willard, an internationally renowned lawyer and educator in cyberbullying, writes in "An Educator's Guide to Cyberbullying and Cyberthreats" (http://www.internet-safetyproject.org/wiki/center-safe-and-responsible-internet-use) that the harm caused by cyberbullying may be even greater than the harm caused by most other forms of bullying for the following reasons:

- Online communications can be extremely vicious.
- There is no escape for those who are being cyberbullied; victimization is ongoing and can take place at any time on any day of the week.
- Cyberbullying material can be distributed worldwide and is often irretrievable.
- Cyberbullies can be anonymous and can solicit the involvement of unknown "friends."

Make a concerted effort to communicate to stakeholders your commitment to addressing and handling incidences of bullying and cyberbullying. Find time to learn about the latest risks and solutions. Educate others and hold them accountable for their own staff development and management of potential concerns. Most importantly, demonstrate a commitment to keep students safe.

Sexting

No discussion on bullying and cyberbullying is complete without consideration and education regarding sexting. "Sexting is the act of sending pictures (or messages) of a sexual nature between cell phones, or other electronic media such as the internet" (AASA). For purposes of this discussion, sexting is an activity between minors. However, one must not forget that "adults" who have turned 18 (or above) also attend high schools and alternative education settings.

Nancy Willard, the head of the *Center for Safe and Responsible Internet Use*, provides a broader definition of the sexting challenge that brings clarity to the gravity of the situation: "Sexting appears to be the result of new technologies that foster impulsive behavior that leaves an electronic trail, raging hormones, and a teen's biological inability to predict potentially harmful consequences."[35] Consider the following story:

> *Early Monday morning, a high school principal is informed that a female student sent a picture of herself naked to her boyfriend, who forwarded the picture to a group of his friends. School personnel do not know how many students the message reached or whether it spread to other schools.*[36]

This is not an unusual story. Numerous sources indicate that one in five students participating in sexting. Twenty percent of teens admit to sexting activity.[37] As teens move into their college years, data indicates increasing prevalence. Furthermore, various research venues report that while students do realize they are engaging in inappropriate activity, they engage in it anyway, often without realizing its potential legal ramifications and devastating repercussions. Like other areas school leaders face with at-risk student behaviors, it is the job of the whole school community to educate, observe, and report suspicious electronic activity.

With an estimated 90–95 percent of students carrying cell phones, this trend cannot be ignored.[38] A 2009 study reported the following key findings:[39]

- Although most teens typically send sexually suggestive content to boyfriends/ girlfriends, others are sending such content to someone they want to "hook up with" or they only know online. (Refer to *Internet Crimes Against Children* under "Resources" at the end of this chapter to learn more about online sexual predator behavior.)
- While teens know it is potentially dangerous to send/post sexually suggestive content, they do it anyway.
- Teens send explicit messages/images even though they know such content is often shared with others besides their intended audience.

- Young people who are recipients of such content are sharing with others.
- Teens admit that engaging in sending/posting such content will have an impact on their behavior.

The Role of the School Resource Officer

Exercise caution in evaluating and reporting sexting activity. Stay above reproach when it comes to investigating and viewing sexually explicit images of minors. Administrators have been prosecuted for observing child pornography. Nancy Willard suggests "it is probable that the only actions an administrator should take are to confiscate suspected cell phones, contact the parents, and contact the police."[35]

Turn to school resource officers (SROs) for assistance. SROs "possess a skill set unique among both law enforcement and education personnel that enables them to protect the community and the school campus while supporting the educational mission."[40] They are trained to investigate social media and are cognizant of right to privacy laws. Some SROs have received specialized training through ICAC. Allow these individuals to determine whether a crime has been committed. If your school does not have an SRO, contact a local police officer or pursue the possibility of constructing a memorandum of understanding that permits access to a neighboring district's SRO.

The Need for Awareness

Attempt to educate the all school stakeholders on the issue of sexting. Build partnerships between school and community that foster safety. Implement the following components.

- Call for accountability.
- Facilitate conversations between stakeholders that move the school community forward.
- Challenge all stakeholders to convey the same message clearly.
- Provide an understanding of the laws governing both school and community.
- Strive to build student character and responsibility with the goal of producing productive, responsible citizens.

Training resources for students, staff, and parents abound. Ask law enforcement personnel to provide instruction. Seek assistance from agencies, such as the Bureau of Criminal Apprehension, and other subject matter experts. Make concerted efforts to bring people together. Resourcefulness pays. Much is at stake.

Do not underestimate the importance of creating and maintaining a healthy school climate. The May 2013 edition of *Principal Leadership* from the National Association of School Psychologists includes this statement: "A positive and supportive school climate that engages the entire school community in efforts to feel safe and engaged, encourages respectful behaviors and attitudes, and builds trusting relationships between students and adults is an essential part of preventing problem behaviors of any kind within a school."[41]

Current laws governing sexting are evolving rapidly. Routinely remind stakeholders that students involved in sexting may face felony charges, including the production and distribution of child pornography. These charges can eventually lead to mandatory registration as a sex offender.[42] Educate people in forums such as parent newsletters, student assemblies, community partner outreaches, district policies, and schoolwide discipline plans.

Sexting represents a very real threat to our students' well-being. Now is the time to be familiar with current information, resources, and case law.

Dating Violence, Stalking and Sexual Assault

When the topic of sexual assault is discussed in American society, very often the image of a stranger raping a woman in a dark alley comes to mind. With domestic violence, one commonly thinks of a husband/adult male abusing his wife/adult female girlfriend who is living with him. With stalking, if the topic comes up at all, one normally assumes it involves a fan obsessed with a celebrity.

Although these situations are devastating and certainly worthy of note, research tells us that a disturbingly high percentage of US middle school and high school students are also victims of sexual assault, stalking, and intimate partner violence. Americans must expand their perceptions of who they believe can be victims of these crimes.

About one in five female victims and one in fourteen male victims of stalking experience these violations between the ages of eleven and seventeen (Centers for Disease Control). Forty-four percent of sexual assault victims are under the age of eighteen (US Department of Justice). From http://www.cdc.gov/violenceprevention/pdf/nisvs_executive_summary-a.pdf, nearly 1.5 million high school students nationwide experience physical abuse from a dating partner in a single year. In fact, one in three adolescents in the United States is a victim of physical, sexual, emotional, or verbal abuse from a dating partner, a figure that far exceeds rates of other types of youth violence.[43]

It should also be noted that battering, sexual assault, and stalking often intersect. For example, a teen romantic relationship with a history of violence could escalate into one that includes stalking, rape, or both. See Figure 5.2 for a visual depiction of the overlap of lifetime intimate partner rape, stalking and physical victimization.

These violations not only affect the victims' personal lives; their academic lives can also suffer. For example, a victim of sexual assault, dating violence, or stalking may be afraid to go to school if she (or he) knows she will see her attacker walking the halls or in class.

Because of this, even if an incident occurs off campus, the victim's school must still take steps to protect the student until the claim is properly investigated by the school, police, or both. Protections for the victim could include providing an escort to ensure he or she can move safely between classes; ensuring the victim and the alleged assailant do not attend the same classes; moving the alleged perpetrator to a different school in the district; providing counseling and/or medical services; and more.

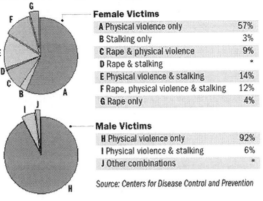

Overlap of Lifetime Intimate Partner Rape, Stalking and Physical Victimization

Female Victims

A	Physical violence only	57%
B	Stalking only	3%
C	Rape & physical violence	9%
D	Rape & stalking	*
E	Physical violence & stalking	14%
F	Rape, physical violence & stalking	12%
G	Rape only	4%

Male Victims

H	Physical violence only	92%
I	Physical violence & stalking	6%
J	Other combinations	*

Source: Centers for Disease Control and Prevention

FIGURE 5.2

At the same time, a school must promptly conduct its own thorough and impartial investigation into the allegations of sexual misconduct and not wait for the conclusion of a criminal investigation, if there is one. This point was reinforced in 2011 by the US Department of Education Office for Civil Rights (OCR) (http://www2.ed.gov/about/offices/list/ocr/docs/qa-201404-title-ix.pdf).

Unfortunately, schools have historically done a poor job of recognizing—let alone investigating—incidents of sexual assault, stalking, and dating violence. Campuses and society as a whole have often blamed the victim, especially when sexual assault is alleged and when the victim and perpetrator know each other. Victim-blaming types of questions discourage victims of sexual assault from coming forward: "Why did you drink?"; "Why did you drink so much?"; "Why did you go to that party?"; "Why did you go into that room with him?"; "Why did you go on a date with him when your parents don't allow you to date in the first place?"

In relationship violence situations, victims also very often do not recognize when they have been abused. With K–12 students, these relationships are usually their first, and they do not have the experience an adult might have to know the difference between healthy and unhealthy behaviors. In other cases, the victims may have had abusive relationships modeled for them in their homes, so they believe abuse is normal.

Stalking is another murky area. What may appear to be stalking by an adolescent boy or girl—hanging out at the object of their affection's locker; calling them repeatedly and then hanging up; looking at their Facebook page; or asking the friends of their crush for more information about the person—might just be common adolescent behavior. It could also be stalking, if the target has expressed a boundary that the pursuer ignores. The behavior must be taken in context. The victim also could be unaware that he or she is being stalked, especially if technology such as GPS or spyware is used by the stalker.

When same-sex relationships experience violence, victims may hesitate to come forward because they do not want to "out" themselves to their families or communities.

LGBTQ victims are also often afraid to ask for help, believing the police or school administrators will not take their relationships seriously. Male victims also struggle to come forward due to America's masculine gender socialization. Additionally, females can be perpetrators. That being said, when men perpetrate violence against women, the physical injuries to women tend to be more serious, possibly requiring medical attention.

So how can a school administrator, teacher, police officer, or volunteer recognize when a student has been the victim of a sexual assault, dating abuse, or stalking? Developing relationships and dialogue with students is the first step. This will help school personnel identify changes in personality or behavior that often occur after a person has been assaulted. Perhaps a normally outgoing student suddenly becomes withdrawn. Falling grades are another good indicator. In cases where dating abuse is occurring, if the staff member witnesses controlling or abusive behaviors by a dating partner, that should raise a red flag.

It should be noted, however, that adults are often the last people to find out about a sexual assault or abusive relationship. A student's friends may be the first. Additionally, a perpetrator's friends may witness behavior before, during, or after an incident that may indicate a crime or inappropriate conduct has occurred. That is why many researchers believe that the bystander intervention approach is the most effective way to address sexual violence on campus. This approach works to change the culture of a school and community so that it no longer supports, either overtly or covertly, inappropriate behavior.

Bystander intervention is based on research by David Lisak that shows there are really a small number of perpetrators on campus, but there are many more people (bystanders) who support sexual violence. Bystanders support sexual violence by failing to intervene when they see something happening or dismissing behaviors altogether, which sends a message to the perpetrators that their actions are permitted. Additionally, if the perpetrator is popular or someone who holds a position of privilege, fellow students may turn against the victim and blame that person rather than holding the perpetrator accountable and reporting him or her (http://www.davidlisak.com/wp-content/uploads/pdf/PredatorsUncomfortableTruths.pdf).

The Mentors in Violence Prevention (MVP) program serves as one example of the bystander model. MVP works to empower students to take an active role in promoting a positive school environment. Started in 1993, it was designed to train male college and high school student athletes and other student leaders to use their status to speak out against rape, battering, sexual harassment, gay bashing, and all forms of sexist abuse and violence. It has since expanded to include female students. Unfortunately, the financial support for programs like MVP has been minimal at best. That being said, even schools with robust bystander intervention programs will still most likely face the daunting task of investigating dating abuse, sexual assault, or a stalking incident because they are so common.

The US Department of Education's Office for Civil Rights' April 4, 2011, "'Dear Colleague' Letter," which outlines K–12 school and district duties under Title IX, has provided some fairly clear guidance on how schools should investigate claims of sexual violence. This letter, as well as other resources, can be found on the Department of Education's website.[44] Simply reviewing this material, however, is not sufficient for the reader to gain

the full understanding of this topic. Indeed, school administrators, law enforcement, security, counselors, and other personnel should receive extensive training on how they can
comply with OCR's Title IX's sexual violence guidance.

Instruction makes sense considering the trends institutions of higher education have
been experiencing with this issue. As this book goes to print, more and more college students who have been sexually assaulted are claiming their schools are not complying with
OCR's sexual violence guidance for Title IX. It remains to be seen if K–12 victims will pursue a similar course of action in the future against their schools and districts. It is highly
advisable for school and district administrators to familiarize themselves thoroughly with
the provisions of Title IX as they apply to sexual misconduct.

In summary, consider the following key points.

- Understand that dating violence, sexual assault and stalking do occur in K–12
  environments, both on and off campus.
- Provide adequate training to counselors, teachers, nurses, coaches, administrators, and
  others on how to respond to reports of these types of incidents.
- When an incident is reported, start your administrative investigation immediately. Do
  not wait for law enforcement to complete its inquiry.
- Review and revise your drug and alcohol policy so it does not discourage victims from
  reporting assaults.
- Be certain to let students know how they can report incidents and educate them on your
  policies on sexual assault, dating violence, and stalking.
- Ensure that designated investigators are competent and the investigation process is
  appropriate so victims are assured their claims will be handled properly.
- Do not use victim-blaming language or adopt policies that could be perceived as victim
  blaming.

Conclusion

Addressing issues involving bullying, sexual abuse, and drug problems has always been
part of K–12 security. Too often, however, we have only dealt with the few problems that
erupt in public—a bully victim coming home with a black eye, for instance. Yet there are
many other instances of bullying, sexual abuse, and drug use that may go unseen.

Consider the statistics: the National Education Association estimates say that 160,000
children stay home from school daily because they fear being attacked by other students.
According to the National School Safety Center, there are 2.1 million bullies and 2.7 million
bullying victims in U.S. schools today. According to a 2011 survey by the Centers for Disease Control and Prevention, 9.4 percent of high school students report being hit, slapped,
or physically hurt on purpose by a boyfriend or girlfriend during the 12 months prior to
the survey.

Surveys conducted in 2013 by the National Institute on Drug Abuse arm of the National
Institutes of Health indicated that 7 percent of eighth graders, 18 percent of tenth graders, and 22.7 percent of twelfth graders used marijuana in the month before the survey.

In 2013, 15 percent of high-school seniors reported using a prescription drug for non-medical purpose in the past year.

Today, we understand that these problems exist but are hidden. We know that we must actively search for victims and victimizers and help them. Over the years, we have also learned that no one sets out to become a bully, drug user, or sexual predator. These are learned behaviors. Educational programs can inform students about these behaviors and help them to avoid falling prey to them (http://www.drugabuse.gov/publications/drugfacts/high-school-youth-trends).

References

1. http://www.bullyingstatistics.org/content/bullying-statistics-2010.html.

2. Arthur Kelly, US Department of Education, School Safety Conference, Office of Safe and Drug Free Schools, Threat Assessment Training. 2009.

3. Karen M. Hawkins, Safe and Secure Schools, *Research Roundup* 21 no. 1 (Fall 2004).

4. Stan Davis and Julia Davis, *Schools Where Everyone Belongs: Practical Strategies for Reducing Bullying*, 2nd ed. (Champaign, IL: Research Press, 2007), 9.

5. Brenda Morrison, 2011. http://safesupportivelearning.ed.gov/sites/default/files/sssta/20110321_PresentationSSSTASCBullyingPreventionwebinar3161711FINAL3.17.11.pdf.

6. Emily C. Williams, "Bully and Victim Characteristics," *Bullying Project*. http://bullyingproject.com/bullies-and-victims/.

7. Bryan Vossekuil, et al., *The Final Report and Findings of the Safe School Initiative: Implications for the Prevention of School Attacks in the United States* (Washington, DC: US Secret Service and the US Department of Education, 2004), 11–12, http://www2.ed.gov/admins/lead/safety/preventingattacksreport.pdf.

8. Neil Marr and Tim Field, *Bullycide: Death at Playtime—An Expose' of Child Suicide Caused by Bullying* (Success Unlimited, 2001).

9. Barbara Coloroso, *The Bully, the Bullied, and the Bystander*, 2nd ed. (New York, NY: HarperCollins Publishers, 2008), xix.

10. Ibid.

11. "Bullying Statistics 2010," *Bullying Statistics*. http://www.bullyingstatistics.org/content/bullying-statistics-2010.html.

12. Susan Strauss, "Bullying vs. Sexual Harassment—Do you Know the Difference?" *Ms. Magazine*, November 15, 2011.

13. "Checklist for a Comprehensive Approach to Addressing Harassment," *US Department of Education*, last modified September 22, 2003, http://www2.ed.gov/policy/rights/guid/ocr/checklist.html.

14. Youth courts are juvenile justice diversion programs in which young people are sentenced by their peers. Street Law, Inc., developed lessons for youth courts to use when training youth volunteers or for use as a sentencing option for youthful offenders. "Youth Courts: Educational Workshops," *Street Law, Inc.* http://www.streetlaw.org/en/publications/youth_courts_educational_workshops/.

15. *Street Law for Youth Courts: Educational Workshops* (Street Law, Inc., 2006), 215–216, http://www.streetlaw.org/document/199/.

16. Allan L. Beane, *Protect Your Child from Bullying: Expert Advice to Help you Recognize, Prevent and Stop Bullying Before Your Child Gets Hurt* (San Francisco, CA: Jossey-Bass, 2008).

17. National Youth Violence Prevention Resource Center, 2006.

18. Teachsafeschools.org.

19. Nancy Riestenberg, *Safe and Healthy Learners E-Newsletter*, Minnesota Department of Education, November/December 2013.

20. James M. Kauffman, "Violence and Aggression of Children and Youth: A Call for Action," *Preventing School Failure: Alternative Education for Children and Youth* 38 no. 3 (1994), 8–9.

21. Davis, *Schools Where Everyone Belongs*.

22. Kent Peterson (1998) "Establishing effective schoolwide behavior management and discipline systems" (Reform Talk, 10), Wisconsin Center for Education Research (WCER), School of Education, University of Wisconsin-Madison. Retrieved January 18, 2004 from http://www.wcer.edu/ccvi/pub/ReformTalk/Year_1998/Oct_98Reform_Talk_10.html.

23. Margaret Wheatley, *Turning to One Another: Simple Conversations to Restore Hope to the Future* (San Francisco, CA: Berrett-Koehler Publishers, 2002).

24. Ibid.

25. Coloroso, *The Bully, the Bullied, and the Bystander*, 174.

26. Bonnie Bernard, 1995.

27. Coloroso, *The Bully, the Bullied, and the Bystander*.

28. Justin W. Patchin, "Summary of our Research (2004–14)," April 9, 2014, http://cyberbullying.us/summary-of-our-research/.

29. Ibid.

30. Katherine Lee, "Cyberbullying and Grade School-Age Kids: What You Do Now to Guard Your Children Against Cyberbullying," *About.com*. http://childparenting.about.com/od/technologyentertainment//a/Cyberbullying-And-Grade-School-age-Kids.htm.

31. Ibid.

32. Beane, *Protect Your Child from Bullying*, 131.

33. Ibid., 134.

34. Coloroso, The Bully, the Bullied, and the Bystander.

35. Nancy Willard, "Sexting Guidance for School Leaders," Center for Safe and Responsible Internet Use, May 22, 2010, http://www.csriu.org/.

36. Morgan Aldridge, Susan Davies, and Kelli Jo Arndt, "Is Your School Prepared for a Sexting Crisis?" *Principal Leadership* 13 no. 9 (2013), 12, http://www.nasponline.org/resources/principals/May_13_Sexting.pdf.

37. Ibid.

38. "Sexting," *Internet Safety 101*. http://www.internetsafety101.org/sexting.htm.

39. The National Campaign to Prevent Teen and Unplanned Pregnancy, *Sex and Tech: Results from a Survey of Teens and Young Adults* (Washington, DC: National Campaign, 2008), 2–3. http://thenationalcampaign.org/sites/default/files   /resource-primary-download/sex_and_tech_summary.pdf.

40. "NASRO Testimony Before the Senate," *National Association of School Resource Officers*. https://nasro.org/nasro-testimony-senate/.

41. Aldridge, "Is Your School Prepared for a Sexting Crisis?" 12.

42. "Ibid., 14.

43. "Dating Abuse Statistics," *Love Is Respect*. http://www.loveisrespect.org/is-this-abuse/dating-violence-statistics/.

44. Russlynn Ali, "'Dear Colleague' Letter," US Department of Education, Office for Civil Rights, April 4, 2011, http://www2.ed.gov/about/offices/list/ocr/letters/colleague-201104.pdf.

Appendix A: Sample Bullying Policy

This appendix includes an actual school district bullying prohibition sample policy and filing procedures for both students and staff for your reference and use. The term ISD stands for [Independent School District], but it can be substituted for the name of your institution or school district.

POLICY _____

<SCHOOL DISTRICT NAME>

506.1   BULLYING PROHIBITION

I.   PURPOSE

A safe and civil environment is needed for students to learn and attain high academic standards and to promote healthy human relationships. Bullying, like other violent or disruptive behavior, is conduct that interferes with students' ability to learn and teachers' ability to educate students in a safe environment.

[Insert School Name] is committed to fostering and maintaining a safe and civil educational environment in which all members of the school community are treated with dignity and respect. The school district prohibits bullying, harassment, and any other attempts to victimize others.

The school district cannot monitor the activities of students at all times and eliminate all incidents of bullying, particularly when students are not under the direct supervision of school personnel. However, to the extent such conduct effects the educational environment of the school district and the rights and welfare of its students and is within the control of [Insert School Name] in its normal operations, [Insert School Name] intends to prevent bullying and to take action to investigate, respond, remediate, and discipline those acts of bullying that have not been successfully prevented.

The purpose of this policy is to assist [Insert School Name] in its goal of preventing and responding to acts of bullying, intimidation, violence, retaliation, and other similar behaviors.

II.   DEFINITION

A.   "Bullying" means written or verbal expression, physical act or gesture, and pattern thereof, by a student that is intended to cause or is perceived as causing distress to a student or a group of students and which substantially interferes with another student's or students' educational benefits, opportunities, or performance.

Bullying includes, but is not limited to, conduct by a student against another student that a reasonable person under the circumstances knows or should know has the effect of:
1.   harming a student or a group of students;
2.   damaging a student's a group of students property;
3.   placing a student a group of students in reasonable fear of harm to his or her person or property;
4.   creating a hostile educational environment for a student a group of students; or,
5.   intimidating a student or a group of students.

B.   "Immediately" means as soon as reasonably possible.

C.   "On school district property or at school-related functions" means all school district buildings, school grounds, school property, school bus stops, school buses, school vehicles, school contracted vehicles, or any other vehicles approved for school district purposes, the area of entrance or departure from school grounds, premises, or events, and all school-related functions, school-sponsored activities, events, or trips. While prohibiting bullying at these locations and events, the school district does not represent that it will provide supervision or assume liability at these locations and events.

FIGURE 5.A.1

III.   **GENERAL STATEMENT OF POLICY**

A.   An act of bullying, by either an individual student or a group of students, is expressly prohibited on school property or at school-related functions. This policy applies not only to students who directly engage in an act of bullying but also to students who condone or support another student's act of bullying. This policy also applies to any student whose conduct constitutes bullying that interferes with or obstructs the mission or operations of the school or the safety or welfare of the student, other students, or employees or volunteers. The misuse of technology including, but not limited to, teasing, intimidating, defaming, threatening, or terrorizing another student, teacher, administrator, volunteer, contractor, or other employee of the school district by sending or posting e-mail messages, instant messages, text messages, digital pictures or images, or website postings, including blogs, also may constitute an act of bullying.

B.   No teacher, administrator, volunteer, contractor, or other employee of [Insert School Name] shall permit, condone, or tolerate bullying.

C.   Apparent permission or consent by a student being bullied does not lessen the prohibitions contained in this policy.

D.   Retaliation against a victim, good faith reporter, or a witness of bullying is prohibited.

E.   False accusations or reports of bullying against another student are prohibited.

F.   A person who engages in an act of bullying, reprisal, or false reporting of bullying or permits, condones, or tolerates bullying shall be subject to discipline for that act in accordance with school district's policies and procedures. [Insert School Name] may take into account the following factors:

1.   The developmental and maturity levels of the parties involved;

2.   The levels of harm, surrounding circumstances, and nature of the behavior;

3.   Past incidences or past or continuing patterns of behavior;

4.   The relationship between the parties involved; and,

5.   The context in which the alleged incidents occurred.

Consequences for students who commit prohibited acts of bullying may range from positive behavioral interventions up to and including suspension and/or expulsion. Consequences for employees who permit, condone, or tolerate bullying or engage in an act of reprisal or intentional false reporting of bullying may result in disciplinary action up to and including termination or discharge. Consequences for other individuals engaging in prohibited acts of bullying may include, but not be limited to, exclusion from school district property and events and/or termination of services and/or contracts.

G.   [Insert School Name] will act to investigate all complaints of bullying and will discipline or take appropriate action against any student, teacher, administrator, volunteer, contractor, or other employee of [Insert School Name] who is found to have violated this policy.

H.   Reports of bullying are classified as private educational and/or personnel data and/or confidential investigative data and will not be disclosed except as permitted by law.

I.   Submission of a good faith complaint or report of bullying will not affect the complainant's or reporter's future employment, grades, or work assignments, or educational or work environment.

J.   [Insert School Name] will respect the privacy of the complainant(s), the individual(s) against whom the complaint is filed, and the witnesses as much as possible, consistent with [Insert School Name] obligation to investigate, take appropriate action, and comply with any legal disclosure obligations.

FIGURE 5.A.1 Cont'd

REPRISAL

[Insert School Name] will discipline or take appropriate action against any student, teacher, administrator, volunteer, contractor, or other employee of [Insert School Name] who retaliates against any person who makes a good faith report of alleged bullying or against anyperson who testifies, assists, or participates in an investigation, or against any person who testifies, assists, or participates in a proceeding or hearing relating to such bullying. Retaliation includes, but is not limited to, any form of intimidation, reprisal, harassment, or intentional disparate treatment.

TRAINING AND EDUCATION

A.   [Insert School Name] will provide information and any applicable training to staff regarding this policy.

B.   [Insert School Name] annually will provide education and information to students regarding bullying, including information regarding this policy prohibiting bullying.

C.   The administration of [Insert School Name] will respond to bullying in a manner that does not stigmatize the victim, and make resources or referrals to resources available to victims of bullying.

D.   [Insert School Name] may implement violence prevention and character development education programs to prevent and reduce policy violations. Such programs may offer instruction on character education including, but not limited to, character qualities such as attentiveness, truthfulness, respect for authority, diligence, gratefulness, self-discipline, patience, forgiveness, respect for others, peacemaking, and resourcefulness.

NOTICE

[Insert School Name] will give annual notice of this policy to students, parents or guardians, and staff. and this policy shall appear in the student handbook.

School Board Adoption: July 15, 2013

An Equal Opportunity School District

FIGURE 5.A.1 Cont'd

SCHOOL BOARD POLICY ____: BULLYING PROHIBITION

REPORTING AND RESPONSE PROCEDURE GUIDELINES

A. Any person who believes he or she has been the victim of bullying or any person with knowledge or belief of conduct that may constitute bullying shall report the alleged acts immediately to an appropriate school administrator designated by this policy. A person may report bullying anonymously. However, the school district's ability to take action against an alleged perpetrator based solely on an anonymous report may be limited.

B. [Insert School Name] encourages the reporting party or complainant to use the report form available from the administrator of each building or available from the district office, but oral reports shall be considered complaints as well.

C. The school administrator or administrator's designee (hereinafter building report taker) is the person responsible for receiving reports of bullying at the building level. Any person may also report bullying directly to the superintendent or school board. If the complaint involves the building report taker, the complaint shall be made or filed directly with the superintendent or the school district human rights officer by the reporting party or complainant.

D. A teacher, school administrator, volunteer, contractor, or other school employee should be particularly alert to possible situations, circumstances, or events that might include bullying. Any such person who receives a report of, observes, or has other knowledge or belief of conduct that may constitute bullying should inform a building report taker immediately. School district personnel who fail to inform the building report taker of conduct that may constitute bullying in a timely manner may be subject to disciplinary action.

SCHOOL BOARD POLICY ____: BULLYING PROHIBITION

SCHOOL DISTRICT ACTION

A. Upon receipt of a substantive complaint or report of bullying, [Insert School Name] should undertake or authorize an investigation by a school official or a third party designated by [Insert School Name].

B. [Insert School Name] may take immediate steps, at its discretion, to protect the complainant, reporter, students, or others pending completion of an investigation of bullying, consistent with applicable law.

C. Upon completion of the investigation which verifies that an act of bullying has taken place, [Insert School Name] will take appropriate action. Such action may include, but is not limited to, warning, suspension, exclusion, expulsion, transfer, remediation, termination, or discharge. Disciplinary consequences will be sufficiently severe to try to deter violations and to appropriately discipline prohibited behavior. Action taken by [Insert School Name] for violation of this policy will be consistent with the requirements of applicable collective bargaining agreements; applicable statutory authority, including the Minnesota Pupil Fair Dismissal Act; school district policies; and regulations.

D. [Insert School Name] is not authorized to disclose to a victim private educational or personnel data regarding an alleged perpetrator who is a student or employee of [Insert School Name]. Upon completion of an investigation and/or subsequent disciplinary action, school officials will notify the parent(s) or guardian(s) of students involved in a bullying incident and the remedial action taken, to the extent permitted by law.

FIGURE 5.A.1 Cont'd

Preparing Your People

Introduction

People determine protection effectiveness. Commitment is evidenced by staff attitudes and behaviors that reflect awareness, concern, and a professional responsibility for a safe learning environment. Staff is defined as all school employees, including but not limited to teachers, aides, administrators, counselors, drivers, facilities personnel, administrative assistants, nurses, and security personnel. How would you rate your staff's commitment to maintaining a safe learning environment? What level of awareness do they have regarding security? How prepared are your staff members for emergencies? Are they contributing to or detracting from providing a safe learning environment?

It is important to communicate to staff members that security is almost never convenient, and convenience quite often compromises security. Security products and practices are only as good as the staff members that implement them. In reality, staff members form your security program's first line of defense. School administrators often complain that staff members will not follow security practices. Administrators feel frustrated when teachers prop open exterior doors, leave valuables unattended, or fail to utilize two-way radios while monitoring exterior activities. They accuse staff members of adopting a "Mayberry mentality"—the mistaken notion that the school resides in the fictional community where Sheriff Taylor (Andy Griffith) faced virtually no risk of criminal activity.

One approach suggests appealing to emotions. In other words, when speaking to teachers and staff about security responsibilities, make it personal. Say something like, "Bad things should not happen in school. But as we all know, bad things do happen in school. Promise yourself that nothing bad will ever happen because you left a door propped open or did not question a stranger or did not live up to some other responsibility of yours for keeping the people around you safe."

Another approach seeks to terrify teachers and staff. Push the envelope even further by saying, "You are right. Nothing bad will happen this time. But one day, sometime off in the future, someone may walk through the door you propped open and steal someone's purse or shoot someone in the head. It will be your fault, and you will have to live with it. Wouldn't it be easier to live with the small inconvenience of keeping the door locked?"

Good people may disagree about the extremity of the approach. Nevertheless, security training must take place. Routine, application-oriented instruction is the key to providing a safe learning environment. It is also the remedy for the Mayberry mindset's false sense of security. Improve the safety of your learning environment by establishing an instructional program that addresses the following areas.

Staff Surveys

Solicit the input of teachers and staff by distributing clear and concise surveys. Ask these important stakeholders to offer their perspective on the security program. Even if perception is not always reality, you need to know what teachers and staff are thinking.

Be careful with surveys. Poorly written surveys make staff members frustrated. Inapplicable surveys also pose a problem. People cannot afford to waste time. Beware of evoking emotions that cause people to feel fearful. Effective safety and security surveys both gather important information and raise security awareness in a healthy manner. Effective surveys support the maxim "information eases anxiety." What constitutes important security information? How can surveys raise security awareness without causing fear? Consider the following sample questions:

- Are functional communication systems, such as telephones, intercoms, and two-way radios, available in your area and throughout the school? Please comment.
- Are students, staff, and visitors in the building readily identifiable through identification badges, uniforms, and passes? Please comment.
- Have all staff members been trained in security practices and emergency procedures? Please comment.

Make collaborative decisions regarding survey details. In terms of the format, are you looking to obtain ratings on current conditions, receive comments about security concerns, or both? Remember, the format should be simple and brief. In terms of the method of delivery, will you be using hardcopy surveys or an electronic method, such as SurveyMonkey? Will the survey be completed on personal time or at a scheduled meeting? In terms of timing the dissemination, what time of year would be most strategic and how often should surveys be conducted? Well-timed surveys can alleviate concerns, raise security awareness, and set a tone that positively impacts the culture.

In your collaborative survey development efforts, do not attempt to reinvent the wheel. Find examples of successful campaigns. Make use of relevant resources, such as search engines, to identify best practices. Move forward with confidence.

The Staff Skills Survey and Inventory (Figure 6.1) provides an excellent example of a survey that gathers important information and raises awareness. In a few minutes, you will know what kind of skills staff members possess. This information could be strategic in completing the school's incident command structure (see chapter 7, "Managing Emergencies"). In addition to skills and safety certifications, results will inform you as to who currently carries emergency supplies in personal vehicles. Such information may even encourage others to begin doing so. Share pertinent results with staff. People will feel safer knowing that those around them possess strategic skills.

Student Problem Indicators

The vast majority of students want to learn in a safe environment. Unfortunately, a number of factors, including sheer school population size, make this stakeholder group most likely to perpetrate crimes. How can staff members recognize the potential for incidents and intervene before they occur?

Problem indicators consist of a number of elements that may suggest when students are at risk for drugs, gang influence, and violence. While no one indicator is highly predictive, combinations of indicators enhance at-risk predictability. Call upon your own subject matter experts, such as social workers and community responders, to equip staff to recognize and address risk factors.

In June 1999, following the Columbine High School tragedy, the US Secret Service and the US Department of Education launched the Safe School Initiative. This collaborative effort attempted to answer questions surrounding student-led school attacks. The Safe School Initiative conducted an extensive examination of 37 incidents of targeted school shootings and

Staff Skill Survey & Inventory

During any disaster situation, it is important to be able to draw from all resources. The special skills, training, and capabilities of the staff will play a vital role in coping with the effects of any disaster incident. They will be of paramount importance during and after a major or catastrophic disaster. The purpose of this survey/inventory is to pinpoint those staff members with equipment and special skills that might be utilized in the case of a crisis. Please indicate the areas that apply to you and return this survey to your administrator.

Name: _____   Department: _____

Directions: Please check any of the following areas in which you have expertise or training
and circle "yes" or "no" where appropriate.

____First aid (current certification: yes/no)	____Mechanical ability
____CPR (current certification: yes/no)	____Structural engineering
____Triage	____Bus/truck driver (Class 1/2 yes/no)
____Firefighting	____Shelter management
____Construction (electrical, plumbing, carpentry)	____Survival training and techniques
____Running/jogging	____Food preparation
____Emergency planning	____Ham radio operator
____Emergency management	____CB radio operator
____Search and rescue	____Journalism
____Law enforcement	____Camping
____Bi/Multi-lingual	____Waste disposal
Specify language/s: _____	____Recreational leader

➤ Do you keep a personal emergency kit? _____ In your car? _____ In your room? ____
➤ Do you have materials or equipment in your room that could be of special use during an
emergency? Yes_____ No _____

If yes, please list the materials/equipment: _____

```
Additional Comments/Information:



```

FIGURE 6.1

school attacks that had occurred in the United States, beginning with the earliest identified incident in 1974 and extending through June 2000. They focused on examining the thinking, planning, and other behaviors in which students who carried out school attacks engaged. Particular attention was given to identifying pre-attack behaviors and communications that might be detectable (or "knowable") and could help in preventing some future attacks.

The findings of the Safe School Initiative[1] suggested that there are productive actions that educators, law enforcement officials, and others can pursue in response to the problem of targeted school violence. Specifically, Initiative findings suggested that these officials may wish to consider focusing their efforts to formulate strategies for preventing these attacks in two principle areas: 1) developing the capacity to pick up on and evaluate available or knowable information that might indicate that there is a risk of a targeted school attack; and 2) employing the results of these risk evaluations or "threat assessments" in developing strategies to prevent potential school attacks from occurring.

Support for these suggestions was found in 10 key findings of the Safe School Initiative study. These findings were as follows:

1. Incidents of targeted violence at school rarely were sudden, impulsive acts.
2. Prior to most incidents, other people knew about the attacker's idea and/or plan to attack.
3. Most attackers did not threaten their targets directly prior to advancing the attack.
4. There is no accurate or useful "profile" of students who engaged in targeted school violence.
5. Most attackers engaged in some behavior prior to the incident that caused others concern or indicated a need for help.
6. Most attackers had difficulty coping with significant losses or personal failures. Moreover, many had considered or attempted suicide.
7. Many attackers felt bullied, persecuted, or injured by others prior to the attack.
8. Most attackers had access to and had used weapons prior to the attack.
9. In many cases, other students were involved in some capacity.
10. Despite prompt law enforcement responses, most shooting incidents were stopped by means other than law enforcement intervention.[2]

According to Initiative statistics, at least one other person had some prior knowledge of an attacker's plan in 81 percent of incidents. In 59 percent of incidents, more than one other person had some prior knowledge. Of those incidents where another person knew about the attack in advance, 93 percent of those people were the attacker's friend, schoolmate, or sibling. There is no substitute for forming good, healthy relationships with students. Encourage staff members to invest in cultivating these kinds of relationships.

Visitor Management

Too often it seems that, when visitors walk through school hallways, very few staff members attempt to engage them. Why is that? Could it be that staff members have never been taught how to appropriately engage visitors? We suggest teaching staff members the "Wal-Mart Approach." Using the Wal-Mart Approach, staff members assertively greet visitors with the phrase, "Hi! How can I help you?" This simple phrase accomplishes two objectives. First, the visitor must state a reason for being in the building. Second, the visitor no longer operates under a cloak of anonymity. He or she has been ushered into a personal encounter that also makes it more likely that he or she can be identified, if necessary. Visitor management quickly becomes ineffective if the "how" is dropped in favor of asking a yes/no question, such as "Can I help you?" or "Do you need help?" Yes/No questions do not require visitors to make eye-contact and can be answered, if not dismissed, with a simple, "No, thank you." The Wal-Mart Approach places staff members in control of the situation. They are able to exercise their position of authority in a helpful, customer-focused manner.

Consider incenting staff members to adopt this approach. Announce that a secret shopper will be testing the visitor management system. The secret shopper will make note of the staff members that used the Wal-Mart Approach and communicate those name to the designated administrator. That administrator will reward successful staff members with prizes, such as coffee shop gift cards. Security practitioners have traditionally motivated compliance through negative incentives. Perhaps the use of positive incentives will improve the success rate and make an impact on the school's culture.

Security Awareness

As mentioned earlier, school administrators can be quick to complain that staff members will not follow security practices. Be careful not to adopt a defeatist mentality when it comes to equipping staff with security protocols. Do not underestimate what people can do when properly equipped! Make use of the advanced technology and immediate communications at your disposal. A heightened sense of security awareness can greatly improve your security program. Consider implementing the following awareness raising methods.

Electronic Correspondence

Staff member awareness levels can be increased through monthly electronic (e-mail) correspondence. For example, you might send an e-mail with "Security Notice" in the subject line that states, "FYI–For your safety and the safety of the children, please continue to ensure that all exterior doors are kept closed and locked as part of our closed campus policy. Thank you for your commitment to keeping our school safe." If the government of the United States can deliver homeland security alerts regarding matters of national security to every home in the country, administrators should feel confident in informing and reminding staff members about school security.

While there is no substitute for a proactive approach, electronic correspondence after an incident can also prove helpful. Consider, for instance, the following lessons-learned notification.

"Yesterday afternoon, a staff member's vehicle was broken into. A district-owned, electronic device was stolen along with other personal items. Please remember to keep all valuables secured and out of sight in vehicles, offices, classrooms, etc. This will reduce your chance of being victimized. Please report all suspicious activity to _____ at extension XXXX. Contact _____ at that extension or via e-mail (xyz@xschool.org) with questions. Thank you."

Regular Briefings

Another method that can be implemented to heighten security awareness we refer to as the "Hill Street Blues Method." Remember the television drama series of the 1980s called *Hill Street Blues*? In the opening few minutes of the program, the old sergeant would take his place at the podium during roll call and inform Chicago's finest of the various activities and operations occurring in the community. After a couple minutes of targeted information delivery, he would conclude the teaser segment with the words, "Now … let's be careful out there!" In the same way, you can successfully manage the awareness portion of your security program by taking a few minutes at some point during each staff meeting to deliver useful information, such as recent security incidents, existing emergency procedures, and upcoming events. A few easy ways to begin cultivating a culture of awareness among your staff are listed below.

Pop Quiz

Surprise the staff with a security pop quiz. Ask a thought-provoking question. Consider the following examples:

- What security systems and products does this school have? Let people answer by show of hands. You will be surprised by the impressions staff members have. With differing guesses and curiosity piqued, take advantage of the instructional moment.
- What emergency supplies that are not required by code (i.e., supplies other than first aid kits, AEDs, fire extinguishers, etc.) does the school have and where are they kept? As with the first questions, answers will vary. This question also affords the opportunity for staff members to potentially break through psychological barriers by actually handling the supplies.
- Where about the premises do you feel least safe and why? This question may elicit responses that provide you with important information. It may also present an opportunity to dispel myths (e.g., "I heard the lighting in the back parking lot is inadequate") and educate staff about recent security improvements.
- When is it appropriate for staff to call police? Frequently, teachers and staff feel as though reporting protocols dictate that only administrators can call police. There are, however, a number of situations, especially those that are time-sensitive, which warrant immediate contact with emergency responders. Examples would include situations where a staff member witnesses a crime, discovers a weapon, or needs immediate medical attention.

Remember, the goal of these pop quiz questions is to create a culture of raised security awareness.

Administrators can simultaneously deliver quiz questions using the Hill Street Blues method and current technology. Why not raise security and technology awareness at the same time? For example, PollEverywhere.com is an audience response system that utilizes cellular phones and the web. The PollEverywhere.com system can be embedded in a PowerPoint presentation. Participants see a multiple choice or true-false question on the PowerPoint slide that directs them to text a response code to a five-digit phone number. Results are tallied on a slide on the graph in real time.

Video Awareness Tests

An engaging way to get teachers and staff to think about security awareness is to show them a brief video, such as the "selective awareness test" on YouTube (http://www.youtub e.com/watch?v=vJG698U2Mvo). This awareness test presents a video that asks the viewer to count how many times a basketball is passed between team members that are actively moving across the screen. In a classic misdirection maneuver, a person in a gorilla suit walks through the group of people passing the ball, stops to pound his chest, and ultimately walks away. Most people that watch the video can account for the correct number of passes, but entirely miss the gorilla. The video, then, ask viewers to look for the gorilla during a replay of the scene. This entertaining exercise helps staff to think about paying better attention to things that they see. In just a few minutes, security awareness can be increased.

Emergency Procedure Specifics

The typical staff meeting will never provide enough time to address all emergency procedures. As a result, we recommend that administrators address important procedural distinctions and specific protocols in brief segments. For example, ask staff, "What is the difference between a tornado watch and a tornado warning?" or "What distinctions are made between a lockdown when the threat is in the building as compared to when the threat is outside the building?" Permit staff members to think about the question. Invite them to answer on the spot. Considering and articulating answers to such questions often causes staff members to take ownership of emergency plans and responses.

Going over these questions and answers in a group setting is important. Staff members get a glimpse of what their colleagues know. They can think through specific scenarios in a controlled environment. Even though the answers might seem simple or obvious, we often find in trainings that staff members are unclear on the distinctions. Clarifying these kinds of distinctions proactively may make all the difference in an actual emergency.

Photograph Identification

This particular technique is both challenging and entertaining. Project a photograph of a school parking lot or hallway scene on a screen and ask teachers and staff to look at the photo. After a few moments, remove the photo. Ask staff members, by show of hand, to name just one thing from the scene. Once most aspects of the scene have been identified, ask people to be more specific. You will find that most people are not confident in what they saw. Sometimes people will describe details that are incorrect. After some healthy interchange, put the photograph back on the screen and point out areas for the purposes of affirming and correcting. With each photo identification exercise, staff members will become more accurate because this type of awareness exercise improves perception.

In-Service Training and Annual Presentations

School violence incidents often motivate schools to prioritize security. When this occurs, take advantage of the promotion from after-thought to priority. Think of it as an opportunity to set the tone for the semester and beyond. When addressed appropriately, the topic of security can have significant and lasting effects. If security becomes a priority, what is the best way to address it? Whose voice should deliver the message?

Involving Emergency Responders

It is imperative that schools establish and maintain good relations with emergency responders. Strive to promote a sense of teamwork. Take steps to demonstrate appreciation for their services and cause them to feel welcome on your property and in your building. Invite emergency responders to provide instruction at an appropriate level and frequency.

Numerous determining factors affect the amount of time and reach emergency responders should be granted. On the positive side of the ledger, responders carry a certain degree of authority. Emergency vehicles and uniforms inspire confidence and trust. As part of the community, these individuals demonstrate an admirable investment in the school. On the potentially negative side, some emergency responders do not possess skills in public speaking. Additionally, some may not understand or know how to speak to the teacher and staff mindset.

Simply by virtue of position, emergency responders should routinely participate in security training and drills. Exercise prudence in deciding how much time and at what level they will participate.

Subject Matter Experts

Whether delivering a keynote address or a targeted workshop, many schools benefit by bringing in a subject matter expert. In terms of selecting the right person, schools can afford to be much more discriminating than they are with emergency responders. Attempt to choose a subject matter expert who is a known quantity in terms of content and speaking skills. Whereas emergency responders come with no price tag, a good subject matter expert can be expensive. Look for someone who effectively communicates principles and equips staff to take ownership of the security program. Excellent training will be application-oriented and stand the test of time.

Annual or Special Presentations

Once or twice a twice a year, make a presentation that summarizes security goals and the ways in which you intend to achieve those goals. Safety consultants that train workers to use dangerous machinery say that effective safety training must be personal and frightening. Taking a cue from that approach, the following presentation frames the goals of security in personal terms, makes the stakes clear, and urges continuing collective vigilance:

Taking Personal Responsibility (Sample Presentation Script)
Security is our responsibility. Not just my responsibility but our responsibility. If we live up to our collective responsibility properly today, all of our students will make it home from school safely this afternoon. That is the goal of security here at our school: making sure that every student gets safely home to his or her family every day.

If we miss something, if, for instance, we give a visitor who should not be in the building a badge, most of the time nothing bad will happen. The visitor will probably turn out to be on legitimate business after all. If not, then one of us will notice some kind of problem taking shape and step in by calling a colleague or me or the police. Security is our collective responsibility, and we all have to remain alert and investigate things that look wrong or out of place. Believe me, you don't want to have to live with being the one that let someone with a gun or knife or other weapon into the building. Most of the time, of course, that will not happen, even if you make a mistake. But it does happen. Every year, someone with a gun comes into a school somewhere in the United States and starts shooting. Here is what that looks like afterward. (Move through slides of the most recent school shootings or other security catastrophes.)

These are the stakes. This is what we want to prevent. Can we be 100 percent sure that we will prevent this if it comes our way? No. But we can give ourselves a chance if we each accept personal responsibility for making sure that all of our kids get home safely every day. Thank you."

Personal Crime Prevention

Theft of personal belongings, such as electronic devices, purses, clothing, and school items such as building keys, technology equipment, and electronic information tends to occur more frequently when we grow careless from a security perspective. Visibly carrying or counting cash, leaving valuables unattended, and leaving vacant classrooms unlocked invites trouble. Anybody, given the right opportunity, can act on the temptation to steal. Eliminate opportunities.

The same principle governs vandalism. Door propping devices such as bricks and chairs placed near exterior doors, poorly lit areas around the campus, and shrubbery that permits concealment encourage potential vandals. The risk of experiencing these kinds of crimes decreases as we "harden" potential targets. Staff members can and should be taught to lock file cabinets, desk drawers, and interior rooms. They should also be instructed to promptly report burnt-out lights, graffiti/tagging, broken windows, defective security equipment, and other potentially unsafe conditions. Custodial staff can and should be equipped with duty checklists that require the securing of unmonitored areas, such as vacant classrooms, utility rooms, and the faculty lounge. These checklists can also require the removal of door propping devices, immediate replacement of non-functional lighting equipment, and repair of defective door hardware. Routinely remind all stakeholders, including students, to follow crime prevention practices, such as reporting suspicious activity and refraining from displaying valuable items in vehicles (see Figure 6.2). An operational commitment to the regular trainings and briefings described above will heighten awareness and foster a culture of safety and security.

Personal Safety

Why do people advertise themselves as potential victims? Whether battling the Mayberry mentality or simple ignorance, attempt to help staff members before they are victimized. Closely aligned to personal crime prevention, personal safety can be improved by keeping the following, simple tips in mind.

Situational Awareness

Stay aware of your surroundings and the people around you. Inside the building, identify an accountability partner, safe places, and paths of egress. If you saw something suspicious or felt uneasy, whom would you contact? Through what means? If you had to move, where would you feel safest? Where about the property do you feel least safe? Why? In an actual emergency, how would you notify others?

Move about the exterior of the campus only in well-lit areas and away from foliage that conceals. Make a note of areas that are unsafe. Report the issues to those in authority. Document your concerns, if necessary.

FIGURE 6.2 Vehicle with laptop in plain view

Avoid working and walking alone. The two-person rule is a basic tenet of security. If alone, contact the main office or facilities personnel to request an escort to your vehicle. Carry your car keys in your hand as you approach your vehicle. Use your cellular phone to converse with an accountability partner as you move between the building and the vehicle.

Trust your safety instincts when suspicious about a person or situation. Consider fear to be a legitimate feeling. Act decisively. Follow pre-determined protocols. Do not be afraid to call for assistance. In fact, communicate your suspicions immediately. With the exception of nuisance alarms, emergency responders would rather find someone sincerely erring on the side of caution than someone who has already been victimized.

Safety Tools

Encourage staff members to be prepared for emergencies. Assist them in storing emergency items such as wind-up flashlights, Mylar blankets, and first aid supplies in classrooms and vehicles. Make sure that staff members are familiar with the locations of first aid kits and automated external defibrillators (AEDs) in your building.

Recommend that staff members program emergency contact numbers into speed dial locations on cellular phones. Tell them to store "In Case of Emergency" (ICE) information in cellular phones. They can find an ICE application for their smartphones or manually program ICE numbers into their contact lists if they do not have smartphones.

Encourage staff members to carry a whistle or another sound making device to attract attention in danger. Similar to an insurance policy, knowledge of the resource promotes peace of mind even if it is never used.

Conflict Resolution

If at all possible, staff members should not enter into physical altercations, such as student fights. Behavior management organizations focus on taking every step possible to safely diffuse escalating and assaultive situations. These nonviolent strategies seek to prevent injuries and avoid liability.

Even the most safety conscious individual, however, may not be able to avoid an occasional encounter with a disgruntled person. Keeping in mind that physical confrontation should never be an option, the following principles may prove useful in diffusing a situation.

First, understand the disgruntled mindset. Why is this person at an elevated level? The disgruntled person is often operating at an elevated level of anxiety because previous attempts to resolve an issue have not resulted in a satisfactory outcome.

Second, resist the urge to join the disgruntled person at an elevated level. Make every effort to stay calm and maintain composure. Never lock eyes or square your shoulders with a person in an agitated state. Resolution, not winning the battle, should be the goal.

Third, verbally acknowledge the fact that the person is operating at an elevated level without provoking further escalation. For example, you might calmly state, "I can see that you have a concern." Spoken in a non-threatening manner, this statement provides a mirror of sorts that displays escalation of which the person may not be aware. It also communicates an acknowledgement or understanding that a legitimate issue exists.

Fourth, quickly follow your initial statement with a second statement that attempts to communicate hope. Say something like, "We can try to fix this."

Fifth, if other people are in the immediate area, take steps to lead the person to a safer place. This can be accomplished through a non-threatening command such as, "Follow me." Without waiting for a response from the disgruntled person, deliberately proceed toward the area of safety. In most cases, the disgruntled person will follow. Keep the individual in your peripheral vision. As the result of movement, adrenaline levels will begin to decrease. Make certain that you lead the person to an area that is indeed safer.

Please understand that this list is by no means exhaustive and should only serve to provide guidelines to develop a plan of resolution. For more detailed instruction or formal certification in conflict resolution, seek out organizations that provide on-site, web-based, and/or video training in nonviolent responses to conflict.

Online Training

In consideration of time and scheduling difficulties, many schools have turned to web-based and software-based security training for teachers and staff. Depending on the platform, web-based training offers staff members the ability to receive the instruction on demand. It may also provide administrators with an accountability audit trail as systems automatically log successfully completed programs. The audit trail may also serve administrators from a liability standpoint in demonstrating the reasonable efforts taken to instruct staff members.

Scenario Learning, the largest online safety training provider, published studies finding that the amount of time it took staff members to complete an interactive, self-paced course was between 25 and 75 percent less than a classroom course. The time it took for employees to master the content presented to them in a multimedia environment was 60 percent faster than those in a classroom environment. Studies also found that staff members receiving multimedia instruction had a 25–50 percent higher retention rate over those receiving the content through classroom instruction. Retention rates are a measure of how much content reaches long-term memory. They reflect the employee's ability to recall information days, weeks, or months after the training is completed.

The variance in content delivery with multimedia training was 20–40 percent less than instructor-led training. The range of percentage can be attributed to the different choices available to staff members as they made their way through interactive courses. Finally, the studies reported high employee satisfaction associated with multimedia training because employees felt they could learn at their own pace, could take training at their convenience, were more involved in their own learning process, and had privacy during training sessions.

Web-based training options also include very brief, cost-effective instructional vignettes, such as the security tutorials found at http://www.RetaSecurityOnline.com/. Designed to heighten staff member awareness of risk exposures, the platform prepares subscribers to address effectively and/or prevent specific hazards from occurring. Each training program runs approximately one to three minutes in length, with key points presented in video format. Following the video, the subscriber takes a short, interactive quiz that reinforces the important elements pertinent to each topic. Upon successful completion of all 12 programs, a final exam is administered to reinforce complete understanding of the series. The training program includes topics such as visitor management, exterior activity monitoring, and lockdown procedures.

Motivation

Never do we feel more motivated to protect our schools and children than in the immediate aftermath of a tragedy. Outrage, fear, and disgust are powerful motivators, yet these emotions dissipate as time passes. Public outcry for change will always wane as time goes on, only to come surging back with the next catastrophe. With the aforementioned inconvenience of following school security practices, it can be easy for staff members to lose consciousness of the great importance of protecting those for whom they have been entrusted to care. Utilize motivation to effectively remind staff members just why their daily security effort is necessary and valuable. These motivational techniques serve not as "shock and awe" measures, but as ways to tap into the powerful emotions that can be such great motivators. To this point, you have trained your staff in the "how" and the "what." The following techniques will demonstrate the "why."

Cultural Touchstones

There is powerful imagery to be seen in the wake of national disasters that demonstrates our collective resolve as a country. Think back on President Bush throwing a first pitch strike in Yankee Stadium during the first World Series game in New York after 9/11. Remember when Paul Simon christened the 9/11 memorial 10 years later with a rendition of "The Sound of Silence?" Consider the rarity and tenderness of seeing a nation's leader shed a tear on live television, as President Obama did in the aftermath of Sandy Hook. Were you moved by Neil Diamond and a capacity crowd at Fenway Park singing "Sweet Caroline" following the explosions at the Boston Marathon? Boston strong, indeed! Seek out special moments that resonate with you and share them with your staff on a periodic basis.

Testimonials

Chances are that someone on your staff has a relevant story of survival to share with the rest of the team. Perhaps the staff member was part of a situation in which he or she witnessed effective measures being used to prevent a disaster. Maybe that person, or a close contact, experienced loss as a result of a security incident. If that staff member is willing to relate helpful stories, give that person an opportunity to impact others. People benefit from hearing relevant information from their peers. Actively seek out members of your staff that have special insights to give and encourage those people to share lessons learned with the rest of the team.

Affirmation

Staff members may not feel confident about their grasp of emergency procedures until they receive personal affirmation. They may not take ownership in making correct security decisions without positive reinforcement. Avoid generic platitudes such as, "Good job, everyone!" Take the time to observe and make note of specific actions that warrant affirmation. Commend individual team members for those actions. Tangibly reward behaviors that contribute to a safe learning environment. Incent people to take steps in the right direction. Great motivators have gleaned hours upon hours of excellent performance from their teams with nothing more than a bag of mini-candy bars and carefully chosen words of praise.

A commitment to affirmation can change the school's culture. Take a first step. Find a staff member doing something right. Tell that person what he or she did and why it was the right thing to do. Even if he or she was unaware of the specific behavior, he or she will appreciate the fact that you noticed it. Tangibly reward that person. The specific reward may be irrelevant. Importance is derived from the fact that there is a reward. Make it a habit to find someone on your staff and hand out one of these rewards on a regular basis. You will experience a cultural change in terms of security awareness and your staff will feel appreciated for their contributions. There are no losers in this exercise.

Documentation

The value of documentation should not be underestimated, especially from a liability perspective. Without a paper trail, it can be very difficult to demonstrate reasonable efforts to address vulnerabilities. Instruct staff in the value of documentation. Place emphasis on the following areas.

Work Orders

Too often, facilities personnel complain that staff members have neglected to complete a work order. The claim is that unsafe conditions, such as doors that do not latch and lighting that is no longer functional, could have been avoided if someone had followed the right process. Since staff members provide this important, frontline reporting service, make the work order process clear. Provide detailed instruction in how to submit work requests, assure them of the importance attached to work orders, and give them a timeframe for response.

Keep staff apprised of current reporting practices. As work order processes evolve, remind staff members that former procedures, such as voicemails and in-person reporting, no longer apply. Send electronic correspondence that says, "The Facilities Department would like to remind you to submit all current work requests via e-mail. Methods used in the past will not be recognized. If you currently have a verbal or voicemail request for maintenance, please re-enter your request via e-mail. We value your input. Thank you for your cooperation."

SchoolDude, the leading education platform of cloud solutions for schools, has automated the work order process. Staff members can submit reports through a computer software program or via a proprietary application from any portable device. The reporting staff member can see the process unfold from reception and task assignment to scheduling and project completion.

Discipline Reports

Staff members responsible for student discipline have titles such as paraprofessionals, hall monitors, safety monitors, transportation personnel, and security personnel. No matter the title, the likelihood of one of them completing a discipline report can vary wildly. Some staff members avoid writing reports in an attempt to court the favor of students. Some simply find completing a report to be tedious. A small percentage of personnel write reports with a military grade frequency.

Set clear expectations. Strive for uniformity. Review performance. Hold people accountable. Students resent or take advantage of unfair treatment. Those responsible for student discipline can set the tone for the security program. Consistent reporting practices go a long way toward earning the respect of students and staff.

Administrator Documentation

Administrators often complain that staff members will not comply with security practices, such as the directive to avoid propping exterior doors. They reason that the building has too many exterior doors, that too many staff members engage in propping those doors, and that there have been too many conversations without change. Administrators often give up and stop trying to fix the problem. Instead of acquiescing to this violation of security practices, consider adopting the following suggested sequence:

- Disseminate a clear directive to all staff that prohibits door propping as part of on-going efforts to furnish a safe learning environment.
- If the administrator finds an exterior door propped open and has the opportunity to find the staff member responsible, diplomatically engage in a personal conversation with the offending staff member. Ask if the individual has received the directive. Request a personal commitment to comply with the security practice for the sake of furnishing a safe learning environment.
- If the administrator finds the behavior repeated, take a copy of the directive to the offending staff member. Ask the individual if there is a willingness to comply. Request a signature on the copy of the documented security practice.

The idea is to avoid going down the path of an official employee discipline situation.

Attendance

Keeping track of student attendance is one of the most overlooked components of school security. Instruct staff members to take this period-by-period reporting requirement seriously. Establish a clear expectation of immediate reporting and hold teachers accountable.

Too often, staff members take attendance late in the period. Sometimes they even wait for an "off period" to enter several classes of attendance with the mistaken notion that the information is not time sensitive. On rare occasions, staff members wait until after the school day to report the entire day's attendance at once. Delayed reporting preys on memory limitations. Mistakes can be costly.

Consider how attendance information is processed. During each school day, every student has a set schedule. Deviations from the set schedule, such as special music lessons, get entered daily. Attendance software, for the most part, only identifies exceptions. In other words, the program only reports deviations from the normal schedule. If only one student is reported missing from Room 103 during first period, all of the other students are assumed to be present.

The purpose of attendance reporting goes far beyond identifying student absences due to illness or determining discipline issues such as skipping class. Accurate and timely information becomes especially important during an emergency. Follow this hypothetical situation: Period one: staff member Ms. Hetrick does not enter attendance during the period. As a result, attendance office personnel cannot account for any of those students. One student, Amanda, is absent during the period, but the office has not been informed. Period two: Amanda misses physical education, but those teachers never enter attendance until the end of the day. Period three: The substitute teacher marks Amanda absent on a hardcopy report because the school does not grant substitutes access to the attendance software. The hardcopy report will be submitted at the end of the day. Period four: Amanda misses lunch, but attendance is never taken during lunch. Period five: Amanda's teacher reports her absence. This report marks the first indication the attendance office receives that Amanda may not be at school. Immediately, the attendance office must attempt to locate Amanda. Why wasn't she reported absent in the first four periods? Was she in school earlier and permitted to leave for some reason? Did she sign out? Did she cut fifth period? Attendance personnel access Amanda's schedule. They can see Amanda's classes and find that none of them have reported attendance yet. While investigating, the attendance office receives information from Ms. Hetrick, Amanda's first period teacher. Catching up during her free period, she has just entered attendance information for her first three classes. But Amanda was not reported absent. The attendance officer calls Ms. Hetrick for confirmation. She apologetically indicates that she may be mistaken about her attendance. Next, the attendance officer calls the substitute teacher from period three. She checks her written attendance sheet and indicates that Amanda was not in class during period three. Attendance personnel now review the music lesson list. Amanda is not scheduled to be out of any classes today. As the investigation continues, period six begins. The teacher reports that Amanda is absent. The attendance office now verifies that Amanda did not sign out during the day. An attendance office staff member calls Amanda's home to notify her parents that she is not in school today. Amanda's mother indicates that she sent her daughter to the bus stop this morning. Amanda is missing and the school did not discover that fact for almost five hours.

Based on an actual scenario, this hypothetical situation raises numerous questions. How important is student accountability? If student accountability is important, what steps can be taken to improve it? How can information be reported more accurately and in a timelier fashion?

Unless all staff members report attendance information at the beginning of each class, the attendance office cannot identify the actual location of every student at any given time throughout the day. In an emergency, specific information can mean the difference between life and death. In any emergency, such as a fire, lockdown, or abduction, student accountability is of paramount importance. Teachers, administrators, and responders must know the precise location of students. They must know who is missing.

Educate staff members on the vital responsibilities carried out in the attendance office. Document and disseminate attendance reporting policies. As mentioned, require teachers to take attendance at the beginning of every period. Require them to report updates if attendance changes during the period. Enforce those policies.

Pursue collaborative solutions for atypical classes. Some classes, such as physical education, and settings, such as the lunch room, present significant challenges. In situations where student to staff ratios make monitoring difficult, consider utilizing wireless devices, such as a tablets, to take attendance.

Security Systems

People determine the value of security systems. An investment in exterior door locking mechanisms fails to pay dividends when a staff member props a door open and leaves it unmonitored. Recent school security incidents demonstrate that electronic access control systems fail when credentialed personnel inadvertently permit "piggybacking" (allowing someone else to enter before the door closes and latches). Effective staff training optimizes security measures.

Provide instruction in the correct use of security systems and products. Explain to staff members how careless actions defeat systems. Demonstrate the actions that compromise and expose vulnerabilities. Ask for personal commitments to follow safe practices.

Routinely remind staff members that school security systems protect students and personnel. Challenge them to take ownership in ensuring that systems are functional. Periodically ask them to identify the number and locations of cameras. Offer opportunities for staff members to make test announcements over the public address system. Assign individuals the task of opening a first aid kit and handling the supplies. This kind of training helps people crash through psychological barriers and prepares them for emergencies. Remember the maxim: information eases anxiety.

Emergency Preparedness

Numerous states require schools to conduct emergency drills, such as fire drills, lockdown drills, shelter-in-place drills, and bus evacuation drills. There is no substitute for participating in these kinds of exercises. Whether or not your state issues mandates, commit to engaging staff members in routine emergency drills.

Some government agencies, such as the Georgia Emergency Management Agency, provide free training DVDs to schools that request them. Training videos can be used in new staff orientation, as a method of refreshing past learning, and as a department-specific tool. "School Bus Security: A 21st Century Approach" serves as an example of a department-specific training video. Ensure that substitutes, part-time staff, and outside organizations that utilize building space participate in emergency drills and benefit from training videos as well. When operational obstacles prohibit inclusion, pursue collaborative solutions.

Substitutes and Part-Time Staff

Do not forget to equip substitute teachers and part-time staff when it comes to security training and emergency preparedness. Even an abbreviated amount of instruction can make a significant difference in preventing or mitigating an incident. If one of these individuals cannot attend a security workshop, consider requiring that person to complete an assigned online training module that highlights key concepts. If a substitute cannot participate in a lockdown drill, perhaps that person can receive an emergency flipchart that describes response protocols upon entering the building.

Security Personnel

School security personnel can either refer to school employees—such as security officers, paraprofessionals, and safety monitors—or outsourced officers from a contract security firm, such as Whelan Security. Sometimes schools utilize a blended force that is comprised of in-house personnel during the school day and outsourced personnel for nights and weekends. Whatever the case, make the training requirements for security personnel consistent. At minimum, address the following areas.

Scheduling

Collaboratively determine security personnel scheduling so that it will coincide with school operations. Why would the facilities department unlock exterior doors for student arrival at 6:00 am when security personnel do not arrive until 6:30 am? What thought process goes into deciding when security personnel will leave for the day? How many individuals does it take to adequately monitor the cafeteria during lunch periods? Do not permit tradition or apathy to drive your schedule. Proactively review and develop your security personnel scheduling.

Duties

Schools that do not hire security personnel based on a clear job description are asking for trouble. Administrators experience difficulty in disciplining and terminating personnel against a backdrop of vague requirements. Students do not respect personnel that cannot perform basic duties, such as moving up and down stairs in a reasonable amount of time. Students also want rules to be applied evenly. Craft a clear job description and specify responsibilities. Prohibit fraternizing and inappropriate behavior. Ensure that communication with students and staff members is above reproach.

Adequately equip your security personnel. Standardized uniforms serve to deter crime and help stakeholders identify assistance. Maintain a consistent visual security presence. Personnel should carry two-way radios, first aid supplies, and reporting tools. Establish strategic post locations and patrol routes. Deliver detailed post and patrol orders. Require consistent practices.

Training

Since security personnel are strategically positioned at posts and assigned patrol routes, provide them with the training they need to effectively respond. Do they have basic first aid, CPR, and AED training? Have they been certified in conflict resolution? What specific two-way radio communication instruction have they received? Enlist the help of local law enforcement in establishing security practices and correct responses to emergency situations.

Conclusion

Remember, teachers and staff members form your security program's first line of defense. Since security products and practices are only as good as the teachers and staff members who implement them, it is important that they receive routine training. Whether you adopt a specific method of raising collective security awareness or periodically appeal to emotions, resolve to provide security instruction. Failure to do so often results in the collective adoption of a Mayberry mentality. Do not permit individuals to trade security for convenience. You can change the culture of your school from a lack of security awareness to one that fosters a safe learning environment.

References

1. B. Vossekuil et al., *The Final Report and Findings of the Safe School Initiative: Implications for the Prevention of School Attacks in the United States.* (Washington, DC: US Department of Education and US Secret Service, 2002), n.p.

2. Ibid, n.p.

Managing Emergencies

Introduction

His first day! The new substitute teacher smiles nervously at the class of eighth graders in front of him. The kids stare back, a couple obviously contemplating pranks designed to cause trouble for substitutes. Suddenly, an announcement crackles from the loud speaker: "Attention: Code Orange. Code Orange."

The substitute looks blankly at his students. He shrugs and raises his palms toward the ceiling as if to ask for assistance. "We need to lock the door, turn off the lights, and get to the back of the room away from the door and windows," shouts one of the students.

The substitute leaps to the door, turns off the lights, and fumbles with the doorknob, looking for some sort of button to push or turn. Instead, he finds a key cylinder. Unfortunately, no one had given him a key when he checked in that morning. Quickly, he herds the class to the back of the room, tells them to turn the desks over and get behind them. "Does the teacher keep an extra key in the room?" he asks. No one knows. Staying low, the substitute drags his desk over to block the door. Then he gathers some books and his desk chair. He is ready to start flinging things at anyone that opens the door. He takes a deep breath and watches as the knob starts to turn.

Thinking about how an emergency might play out and developing a plan to manage the emergency—before there is an emergency—is a life-saving activity. Drilling and practicing the plans will save lives, too, by highlighting flaws in the plan—such as forgetting to give a substitute teacher a classroom key—and enabling planners to set things right before the real incident happens.

In developing an emergency plan, remember that the reason for planning is to save lives, prevent injuries, and reduce property damage. Many schools create a written emergency operations plan because of a state requirement. Resist the urge to write a plan that simply complies with regulations. Plans tend to be incomplete. Do not forget to consider, for example, individuals with disabilities and others with access and functional needs. Plans quickly become outdated. Formalize a planning team and commit to a routine meeting and review process. Plan as if lives depend on it, because, in fact, lives do depend on it.

A comprehensive emergency plan involves the following components:

- Plan Purpose Statements and Principles
- Plan Procedural Specifics
- Plan Training and Preparedness

Preparing to Get Started

Think of your school's emergency plan as a living document. It requires routine review and updating. Procedures evolve. Key contacts change. New threats surface. State requirements get passed.

Your school must take ownership of the plan. You may benefit from the assistance of local emergency responders and state agencies, but do not transfer ownership. Chapter 9 ("School Security Resources & Conclusion") provides helpful guides and sample templates, but resist the temptation to merely fill in blanks. The development process is important.

Emergency Planning Team

Developing an effective emergency response plan requires collaboration. Do not confuse the Emergency Planning Team with the Security Planning Team described in chapter 2 ("How Safe Is Your School"). The Emergency Planning Team should comprise administrators, teachers, nurses, facility managers, school psychologists, transportation managers, food personnel, and family services representatives. This planning team should also include student and parent representatives, those that represent individuals with disabilities and special needs, and racial minorities and religious organizations, so that specific concerns are included in the early stages of planning. In addition, the planning team should include first responders, local emergency management staff, and others who have roles and responsibilities in school emergency management before, during, and after an incident. This includes local law enforcement officers, emergency medical services personnel, school resource officers, fire officials, public and mental health practitioners, and local emergency managers.

US Department of Education Guide

Align your emergency response plan with the nation's approach to preparedness. National, state, and local response agencies follow consistent practices and principles in their emergency planning efforts. According to the US Department of Education's *Guide for Developing High-Quality School Emergency Operations Plans*, Presidential Policy Directive 8 defines preparedness around five mission areas: prevention, protection, mitigation, response, and recovery.

- Prevention means the capabilities necessary to avoid, deter, or stop an imminent crime or threatened or actual mass casualty incident. Prevention covers the actions schools take to prevent an incident from occurring.
- Protection means the capabilities to secure schools against acts of violence and human-made or natural disasters. Protection focuses on ongoing actions that protect students, teachers, staff, visitors, networks, and property from a threat or hazard.
- Mitigation means the capabilities necessary to eliminate or reduce the loss of life and property damage by lessening the impact of an event or emergency. Mitigation also means reducing the likelihood that threats and hazards will happen.

- Response means the capabilities necessary to stabilize an emergency once it has already happened or is certain to happen. Establish a safe and secure environment, save lives and property, and facilitate the transition to recovery.
- Recovery means the capabilities necessary to assist schools affected by an event or emergency in restoring the learning environment.[1]

Your emergency planning team should be familiar with these mission areas.

ADA Compliance

Plans must comply with the Americans with Disabilities Act (ADA), among other prohibitions on disability discrimination, across the spectrum of emergency management services, programs, and activities, including preparation, testing, notification and alerts, evacuation, transportation, sheltering, emergency medical care and services, transitioning back, recovery, and repairing and rebuilding. Plans should include students, staff, and parents with disabilities. Among other things, school emergency plans must address the provision of appropriate auxiliary aids and services to ensure effective communication with individuals with disabilities, such as interpreters, captioning, and accessible information technology. Ensure individuals with disabilities are not separated from service animals and assistive devices, and can receive disability-related assistance throughout emergencies, such as assistance with activities of daily living and administration of medications. Comply with the law's architectural and other requirements. Information and technical assistance about the ADA is available at http://www.ada.gov.

Language Access Compliance

Effective communication with individuals with limited English proficiency, including students and parents, is an essential component of emergency planning and response. Plans must comply with applicable legal requirements on language access, including Title VI of the Civil Rights Act of 1964 (available at http://www.justice.gov/crt/about/cor/coord/title vi.php) and the Title VI regulation of the Civil Rights Act of 1964 (available at http://www.justice.gov/crt/about/cor/fedagencies.php).

Plan Content

The school Emergency Operation Plan (EOP) begins by explaining the plan's basic purpose and why the EOP is necessary, citing threats and hazards that are a risk to the school. The next section gives an overall picture of how the school will protect the students, staff, and visitors, while the third section provides an overview of the broad roles and responsibilities of school staff, families, and community partners during all emergencies. Annexes are the parts of the EOP that begin to provide specific information and direction. These focus on operations: what the function is and who is responsible for carrying it out.

Plan Purpose

Every emergency document should begin with something similar to a mission statement that describes an intention to lessen the effects of an emergency, the steps that will be taken to accomplish that goal, and how it will be communicated to relevant stakeholders. This section of the plan should be brief. Devote it solely to the basic task of developing a plan and identifying the people who will be in charge of organizing, coordinating, and revising it going forward.

Write something like, "The objective of the school Emergency Operations Program is to protect the lives and well-being of students, staff, and visitors through the prompt and timely response of trained school personnel should an emergency affect the school. To meet this objective, the school will establish and maintain a comprehensive emergency operations program that includes plans and procedures, hazard analysis, security audits, training and exercises, and plan review and maintenance."

Make the first component very basic. Begin with a heading such as, "Description of the school's overall approach to emergency operations." This description of the school's emergency operations strategy is vital because it provides emergency responders, administrators, staff, teachers, and eventually parents and students with a general idea of how to respond in an emergency.

Write a description such as, "The purpose of our school Emergency Operation Plan is to identify threats and hazards, then plan how to respond to a variety of incidents by outlining the responsibilities and duties of our school and its employees. Developing, maintaining, and exercising the plan empowers employees and other stakeholders to act quickly and know their roles and responsibilities before, during, and after an incident. This plan provides parents and other members of the community with the assurances that our school has established guidelines and procedures to respond to incidents in an effective way."

The second component involves a statement about how and when the emergency plan will be implemented. This is very simple and relates to the first part of this section because the two are intertwined. While the first is a description of an overall approach to emergencies, the second details what the first left out. It is the specifics of the plan rather than the total concept.

Write something like, "The basic plan and the functional and hazard-specific annexes outline an organized, systematic method of mitigating, preventing, preparing for, responding to, and recovering from incidents. Teachers and staff have been trained to assess the seriousness of incidents and respond according to these established procedures and guidelines. The school regularly schedules emergency preparedness in-service training for teachers and staff."

The third and fourth sub-points of this section are directly related. They both seek to identify individuals who will be leaders and organizers of the previously mentioned steps in the present and in the future. The first of these seeks to identify who will coordinate with first responder agencies and how the coordination will take place. At this point, the school may also decide to add this responsibility to an administrator's job description.

This individual will be in charge of communicating with police, fire, and medical officials if an emergency were to occur. The final part of the first section seeks to identify who will be responsible for revising the school's EOP and for disseminating the updated plan to all agencies, such as principals and first responders. Once again, it is imperative to identify someone who will oversee the emergency plan itself. This may involve adding responsibilities to an existing administrator's position or perhaps creating a new position altogether. It is important to be constantly updating and revising emergency plans, but it is also vital to keep first responders, teachers, staff, parents, and students in the loop when it comes to existing plans and updates.

Plan Procedural Specifics

The second section of the EOP addresses definitions and assignment of roles and responsibilities. This section accounts for the real substance of the plan. While the first section dealt with creating a plan and organizing how it will be put into effect, this section is far more detailed and focuses on specifics within the emergency operations plan. This section begins with a school emergency management organization that follows the Incident Command System (ICS).

The ICS is part of the National Incident Management System (NIMS). Developed in the aftermath of 9/11, NIMS is a consistent framework used by all agencies to respond to disasters. The ICS is a NIMS tool developed for the command, control, and coordination of emergency response. In other words, the ICS specifies individuals within the school who are tasked with managing a crisis. Some administrators assume that first responders will meet this need, but responders often cannot arrive immediately, which means an in-house group must initially manage the incident. For many schools, the principal is the natural choice to fill the role of incident commander, but the ICS requires redundancy. Who will serve as the incident commander's backup? Who will serve as that person's backup? In addition to the incident commander, schools must document positions such as public information officer, safety officer, liaison officer, operations, logistics, planning, and finance and administration. The goal is to have two alternates at every response position.

Collaboratively complete the ICS form utilizing personnel that are available during the school's normal operations, such as 7:30 am to 3:30 pm. This exercise can be challenging, but will pay dividends. The more difficult task surfaces in attempting to complete the ICS structure during the often-forgotten, after-hours timeframe. Many administrators question the feasibility of finding qualified individuals during this timeframe, but the need for a game plan to manage an after-hours emergency cannot be denied. To assist in addressing this need, we recommend asking staff members to complete a staff skills survey (Figure 7.1) that identifies qualifications, credentials, training, and skills individuals possess. Once results are compiled, administrators often find that there are staff members working after-hours who have the skills to fill ICS positions.

To assist in preparing emergency plans, the federal government has developed a course (IS-100.SCA: Introduction to the Incident Command System for Schools) to familiarize school administrators with how ICS principles can be applied in school-based incidents

Staff Skill Survey & Inventory

During any disaster situation, it is important to be able to draw from all resources. The special skills, training, and capabilities of the staff will play a vital role in coping with the effects of any disaster incident. They will be of paramount importance during and after a major or catastrophic disaster. The purpose of this survey/inventory is to pinpoint those staff members with equipment and special skills that might be utilized in the case of a crisis. Please indicate the areas that apply to you and return this survey to your administrator.

Name: _____   Department: _____

Directions: Please check any of the following areas in which you have expertise or training and circle "yes" or "no" where appropriate.

____ First aid (current certification: yes/no)   ____ Mechanical ability
____ CPR (current certification: yes/no)   ____ Structural engineering
____ Triage   ____ Bus/truck driver (Class 1/2 yes/no)
____ Firefighting   ____ Shelter management
____ Construction (electrical, plumbing, carpentry)   ____ Survival training and techniques
____ Running/jogging   ____ Food preparation
____ Emergency planning   ____ Ham radio operator
____ Emergency management   ____ CB radio operator
____ Search and rescue   ____ Journalism
____ Law enforcement   ____ Camping
____ Bi/Multi-lingual   ____ Waste disposal
____ Specify language/s: _____   ____ Recreational leader

➤ Do you keep a personal emergency kit? ____ In your car? ____ In your room? ____
➤ Do you have materials or equipment in your room that could be of special use during an emergency? Yes ____ No ____

If yes, please list the materials/equipment: _____

┌───┐
│ Additional Comments/Information: │
│   │
│   │
│   │
└───┘

FIGURE 7.1

and prepare schools to work together with community response personnel. In about an hour or two, school administrators can take this course and obtain professional development CEUs and certification at the FEMA website (http://training.fema.gov/EMIWeb/IS/courseOverview.aspx?code=is-100.sca).

Next, move from the high-level ICS components to more detailed roles and responsibilities. The actual first responder is usually the individual who discovers the emergency situation. For example, a teacher who encounters a fight between students might respond according to the following procedures.

• Notify the school's incident commander immediately and get assistance.
• Do not let a crowd incite participants.

- Disperse onlookers and keep others from congregating in the area.
- Use calm verbal commands to try to break up the fight first.
- Avoid stepping between participants.
- Once assistance arrives, work as team to separate participants.
- When participants are separated, move them quickly; escort the participants to the office and do not allow further visual or verbal contact.
- Document all activities witnessed by staff.

Similarly, your EOP should detail the responsibilities of the incident commander and other members of the emergency team. Continue in this fashion to document the responsibilities of monitors who will ensure the proper execution of the planned response; the responsibilities for communicating with first responders, building occupants, families, representatives of the media, and other members of the community; and the responsibilities for maintaining emergency-related records.

Each response description should include the titles of the people who will lead and assist in the response. Be sure to include the name and contact information of the media contact (public information officer) who will take questions from reporters.

Other common features of each kind of emergency involves evacuation from the building to a predetermined assembly site where faculty will ascertain who may still be in the building. Later may come relocation to another site where parents and students can reunite. Finally, the team leader will brief first responders and shift into a supporting role.

Functional Annexes/Protocols

Functional annexes are critical operational functions or protocols that clearly define and describe the policies, processes, roles, and responsibilities inherent in the various functions before, during, and after any emergency period. These written procedures specify the courses of action for emergency functions that apply across multiple threats or hazards. In other words, these protocols can be implemented in any number of different emergencies. While it may be an oversimplification to assert that all emergency responses boil down to people either needing to stay (e.g., shelter-in-place, lockdown) or go (e.g., evacuate), there is some truth to the assertion. Common functional protocols include the following.

- Evacuation – when conditions outside the facility are safer than inside, the quick and orderly movement of students/staff away from the building.
- Shelter-in-place – when unsafe conditions exist or there is the potential for unsafe conditions, the movement of students/staff into a designated area of refuge within the building. Shelter areas may change depending on the emergency.
- Lockdown – when there is a threat of violence inside the school building or serious incident that could jeopardize the safety of students/staff, all exterior doors and classroom doors are locked, and students and staff stay in their secured offices, work areas, and classrooms.

- Reverse evacuation – when conditions inside the facility are safer than outside, the quick and orderly movement of students/staff back into a facility to protect them from a threat or hazard.
- Reunification – the redirection of building occupants to a secured site that is removed from the scene of the emergency with the goal of reuniting students/staff with their families.

As an example, reunification action steps may be implemented when the facility has suffered some type of structural failure or in the immediate aftermath of an active shooter situation. Functional protocols do not apply to just one kind of emergency. While the following list of specific emergencies requires unique response protocols, functional protocols are also used as part of the action steps.

Severe Weather

Severe weather is probably the most common emergency. Threats for which schools must prepare include thunderstorms and lightning, tornadoes, damaging winds, flash floods, and hail. Other forms of severe weather, such as snow/ice storms and flooding, are generally predictable and cause schools to close for the duration.

According to the National Weather Service (NWS), a severe thunderstorm produces hail at least one inch in diameter, winds of 58 mph or stronger, or a tornado. The NWS has produced a severe weather preparedness guide for schools. It includes safety information for tornadoes. The guide can be accessed at http://rems.ed.gov/docs/NOAA_TornadoSafetyForSchools.pdf.

To stay safe in a severe thunderstorm or tornado, you must first know that the current weather conditions may produce a storm. The NWS Doppler radar network covers the US, and the National Oceanic and Atmospheric Administration (NOAA) maintains a nationwide network of radio stations that constantly broadcast warnings, watches, forecasts, and hazardous weather information. NOAA weather radios are available from brick-and-mortar and online electronics retailers. Every school should have one. Test it monthly and change the batteries annually.

When NWS issues a severe weather warning, all outdoor activities and classes should move indoors immediately. Call for a reverse evacuation. Students, staff, and visitors should shelter-in-place in interior rooms or designated areas—with no windows on the school's lowest level—to wait out the warning or a storm.

On May 22, 2011, Joplin, Missouri was struck by an Enhanced Fujita scale category five (EF5) tornado, resulting in approximately 160 deaths and 1150 injuries. The tornado destroyed thousands of structures, including houses, businesses, and school buildings. Because this catastrophe occurred on a Sunday afternoon, schools were not in session. Nevertheless, video captured by school hallway cameras fundamentally changed the way Joplin schools prepared for tornados. For decades, these schools conducted severe weather drills by pulling students out of classrooms and placing them in interior hallways. Staff directed students to line up against the hallway walls and assume a "duck and cover" position. Hallway cameras showed how hallways quickly became wind tunnels. Large amounts of dangerous debris tumbled and sliced through the halls. In some areas, classroom walls fell into the hallway. Lives would have been lost in hallways had the tornado touched down during school hours. As a result, Joplin schools no longer shelter in hallways. Instead, the district now shelters in basements. In the schools that do not have basements, students shelter in interior rooms that do not have exterior windows, such as locker rooms, rest rooms, and offices. See Chapter 9 ("School Security Resources & Conclusion") for additional options and preparedness planning information.

Fire

When it comes to fires, there are many codes and safety procedures in schools to prevent and reduce risk. The dedication to fire safety, in large part, stems from a 1958 tragedy that claimed the lives of almost 100 people at Our Lady of the Angels catholic school in Chicago. After this incident, fire codes and regulations swept across the education landscape. Evacuation procedures became second nature. As a result of this commitment to fire safety, not a single student has died in a school-related fire since.

That is a record worth preserving. While fire drill evacuations have become part of the routine in K–12 schools, a few additional measures can help firefighters respond faster in the event of a fire. Nothing helps a first responder as much as familiarity with the site. Visit the local fire department and talk with the community-relations officer. Invite the firefighters to the school to look around and make suggestions. Offer the school as a site for drills at night.

Bomb Threat

Bomb threats arrive in the form of suspicious packages or through communication by way of written notes or telephone calls.

According to the Federal Emergency Management Agency, packages that should raise suspicions arrive unexpectedly from an unfamiliar sender, have no return address, and often carry restrictive labels such as "Personal" or "Do Not X-ray." Protruding wires, aluminum foil, strange odors, and stains are suspicious, too.

Compare the postmark and return address on all packages—they should match. Treat packages of unusual size, weight, or shape carefully. Threatening language, unusual labeling, misspellings of common words, incorrect titles, and handwritten or poorly typed addresses should raise suspicions as well.

If you receive such a package, call the police. Likewise, call the police if you come across a package that appears to have been abandoned. Increase staff awareness in areas where mail is handled by posting the US Postal Service's "Suspicious Mail or Packages" guide (http://about.usps.com/posters/pos84.pdf).

Some bomb threats arrive by telephone. FEMA advises keeping a bomb threat caller on the line and getting as much information as possible. Ensure that a bomb threat checklist (Figure 7.2) is visible and positioned within arm's reach of every main telephone. Collect information and notify the police immediately.

If there is an explosion and debris is falling, individuals should take cover under a sturdy piece of furniture. When the debris stops falling, evacuate the building as quickly as possible. Do not waste time retrieving personal belongings and do not use the elevator.

BOMB THREAT CHECKLIST

Description Detail Report

Questions to Ask:

1) When is the bomb going to explode?

2) Where is it right now?

3) What does it look like?

4) What kind of bomb is it?

5) What will cause it to explode?

6) Did you place the bomb?

7) Why?

8) What is your address?

9) What is your name?

Exact wording of the threat: _____

_____

_____

_____

_____

Sex of caller: _____ Race: _____

Length of call: _____ Age: _____

Date: _____ Time: _____

Number at which call was received: _____

_____

Notes:

Callers Voice - Circle as Applicable:

• Calm	• Nasal
• Angry	• Stutter
• Excited	• Lisp
• Slow	• Raspy
• Rapid	• Deep
• Soft	• Ragged
• Loud	• Clearing throat
• Laughter	• Deep breathing
• Crying	• Cracked voice
• Normal	• Disguised
• Distinct	• Accent
• Slurred	• Familiar

If voice is familiar, whom did it sound like?

_____

Background Sounds:

• Street noises	• Factory machinery
• Animal noises	• Voices
• Clear	• PA system
• Static	• Local call
• Music	• Long distance call
• House noises	• Phone booth
• Motor	• Office machinery
• Other	

_____

_____

Threat Language:

• Well-spoken (educated)	
• Incoherent	• Taped
• Foul	• Message read
• Irrational by Threat Maker	

Remarks: _____

_____

_____

FIGURE 7.2

Once outside, stay away from the building, especially windows and glass doors. Clear the sidewalks and streets for emergency officials.

Structural Failure

Severe weather, fires, earthquakes, bomb blasts, and other serious incidents can all create consequences, one being structural damage and, in the worst cases, structural failure. Should a structural failure such as the collapse of the roof or wall occur, building occupants should seek cover. Sturdy desks and tables can help protect individuals from falling debris. When the collapse ends, help those with injuries evacuate the building.

If there has been no collapse but cracked columns, bowed walls, and other building features suggest that a collapse could occur, evacuate the affected area immediately. Take stock of the building during the evacuation. Has a fire started? Are there any water leaks? Is gas leaking?

Call 911 and tell the dispatcher what has happened, the status of the evacuation, and if it is likely that any victims remain in the building. Report anything that has been observed about the condition of the building. Dispatch staff to shut down utilities and to keep people away from the building perimeter. No one should return to the building—or the affected part of the building—until structural integrity has been restored.

Utility Failure

Utility failures include power outages, gas leaks, loss of water service, and interrupted sewage service. While it is often possible to wait for power to be restored, gas leaks require an immediate response, usually an evacuation that leaves windows and doors open to disperse the gas. Loss of water service and interrupted sewage service may also require an evacuation. Lengthy events may cause the school to close. The team leader can help to determine this by calling the affected utility companies to determine when service might be restored.

Bus Accidents

A school bus accident requires action from the bus driver, the school's emergency management leader, and district administrators.

In the event of an accident, the bus driver must protect the students. After turning off the ignition, removing the key, and activating the vehicle's hazard lights, he or she must determine where the students will be most safe—on the bus or on the side of the road. If necessary, the driver will evacuate the bus.

Call 911 and tell the dispatcher about the accident, stating that a school bus is involved and reporting the nature of any injuries. Next, the driver will notify the school's principal, who will pass the information along to the emergency management leader. The leader will send a district representative—or, if necessary, a team—to the scene of the accident. At the scene, it will be important to collect the names of the students on the bus, find out who was injured and how seriously and who was taken to what hospitals. In addition to notifying parents, administration personnel should visit each hospital to track the condition of all injured students. Depending upon how serious the injuries are, administrators may decide to arrange for counseling for the passengers as well as the driver.

Hazardous Materials Incident

While we do not always think about them, hazardous chemicals and materials are never far away. Manufacturing plants that make or use hazardous chemicals or materials operate in most regions of the country. Freight trains and semi-trailers carrying hazardous materials pass within a few miles of most communities. Even closer are the chemicals used in school laboratories, vocational/technical shops, pool areas, and school maintenance areas.

For an outdoor release, the school's emergency management leader will order everyone into the school building to shelter-in-place and direct assistants to call 911, to close all windows and doors, and to shut down the heating, ventilating, and air-conditioning systems.

Should a spill or release occur inside the school, the leader would order an evacuation to an assembly location upwind of the contaminated area. The rest of the procedures would be similar to those employed during an external release. The leader would order assistants to call 911, close all windows and doors, and shut down the HVAC system.

In each case, students, faculty, and staff must avoid the affected area until the first responders determine it is clear.

Intruder Incident

Identification badges on color-coded lanyards worn by students, faculty, administrators, staff, and authorized visitors make it easy to identify and quickly respond to an intruder.

Students seeing an intruder should avoid the individual and report the sighting to an adult. Two or three adults should make a friendly approach, observing the individual closely. Is he or she carrying anything that might conceal a weapon. Does the person's demeanor suggest trouble? If there is any hint of potential violence, back away, call the emergency response leader—on a phone that he or she will always answer—and ask for the police.

In most cases, you will feel fine about engaging the individual: "Hello, how may I help you? I see that you do not have a visitor's badge. Let me show you to the office where you can get one." Most of the time, a supposed intruder will turn out to be an uninformed visitor who will welcome the guidance.

If the intruder refuses to accompany the group to the office, someone might say, "We have a strict policy of calling the police if a visitor refuses to register at the office and get a visitor's pass. You will have to come to the office or leave." If resistance continues, the second or third adult in the group should call the emergency response leader, report the intruder's presence, and ask for the police.

If at any time, the intruder appears to be considering violence, walk away and watch from a safe distance. Inform the emergency response leader, who may order a lockdown.

Public Health Emergency

There are public health emergencies of all kinds. Each demands a specific response. Preparing to manage different public health emergencies, however, follows the same basic steps: research the problem, communicate prevention information and activities, and communicate care and recovery information. Finally, get teachers and student back to school as soon as possible.

The following steps demonstrate how the process might work in the case of the outbreak of an infectious disease, such as the flu. School board health committees and school nurses across school districts should check state and local health department websites and the Center for Disease Control (CDC) website (http://www.cdc.gov/) daily for alerts about infectious diseases—as well as other public health emergencies.

The CDC website has a page devoted to outbreaks. It describes four infectious disease outbreaks that occurred during 2013. It also posts a weekly report on the flu, called Flu-View, which summarizes flu activity around the country. Information flows both ways, from CDC to state and local health departments and from state and local health departments to the CDC.

If the CDC has concerns about a possible or existing health emergency, it will post information on the website and inform state and local officials, who in turn will inform school board health committees, which will pass information along to school nurses. When something big is in the offing, the CDC will issue guidelines to help schools prevent the spread of the disease and to facilitate recovery.

In the case of flu, many of the recommendations are well known. For instance, the CDC recommends that everyone six months of age and older receive a flu vaccine every year. The CDC also recommends publicizing the need for vaccines and the importance of preventive measures such as avoiding sick people, washing hands regularly, and coughing or sneezing into a tissue or your sleeve—and then washing your hands. Of course, those who do get sick should stay home to avoid infecting others.

In the past, treating the flu meant staying in bed, getting plenty of sleep, and drinking liquids. Over the counter medicines could reduce the severity of symptoms. In the end, however, a patient had to wait until the body's immune system killed the virus. While that is still necessary, there are antiviral drugs available today that do not only ease the symptoms but also shorten the duration of the disease.

Part of preparing for public health emergencies or other kinds of emergencies is imagining a worst-case scenario. For example, while preparing for the onset of the H1N1 Swine Flu virus in 2009, many feared that the epidemic could grow severe enough to close schools. Unlike other flu strains, H1N1 affects people between six months and 24 years old more than other age groups. In fact, by the end of October 2009, over 600 schools closed temporarily, causing 126,000 students in 19 states to miss classes.

The CDC recommended that colleges with significant numbers of ailing students consider suspending classes. In response, some schools, such as the Johns Hopkins University School of Nursing, asked faculty members to prepare video and audio classes that students could access online.

That is a good idea for a year that brings a severe flu outbreak, and it can help ailing students during ordinary flu outbreaks. Recovering students often find themselves exhausted upon returning to class. Online classes that enable them to stay home for one or two extra days can help them recover their stamina.

Other Emergencies

As a reminder, the types of emergencies discussed above represent a minimal number of areas that should be addressed. Areas that can be added may include emergencies that involve aircraft incidents, nuclear incidents, state/federal prison incidents, etc.

Available Resources

An effective EOP will catalogue an inventory of resources that are available when responding to emergencies. An emergency contact list (Figure 7.3) is a vital component that identifies persons by title and agency who must be notified in an emergency. This information applies to your formal emergency plan, not to crisis flipcharts that individual staff members receive. Flipcharts are limited in space and only require basic numbers, such as how to contact the school office, the district office, the nurse, the school resource officer, and 911. The formal emergency plan, however, should include direct contact numbers for all public safety agencies, such as local hospitals and clinics, police, fire, and poison control. It should also include contacts at the district level, such as the superintendent, the transportation director, the director of buildings and grounds, food services, health services, and media coordinator. Finally, the plan should include school contact numbers, such as administrators, the school nurse, the counseling office, the school resource officer, and facilities personnel.

The second resource component involves methods for accounting for the whereabouts and status of all children and the process established for releasing students into the care of their parents and others. All schools should have a designated parent reunification site. To avoid an influx of large numbers of people at the scene of an emergency and the possibility of interfering with responding agencies, parents should be made aware of a predetermined, off-site location where students will be released. Document the release of all students and staff (see Figure 7.4).

The third resource component addresses response guidance materials and the methods of providing them to students and staff, including personnel such as bus drivers, secretaries, custodians, and visitors. For example, post accurate evacuation maps in every room in the facility, including restrooms. Evacuation maps should clearly depict the facility diagram, current location, primary and secondary evacuation routes, exterior rally areas, lockdown safe rooms, and designated shelter-in-place areas. Emergency evacuation maps should detail fire evacuation routes (in red), tornado shelter areas (in green), and designated safe rooms (in blue).

Individual crisis flipcharts, or guides, became popular a number of years back when it was common to find alphabetized flipcharts with tabs that were all the colors of the rainbow. These guides should never be alphabetized, as they are not a phonebook. As English readers, we habitually look to the top first. A crisis guide should be organized in order of likelihood to occur. For example, severe weather should be at or near the top. Crisis guides should not have numerous colors. There is no real cognitive value in having numerous color distinctions. Environmental emergencies, such as fires, should be colored red and security emergencies, such as intruder incidents, should be colored blue. We recommend a one page, double-sided, laminated crisis guide. Place all environmental emergencies, in order of likelihood, on one side with a red border. Red is the universal, OSHA-approved, cognitive color for environmental emergencies. Place all security emergencies on the other side with a blue border. Television programs, such as *Hill Street Blues*, *NYPD Blue*, *Blue Bloods*, and *Rookie Blue* remind us that blue is the

Emergency Contact Names & Telephone Numbers

CONTACT	Number
Police Department	911
Non-Emergency..	
Fire Department..	911
Non-Emergency..	
City/Village of	
Public Works..	
Hospital...	
State Road Conditions..	
Statewide Terrorism Intelligence Center........................	
DCFS Hotline...	
Department of Transportation.......................................	
Poison Center..	
Emergency Management Agency	
Gas Company...	
Electric Company..	
Water Company..	
County Regional Office of Education.............................	
State Police Department Safety Education.....................	
County Emergency Management Agency.......................	
County Sheriff's Police Department..............................	
County Health Department..	
Department of Children & Family Services.....................	
Bus Company...	
Director of Facilities...	

FIGURE 7.3

Parent/Family Reunification Form

Fill out at the student site:

Student's Name: _____ Grade_____

Student's Address: _____

Parent's Name: _____

Teacher's Name: _____

Counselor (if applicable): _____

Checked in by _____

Parent(s), legal guardian, or emergency contact signature:

_____

Checked out by: _____

Date: _____

Time: _____

FIGURE 7.4

OSHA-approved, cognitive color for security emergencies. Once again, the emergencies should be ordered in likelihood of occurrence. The benefit of this type of crisis guide is that it can be produced in-house and revised at a relatively low cost when compared to traditional flipcharts.

Document all methods for emergency notification of parents, staff, and students. Mass notification used to be limited to telephone trees, school websites, mass e-mail systems, and television/radio stations. Today's parent notification systems enable administrators to connect quickly and easily with communities in almost any language and on any device. Emergency alerts can be sent via voice, text, e-mail, and social media.

The final resource component lists emergency supplies and equipment (see Figure 7.5). This section addresses maintaining a list of emergency supplies, including first aid kits, AEDs, and fire extinguishers. All of these supplies are code-driven items that schools are required to have by law. Schools should also store additional supplies in case there is a need for locking down or sheltering-in-place for an extended period.

Resource Inventory Form

Please list the number and location of the following types of equipment and supplies: ladders, AEDs, fire extinguishers, power tools, hydraulic lifts, hydraulic carts, hand carts, first aid kits, generators, portable water pumps, portable lighting, extra food, and extra water supply.

Type of Equipment	# of Items	Location

FIGURE 7.5

In addition, we suggest storing emergency supplies in some kind of classroom emergency backpack (Figure 7.6). The ideal backpack includes helpful supplies such as water bottles, hypoallergenic energy bars, windup flashlights (no batteries required), Mylar blankets, and writing supplies. For a more detailed description of supplies, visit http://www.retasecurity.com/pages.asp?pageid=94202. In a best-case scenario, every room would have a classroom emergency backpack. Schools that cannot afford to equip every room with a backpack will occasionally store a tote box full of supplies in the main office. Having a group of supplies in only one area, however, is not good enough. Murphy's Law dictates that the one area where supplies are kept will be inaccessible during an emergency. As a result, we recommend storing supplies in a number of different areas.

Classroom Emergency Backpack

The backpacks have three items that need to be replaced after a period of time. Here are the following items that need to be replaced:

- The water needs to be replaced every two years;
- The light sticks need to be replaced every three years; and
- The food needs to be replaced every five years.

Inventory

- 1 clear backpack
- 1 waterproof tarp (8'x10')
- 2 safety light sticks (12 hour)
- 1 emergency rain poncho
- 6 bottles of water (16 ½ oz.)
- 6 energy bars (non peanut)
- 2 emergency thermal blankets
- 1 red pen
- 1 black pen
- 1 pad of paper (8" x 11½")
- 1 black permanent marker
- 1 wind-up flashlight
- 1 first aid kit
- 2 pencils
- 1 whistle with lanyard
- 1 safety vest
- 1 clipboard
- 2 highlighters
- 1 toilet paper roll
- 2 zip lock bags
- 30 paper cups
- 1 roll silver duct tape (2" x 60')

FIGURE 7.6

Plan Training and Preparedness

This final section of the plan addresses training and preparedness. Begin this section with a description of actions taken to instruct and drill stakeholder groups. The state of Illinois, for example, requires every public and private K–12 school to conduct at least three fire drills each year. One of those drills must be monitored and approved in writing by the local fire department. The state also requires one bus evacuation drill, one severe weather drill, and one lockdown drill. Unfortunately, states vary in types and frequencies of drills.

The next part of this section addresses information that exists about the school, such as hazard analyses, maps/diagrams, site plans, safety reference plans, community agreements, and transportation agreements. The final part of the section details the recording and results of required school safety drills and any optional drills conducted.

Drills and Exercises

There are only two ways we can know if our emergency management procedures are effective. One of those ways involves evaluating them during an actual emergency. Unfortunately, that can be a very inconvenient time to find out that your emergency procedures do not work. The other way we can determine effectiveness is through testing or drilling the plan.

- Tabletop Exercises: Tabletop exercises are small-group discussions that walk through scenarios and courses of action a school will need to take before, during, and after emergencies to lessen the impact on the school community. This activity helps assess the plan and resources and facilitates an understanding of emergency management and planning concepts.
- Drills: During drills, school personnel and community partners (e.g., first responders and local emergency management staff) use the actual school grounds and buildings to practice responding to a scenario.
- Functional Exercises: Functional exercises are similar to drills but involve multiple partners; some may be conducted district-wide. Participants react to realistic simulated events (e.g., a bomb threat or an intruder with a gun in a classroom) and implement the plan and procedures using the ICS.
- Full-Scale Exercises: These exercises are the most time-consuming activities in the exercise continuum and are multi-agency, multi-jurisdictional efforts in which all resources are deployed. This type of exercise tests collaboration among the agencies and participants, public information systems, communications systems, and equipment. An emergency operations center is established by either law enforcement or fire services, and the ICS is activated

Conducting Tabletop Exercises

The first level of testing should take place in a tabletop exercise. This kind of exercise simply requires gathering a few stakeholder representatives, such as an administrator, a custodian, a teacher, and a secretary around a table to participate in a role-playing scenario. The purpose is to engage in problem-solving in a low-stress environment. Stakeholders become acquainted with one another, their interrelated roles, and their respective responsibilities.

To ensure spontaneity, it may be helpful to be prepared with a number of scenarios and draw one out of a hat. Assign someone the task of note taking. As soon as the scenario is drawn, a time-keeping device should begin to audibly count the seconds or mark specific time intervals. This element provides a measure of reality and, at the same time, records the length of the exercise. Exercises can be completed in as few as 30 minutes or extended over a period of hours.

Read the scenario aloud. Give each stakeholder an opportunity to explain the actions that he or she would take. Document responses. The facilitator of the exercise can add updates to the scenario at any time. The facilitator also determines when the exercise is completed. Once completed, constructively evaluate stakeholder responses and adjust procedures. Documentation, before, during, and after the exercise, is critical.

TABLE TOP EXERCISE EXAMPLE
(Enter Date)

(Enter Time)

At _(Enter Time)_ today _____ Police responded to a reported armed robbery at _____ Bank on _____ Street. A 2004 navy blue Ford Taurus, presumably being used as a get-away vehicle by the robbery suspects, was last seen heading toward this area.

_____ Police are notifying local businesses and organizations to be on high alert (optional: the principal is attending an off-site meeting).

You, the school administration and staff, now face a series of decisions.

Administrator – Assume there are some outside activities (i.e., recess, PE). How do you go about alerting your staff? What are your directions for the staff? What do you do next? Do you alert parents? How do you handle pick-up/dismissal of students?

Staff member (inside) – Assume you are conducting class and receive information about this potential crisis. What will you do?

Staff member (outside) – Assume you are supervising an activity on the perimeter of the grounds and receive information about this potential crisis. What will you do?

Secretary – You have just received a telephone call from a concerned parent who heard a breaking news report of the bank robbery on the radio. How will you respond?

Custodian – What are your responsibilities? What actions will you take?

Social worker/counselor – What are your responsibilities? What actions will you take?

Other –

Conducting Drills
A drill is a coordinated, supervised exercise activity. It is usually utilized to test a single specific operation, such as lockdown. The basic level of drilling can involve most, if not all, of your staff.

You may want to set aside some time during a planned in-service to conduct a lockdown drill. Position administrators in hallways and—using plain language—announce a lockdown over the PA system. Each administrator should document the amount of time it takes from the time of announcement for every door in the hallway to be locked. Once the time is recorded, the administrator should check every classroom in the hallway to make sure doors are locked, rooms are completely silent, and occupants cannot be seen.

Any deviance should be recorded and addressed with the responsible staff member later. After each hallway has been checked, the "all clear" announcement should be issued over the PA system and an administrative debriefing session should be held in a conference room.

A more advanced level could involve students, as well. Before pursuing this level, notify parents with a detailed explanation of the lockdown drill.

The highest level of testing involves the participation of local, emergency responders. Plan to test security practices and communication procedures. Attempt to introduce variables that cause staff to make critical decisions. Remember to account for students, staff, and visitors with special needs. Debrief the same day with your teachers and staff. This level should not be attempted without a significant amount of planning, coordination, and parent and community notification.

Conducting Functional Exercises

A functional exercise simulates an emergency in the most realistic manner possible, short of moving real people, equipment, and resources to an actual site. The goal is to test the capability of one or more functions in the context of an emergency event. Appoint someone with experience to manage and direct the exercise. Include stakeholders that would be involved in a real emergency, such as policymakers, emergency coordinators, and operational personnel. Ensure that an official evaluator is assessing performance.

Conducting Full-Scale Exercises

A full-scale exercise is as close to a real emergency as possible. It is a lengthy exercise that takes place on location, using the equipment, personnel, and resources that would be called upon in a real event. It typically tests multiple operational components of the school's emergency plan. A good full-scale exercise can take more than six months to plan. The exercise will involve staff, students, district personnel, community partners, first responders, your emergency management agency, parents, and evaluators.

The Evolution of Active Shooter Procedures

Many of us watched in horror as the tragic Columbine High School incident of 1999 unfolded before our television viewing eyes. We wondered why emergency responders were not storming the building. People unjustly blamed local law enforcement for not taking more immediate action. Those responders were, in fact, following trained procedures—set up a perimeter until a SWAT team arrived and addressed the situation. In the aftermath of that tragedy, law enforcement procedures evolved. The new active shooter response involved rapid deployment. Rapid deployment procedures require officers to quickly locate and neutralize threats. Until the threat is neutralized, they are tasked with moving through unsecured areas without assisting injured victims.

Inside school buildings, teachers and staff adopted lockdown procedures. Plain language, such as "We are now going into lockdown," replaced covert codes such as

"Mr. Green has entered the building" and colors such as "Code Orange." Teachers and staff responded to a plain language announcement by pulling nearby students into classrooms as they locked doors, moving students out of view of classroom door windows, turning off lights, and closing blinds.

Lockdown procedures served as state standards for years. In the mid 2000s, a for-profit company introduced an alternative to lockdown known as ALICE (alert, lockdown, inform, counter, and evacuate). ALICE seeks to keep students and staff from a potential "sitting duck" situation by introducing options to run away from or attack the adversary. This set of procedures represented a school-based evolution in active shooter response procedures. In general, police officers accepted and advocated for this change quicker than school administrators did. In many states, counties, and local municipalities, the sometimes contentious debate between traditional lockdown procedures and ALICE continues. Upon evacuating, to what location(s) will students and staff rally? At what age should students be trained to counter an attacker? What liability concerns arise?

In 2010, the US Department of Homeland Security introduced active shooter response procedures known as "Run, Hide, Fight." An instructional video can be viewed at http://www.youtube.com/watch?v=5VcSwejU2D0. Designed as response procedures that apply to all active shooter incidents, the order of action steps (run, hide, fight) has been questioned in the school arena. In a facility where every room has locking capabilities, should students and staff really be taught to run as the first option? Again, police officers were the first to accept and advocate for this latest evolution in active shooter procedures.

Review your options. Expect further developments. Choose active shooter response procedures based on collaboration and consensus.

Conclusion

Merely possessing an emergency response plan does not guarantee the effectiveness of procedures. In fact, most crisis management plans are incomplete and become outdated soon after they are printed. As noted earlier, most plans are also flawed by details that have been forgotten and procedures that do not get to the heart of the problem. The only way to wring the obsolescence and flaws out of an emergency response plan is to practice and drill.

You can run tabletop drills to clarify response roles, evaluate procedures, develop relationships with responders, assess existing response capabilities, and identify areas for improvement. In some cases, these drills will also satisfy state requirements.

It is also important to hold real-time drills for each of the scenarios covered by an all-hazards plan. Call first responders in to help make real-time drills as realistic as possible. Police officers, firefighters, and EMTs have been through the real thing before. They can critique your plan and help you get it right.

It seems like a lot of work, and it is. But people that have been through drills and then a real emergency report repeatedly that the familiarity with procedures that came from the drills helped them to survive and to help others survive when an actual life-threatening emergency erupted.

Make the plan and practice it, not because regulations require it, but because it might save lives some day.

References

1. US Department of Education, Office of Elementary and Secondary Education, Office of Safe and Healthy Students, *Guide for Developing High-Quality School Emergency Operations Plans* (Washington DC: US Department of Education, 2013), n.p., http://rems.ed.gov/docs/REMS_K-12_Guide_508.pdf.

8 ▪▪▪
  ▪▪▪
  ▪▪▪

Tackling Social Media Risks

Social Media Introduction

Even though it seems like social media risks did not exist just a few years ago, Facebook is now more than a decade old. Students are the primary drivers and victims affected by cyberissues. A tidal wave of inappropriate comments, photographs, and correspondence in an ever-growing sea of social media sites plagues our schools. The word intuitive seems to simultaneously define today's youth and intimidate most adults. An ever-widening technology gap causes adults, including school staff members and parents, to feel left behind. Resolving to avoid social networking altogether, akin to the ostrich approach, is a poor decision. Attempts to ban or rigidly control social media often produce disappointing results. Instead, we recommend that school officials acquire a basic understanding of social media, learn how to use it safely, and positively influence those that use these services.

There is much at stake. Real and fabricated information can go viral in a short amount of time. Student reputations and self-images rise and fall dramatically. Damage feels irreversible.

The term *cyberbullying* has become a blanket term used to describe these types of virtual bullying. StopBullying.gov simply defines it as "bullying that takes place electronically." The National Crime Prevention Council states that cyberbullying occurs "when the Internet, cell phones, or other devices are used to send or post text or images intended to hurt or embarrass another person." Most importantly, US law classifies cyberbullying as a criminal act in some cases, making it imperative for educators to educate themselves on protecting their students. While the anonymity of the Internet makes it hard to trace cyberbullying and technological advances continue to open up new avenues and opportunities for bullying, schools must address this threat as they engage in anti-bullying efforts. This chapter surveys social media types, focuses on identifying some common technology risks, and offers potential solutions for school security personnel and administrators. Numerous students contributed to this chapter. Their insights demonstrate the value of student involvement in school security and will hopefully encourage you to collaborate with your own students.

The cyberworld offers a seemingly unlimited number of social networking websites. The following social networking services may gain or diminish in popularity, yet they provide a representative view of where students and adults spend time and face risk. From a categorization standpoint, consider Twitter and Facebook to be social marketplaces. Think of Instagram, Vine, Snapchat, Tinder, YouTube, Pinterest, and wiki pages as self-contained products that are brought to the social marketplace. The social aspect of dating and gaming sites must also be considered. Individual descriptions of these services follow.

This chapter will then tackle safe ways to address the social media services and related technology.

Twitter

To understand Twitter, it is important to outline the unique form that it takes in the social media landscape. The first thing to be noted is that the message length is limited to 140 characters. These messages are submitted by users and can address anything from politics and religion to the contents of your lunch. Twitter is frequently updated. There are hundreds of millions of tweets each day, sent by well over 300 million active users. As a result, Twitter can be insanely chaotic until organized by hashtags. That term describes the most innovative aspect of Twitter. Hashtags (#s) produce Twitter feeds, which collect all tweets with the identical hashtag in order to create a place for people to talk about one particular thing. These hashtags can be any combination of characters, and can range from the very general to the very specific (e.g., #entertainment #sports #baseball #cubs #castro #goodhit). A subscriber can hashtag as many things in a tweet as capacity allows. Someone might increase the visibility of the tweet by using specific and relevant hashtags.

The follow function of Twitter allows individual users to create a home page Twitter feed that consists only of the tweets from users that they have chosen to follow. In general, following another user is a one-way street. User settings can be changed to allow the user receiving the follow to approve or deny the user attempting to follow them. However, the standard setting, and the least off-putting one, is to allow anyone to follow you and receive your content. This functions differently than other social media. Regardless of whether or not someone grants permission for others to follow, users can still find that individual's content simply by searching that individual's name or discovering that individual's tweet through a different source, such as a hashtag or a retweet (RT).

Twitter's follower function enables this social media giant to become even more powerful. Those individuals and entities that have many followers, such as celebrities or journalistic sources like the *New York Times*, often have astounding numbers of followers. For example, at the moment this was written, President Barack Obama had over 43 million followers. If that individual or entity retweets or favorites a tweet from someone that has fewer followers, that increases the visibility of the original message exponentially.

Twitter's potential for reach and relevancy exceeds that of Facebook and most other social media platforms because it is a public, globally accessible format. Twitter emphasizes short bursts of information (remember, tweets are a maximum of 140 characters) while possessing the capability of servicing any kind of media including text, videos, photos, links to articles, and more. Anything on the Internet can be broadcast to Twitter's 500 million users instantaneously.

The ability to share any kind of information with millions of users is immensely significant because it makes the two traditional barriers of time and space completely irrelevant. Reporting the news, sharing emergency announcements, debating policy, marketing, and any other kind of communication imaginable can be enhanced and exponentially increased by using Twitter.

Like most social media site, Twitter use represents a two-edged sword. On the positive side, Twitter can and will be used as a complementary, if not primary, means of mass notification. On the negative side, this quick and easy flow of information creates a great potential for misuse. Deepen your understanding so that you can stand your ground amidst the tempest of social media!

Facebook

Facebook is a service similar to Twitter, but it is much less concerned about global reach and more interested in communicating, sharing, and connecting with individuals and entities that subscribers already know. With the notable exception of Facebook's Pages service, users are required to friend another user in order to see that person's or entity's information. The accuracy of that statement, however, depends on the correct application of Facebook's privacy settings. Assuming that basic privacy settings are in place, both users must consent to the mutual friendship for either to see each other's content. The service even asks you if you know the person from outside of Facebook prior to accepting a request.

Overall, Facebook is very easy to use to do simple things such as posting on another user's wall or sending a private message to one or a number of people. Most features, such as tagging users in a post or in some other kind of media, are simple to master. As mentioned earlier, this social media site has designed features to be intuitive. The difficult part for many who are new to Facebook is in grasping its wide-ranging—if not overwhelming—versatility. Unlike Twitter, where the user can post any kind of content, such as videos, texts, photos, and links, but is limited to 140 characters per tweet, Facebook users can use countless applications to achieve many different ends that extend beyond simply sharing content.

Facebook users have few limits in terms of versatility of sharing and diversity of applications with which to do so, but they are limited with their global reach because, depending on the share settings in a user's account, only those they choose to friend can see their content. As a result, Facebook and Twitter actually occupy two different niches. Facebook tends to lean toward personal and professional relationships and acquaintances. Twitter can serve the same purpose to a lesser extent, but also allows the user to connect with more individuals and entities than anyone could ever reach on Facebook. Once again, Facebook's Pages feature presents a notable exception.

Potential reach aside, the primary difference between Facebook and Twitter involves the use of applications. The word *application* may be foreign, but the concept is easily understood because we use applications every day in different forms. Facebook offers many different applications to assist the subscriber in experiencing a multidimensional platform. For example, Facebook subscribers can engage in an enormous number of activities, ranging from the trivial, such as posting emoticons, to writing in-depth notes and participating in multiplayer games. In contrast, Twitter maintains strict focus on the 140-character tweet as its primary function. A few examples of Facebook applications include game applications such as Farmville, utilizing Twitter on Facebook, sending virtual gifts, birthday reminders, private messaging, and music applications. These applications enable Facebook to transcend the basic Twitter platform of status updates and news feeds, and permits the user to be immersed in an online, social, multidimensional platform.

Instagram

Everything one needs to know about Instagram can be figured out by learning how Twitter works. Once you understand simple concepts such as global reach, frequent updates, the organization of chaos via hashtags, and followers, you only need to know that Instagram's only purpose involves the sharing of photos and videos.

Rather than sending tweets, Instagram subscribers can only post photos and videos. The appeal of Instagram began with the idea that a user could take a photo with a cell phone and apply filters that would make the photos appear to be professionally taken. This aspect of the service combined with social sharing capabilities is what set Instagram apart from its competitors and led to its $1 billion acquisition by Facebook. Instagram has gone on to widen its photo-sharing capabilities to include 15-second videos, which can also be modified by the classic photo filters that Instagram users love. Photos and videos can also include captions. The Instagram platform also utilizes slightly different terminology than Twitter. But other than differing terminology and Instagram's more focused emphasis on photos, Twitter and Instagram are virtually indistinguishable.

Vine

What Instagram is to photo sharing, Vine is to video sharing. Vine introduced the concept of brevity in video sharing. Videos taken with this application are limited to six seconds in length and can be edited as they are filmed. Users can film multiple "scenes" within a single video by starting and stopping the recording as many times as they wish. This creates an extremely versatile user experience and the videos shared can appear as stop-motion animations or mini-movies.

Vine was acquired by Twitter and that association with the social media giant has only increased the sharing power of their users' videos. Smaller videos equal smaller file sizes and quicker uploads. A subscriber can shoot a "vine" and immediately upload it to his or her Vine feed, Twitter, or Facebook.

Hashtags are also prominent within Vine and its "explore" feature has a list of the most popular trending tags, a concept borrowed from their parent company, Twitter. Despite the fierce competition for market share, the social features of Vine and Instagram are greatly alike.

Snapchat

Snapchat is a photo and video texting service. Think of Snapchat as a photo messaging service for smartphones, but with a small twist. The twist that makes Snapchat unique is the fact that it only allows the person receiving the photo or video to view it for 10 seconds or fewer before it is deleted. In other words, the Snap is gone in a snap. This social media site purportedly deletes these messages from the servers.

It might sound like a frivolous idea, sending something only for it to disappear in a few seconds, but Snapchat seemingly attempts to reverse the trend of popular social media sites that record and store everything indefinitely, if not permanently. In some ways, the Snapchat concept represents a minor revolution in that it hearkens back to the days when people had face-to-face conversations. Without recording devices, the moment something was said, it simply disappeared. This is the concept that Snapchat sold to early adopters. It has since been discovered, however, that Snapchat keeps all information shared via their service, like Facebook does.

In summary, most of the communication on Snapchat consists of subscribers taking photos of their own faces ("selfies") and typing very brief messages (even shorter than the 140 characters permitted on tweets). Just remember, the Snap does not really disappear.

Tinder

Tinder echoes the spirit of one of Mark Zuckerberg's first creations, FaceMash. In creating FaceMash, Zuckerberg compiled the student photos of all Harvard students and invited users to vote "Yes" or "No" to a single photo at a time based on the student's perceived attractiveness. Tinder strikes you as the creation of someone that watched the movie Social Network and decided to update Zuckerberg's idea for the modern world.

Using Tinder is extremely straightforward and simple. Subscribers connect their Facebook accounts to Tinder to provide legitimacy to their profiles. An individual user then selects a photo that he or she has previously uploaded to Facebook and then that photo and his or her name goes out into the ether. Other Tinder users will have the opportunity to see the photo of that user in their individual feeds. Next, they have the option to vote "Yes" or "No." This is not simply a "Am I hot or not?" game, though. If someone votes yes to your photo and you vote yes to that person's photo, then a "match" is created and a feature of the application is unlocked which will allow the two users to text one another.

The idea for Tinder runs concurrently with the overarching themes of social media. It makes the world smaller and the pool of potential acquaintances larger. Some call it a dating application, while others insist that it is simply an opportunity for meeting new friends. Either way, Tinder provides yet another means for people's worlds to intersect.

YouTube

YouTube is the largest video service on the Internet. If you cannot find a "how to" tutorial for even the most specialized interest on YouTube, you are probably not looking hard enough. The most important thing to understand about YouTube is that it actually creates a community. This community is very broad, but is broken up into thousands of different subcultures. The videos produced by these subcultures reflect their uniqueness.

Almost everyone who has access to a computer and the Internet has seen a video on YouTube at one point or another. Once seen, the viewer is almost compelled to pursue a search for additional videos. With very little effort, viewers find that time and productivity levels can be consumed relatively quickly.

The YouTube platform presents an ever-increasing selection of features that may interest subscribers, such as channels for specific artists, playlists created and shared by users, and the ability to stream live events. While it is beyond the scope of this book to describe all of the features, benefits, and quirks of YouTube, think of YouTube as heaven for videos. Just remember that students love to post videos, even those that are incriminating, and that viral videos can be powerful and influential.

School administrators and local law enforcement officers increasingly rely on YouTube videos for investigative purposes. Placing key words, such as the name of a school, into the YouTube search box can yield surprising and helpful results. For example, one school received a telephone call from a parent who had encountered a disturbing video while perusing YouTube. The video, entitled, "Breaking into ____ School," captured the exploits of teenagers demonstrating how to breach school security measures. YouTube is replete with demonstrations of how to defeat security systems, how to build explosive devices, and how to engage in any number of other potentially destructive activities. At the same time, this social media site can be utilized to raise security awareness, train staff members, and demonstrate safe behaviors (see chapter 6, "Preparing Your People").

Wiki Pages

A wiki is simply a website that allows open editing of content and organizational structure. Wikipedia is the best known of the sites engaged in this concept and serves to inform people about almost any subject that people think is worth researching or discussing. Individual wiki pages differ from Wikipedia in that they are not overseen by a large company. The open-sourced page is usually devoted to a single subject or topic and contains whatever content the administrators of that page want to put into it. For example, if you are a gaming enthusiast, you can create a wiki page to help other players of that particular game share their knowledge with those who are unfamiliar with it or interested in learning more. Similar to Wikipedia, the open-source nature of wiki pages allows democratic, collaborative, and constantly updated material to be accessible for any Internet user. This format is different from the social media described above because of the radical freedom that it grants to its users.

Pinterest

Pinterest is an interesting social media site that revolves around sharing photos of things made at home. It is essentially a collection of good ideas submitted by users consisting of anything from recipes to "how to" instructions for making a birdhouse. Used primarily by craft-minded individuals, this medium, while fascinating, has little to do with school security. As will be mentioned later, however, the benefits of this site for schools are untapped and hold great potential for creative staff members.

Dating Applications

You have probably seen commercials for the most popular dating sites on television. Most people are aware of eHarmony and Match.com, and that these sites, designed for adults, require a financial subscription. Another league of sites, however, is free and often accessed by young adults—including high school students. Plenty of Fish and OkCupid do not advertise on television, but that has not stopped them from becoming two of the Internet's most popular dating sites.

All social media sites unite people through common interests. Individuals follow and interact with other subscribers based on posted information such as photos, videos, and personal thoughts. The allure rests in the potential, if not ability, to find people with those common interests whom users might not have found otherwise. In no area is that allure stronger than in the area of online dating. These sites are meant for adults (the minimum listed age is 18) but that does not stop bored and lonely teenagers from subverting the age requirement to join.

Each dating site represents a self-contained entity. Users do not have the ability to share the fact that they met a new person with their Facebook friends. There is absolutely no integration with the other popular applications. As a result, these dating sites are very much less social in nature—and possibly more dangerous.

Gaming Applications

If you have played a game on Facebook or on a smartphone, Zynga probably made it. The gaming giant, whose motto is "connecting the world through games," has produced such titles as Farmville, Mafia Wars, Ruby Blast, and Words with Friends. These games become strangely addicting and have massive fan bases. On the surface, they might seem harmless. Dig a little further, however, and you might form a different opinion.

Detractors of gaming applications will be quick to point out that they are a drain on two of the user's most valuable resources: time and money. Like every social media site, application, and service, games are probably best used in moderation. It is left up to the individual user to decide how much usage is appropriate. Experience often reveals, however, that leaving resource management to the discretion of the user can be dangerous.

Most games follow the buy-in model widely used by many application developers. The game can be downloaded for free. Free sounds good, right? Unfortunately, it does not always turn out that way. Gamers inevitably experience a contemporary twist on an old phrase: "There's no such thing as a free app." Suppose, for example, a user downloads Words with Friends for free and becomes enamored with it. Soon, that user will become bogged down with a variety of advertisements that are specifically designed to agitate the user. The user might have to watch a 30-second video in order to view the game score. That person might have to use a smaller game board in order to accommodate a banner advertisement at the top of the screen. Ultimately, the only reasonable solution to combat the annoyances involves shelling out $3.99 for a version of the game that does not include those annoying ads.

After paying for a game, the user likely feels even more obligated to play. After all, an investment has been made. This line of reasoning contributes to a cycle that keeps users playing free games, buying ad-free games, and then spending more time playing those games.

Addressing Social Media Risks

A few short years ago, schools attempted to prohibit students from carrying cellular phones. Bans failed. Technology personnel installed Internet filtering systems. They were circumvented. Should school administrators give up in their efforts to control social media? Certainly not. The correct approach involves acquiring a basic understanding of social media, learning how it can be used safely, and positively influencing those that use these services. Remember, in order to undertake this approach, students must be involved. We will now revisit the services discussed above from a safety angle.

Twitter

Twitter cannot be censored, contained, or effectively controlled. Despite this fact, not all is lost. The potential for Twitter to make something "go viral" or garner hundreds, thousands, or even millions of hits is both a potential danger and a potential boon.

Stakes are raised exponentially for someone who misuses Twitter. From tweeting an inappropriate photo or video to misrepresenting an organization on an important social issue, risks abound. For example, if a school staff member makes a derogatory comment regarding a community issue, others might infer that the school holds those same views. Countless examples of indiscretion involving athletes and politicians serve to remind us of how fast things can get out of control. These indiscretions can reflect on those who are linked to a tweet in some way, as well. The potential dangers of Twitter compound when ignorance accompanies misuse.

School administrators and security personnel find Twitter useful in a number of ways. For example, they can maintain concise, varied, and unregulated correspondence in settings both large and small. They can get feedback immediately on ideas related to school curriculum. They can monitor student and teacher reactions to district initiatives. The list of potential benefits is virtually limitless.

Many schools are also using Twitter to communicate with students and parents. Rather than having to navigate a school website for news or activity schedule changes, parents can receive a brief message directly from the coach or designated staff member. Parents who want to follow a conversation about their child's specific extracurricular activity can utilize hashtags to focus on that activity alone. Twitter allows those conversations to be viewed by anyone, publicly, and narrows the field of conversation to particular topics. For example, if the school name is Willowbrook High School and the sport is girls' tennis, the hashtag could be #WHSgirlstennis.

Facebook

October 2012 marked a milestone for Facebook, as founder and CEO Mark Zuckerberg proudly announced that his site had finally exceeded the one billion mark for active users (individuals that regularly use their accounts).[1] That number means that an active user base of more than three times the population of the US is regularly using one website. In the midst of connecting with friends, uploading pictures, and posting comments about their lives, many of these individuals are unaware of the risks involving privacy.

A good number of adults have never used social media, including school administrators and staff members. These individuals often intentionally boycott social networking based purely on principle. In many cases, these passive protestors are actually proud that they are not involved in this kind of media and can be critical of social media users. Let me challenge those people to dip their toes in the waters of technology. Those that are unfamiliar with social media are typically unaware of social media risks or unable to comprehend threats presented by technology that they have never seen or used. It is precisely for this reason that we want to inform the social media boycotters. In addition, reformed boycotters may actually come to enjoy some of the many benefits and advantages social media provides. The key is to experience some social media forums to learn different ways to improve cybersecurity. Gaining awareness, increasing understanding, and learning how to provide assistance may be the only way to protect social media subscribers from social networking's two-edged sword.

Since one billion is a number that only seems to come up in national debt discussions, it is worth taking a closer look at the safety settings of the social media site that affects the most people in the world: Facebook.

Secure browsing is the most effective way to protect your information that is shared online. The HTTPS protocol encrypts and protects information that is communicated over the internet. Think of it this way: before HTTPS, all information was communicated in the same language – HTTP. The HTTPS protocol translates your information into a different language while it is being delivered – a language that is incredibly complex and impossible to decipher.

Facebook originally gave users the option to enable "Secure Browsing" by accessing the "Security Settings" section of "Account Settings." Now, that setting is the standard and cannot be disabled. All information shared via Facebook is secured and encrypted. Type "Facebook.com" into your address bar and you will notice that the URL will automatically display https://www.Facebook.com. Secure browsing is enabled for you.

It is important to make sure that secure browsing is activated for all websites that you visit. The responsibility to enable secure browsing falls on the user because some sites will not have HTTPS as the default protocol. Popular browsers such as Google Chrome, Mozilla Firefox and Microsoft Explorer all offer settings where you can enable HTTPS browsing at all times. These browsers can be trusted because it is in their best interest to help their users surf the web safely and securely. Even though browsers vary slightly, each one offers options to utilize the HTTPS protocol when visiting sites. If you ever encounter a site that only has HTTP, you can manually add an "S" to make it HTTPS.

Two-Factor identification ensures that you are always the person accessing your online accounts. Facebook currently offers this level of protection. The first factor is your password. What if it fell into the wrong hands? Two-Factor helps prevent someone else from accessing your account, even if that person has your password.

Many popular and trusted sites that require personal information will offer options for a second factor of identification. For example, the site may ask for your cellular telephone number in order to text you a six-digit code. You, then, enter that code on the site you are attempting to log in to. Facebook uses a Code Generator (Figure 8.1). The Facebook application on your cellular telephone has a code generator that is producing new six-digit codes every 30 seconds. These passwords cannot be stolen and used to access your account because they are constantly changing. If you enable the Code Generator as one of your Login Approvals (this is listed under your Security Settings), it will ask for the six-digit code in addition to your password when you login from an unfamiliar computer. An unfamiliar computer might be your PC at work, a friend's laptop or a new tablet. If it is a location that you have not logged in from before, Code Generator will ask for the six-digit code. As always, this is a minor inconvenience that provides major security benefits.

From the General Account Settings page, move to the left frame and click on Timeline and Tagging. Near the top of the page you will see "Review posts friends tag you in before they appear on your timeline." Click on the Edit link to the right and choose to enable the setting. This will prevent other users from indiscriminately identifying you in unflattering, inaccurate, or inappropriate photos. Instead, any photo another user attempts to tag with your identity will require your permission before it appears. Explore similar security setting to make the Facebook experience as safe as possible. Furthermore, since the Facebook interface changes from time to time, visit retasecurity.com for the latest information on important security settings.

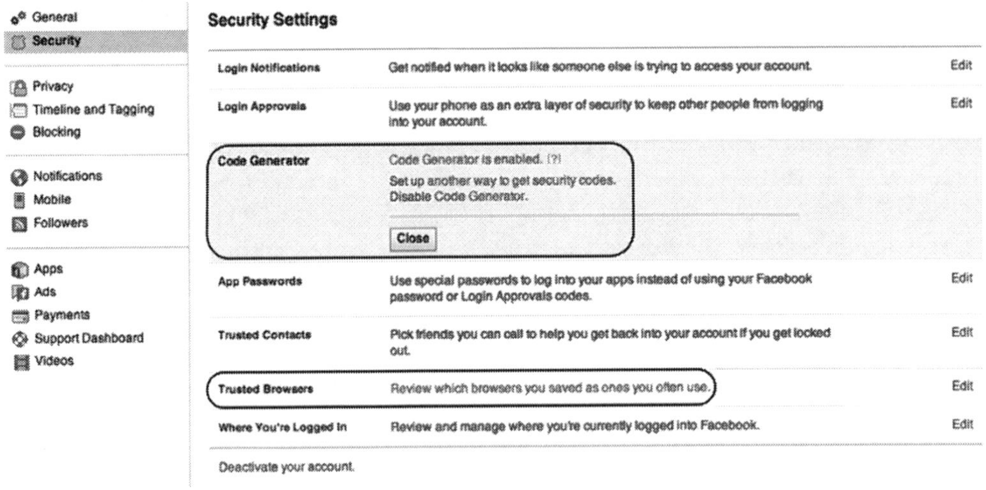

FIGURE 8.1

The term Facebook friends is often a misnomer. Many students and an increasing number of adults have more than 500 or even 1000 friends on Facebook. While possessing large numbers of friends might feel like an ego booster, most subscribers do not really know these friends. This can be dangerous. The term "Facebook creep" has become quite common, as it refers to individuals that virtually stalk others by looking through their Facebook profiles and browsing through the photos. While browsing does not necessarily present a problem—for instance, sharing photos with close friends and family members represents an enjoyable and time-honored tradition—the waters can become murky when individuals begin to fixate on photos of friends with whom they are not very familiar. Students, especially, tend to accept friend requests indiscriminately from those they have never met. Facebook does not permit subscribers to see which friends have been looking at their profiles. This provides an opportunity for people to download photos and stalk individuals anonymously. As a result, we recommend that Facebook users limit their number of friends to trusted contacts, not just acquaintances.

Teach Facebook subscribers to exercise care in posting. In addition to avoiding inappropriate comments and photos postings, users often provide the Facebook community with too much information. They should be cautioned to refrain from status updates that detail upcoming vacation dates and specific location postings. Given the right opportunity, this information can be exploited.

The quest for reducing risk on Facebook may involve pursuing yet another option—creating a page, e.g., facebook.com/safeschools1. The difference between a user account and a page is similar to the difference between a school classroom door that has a window and one that does not. State boards of education generally require all classrooms to have windows so that the room is public. In other words, from the hallway, persons can look into the classroom at any time to see what is taking place. The window provides a measure of accountability. Facebook's user account permits private e-mail correspondence. That situation is analogous to a classroom without a window in the door. A Facebook page, on the other hand, does not permit e-mail correspondence. All posts are public. In that situation, a Facebook page is similar to a door with a window. Many individual school districts and some states have prohibited Facebook correspondence between staff and students as it helps prevent potentially inappropriate interactions that in some cases have resulted in staff being dismissed. All schools should have some kind of documented practice regarding electronic correspondence (see chapter 3, "Developing a Plan"). Creating a Facebook page is an excellent way for an athletic department or extracurricular club to provide a medium for communication with limited risk of inappropriate correspondence.

Instagram

Instagram functions almost exactly the same as Twitter, and thus the security concerns are similar. The difference between the two is the emphasis on photographs and videos as the primary medium of communication. As such, the potential for sharing inappropriate pictures abounds. Examples involving students who have been haunted by the circulation and permanence of inappropriate photos, thanks to social media, can be directly applied to Instagram.

Instagram can also be used in the same way for good, as has been described in the Twitter section. Please notice that these two social mediums are extremely similar. Instead of using Instagram to relay important messages, however, schools can keep parents up to date on sports teams, special events, and other activities using photos and videos.

Vine

Vine's security concerns follow a similar trajectory to those encountered with Instagram. Whereas Instagram involves photos and videos, Vine only involves videos. In fact, Vine was initially plagued by a slew of subscribers that used the six-second video format to produce high volumes of pornographic material. While this was quickly combated and effectively removed from the application, the concern remains the same. Vine users can upload videos instantly. It is difficult to ensure that every video complies with security policies. As a result, there is a risk that things can slip through the cracks.

Vine relies on hashtags to block inappropriate material. Both Vine and Instagram require users to search and explore the application's content exclusively via the hashtag. The purpose of this requirement centers on quality control. Vine's security policy is frequently updated to prohibit hashtags that reference inappropriate subjects. In many cases, however, by the time an inappropriate term has been identified and banned, unscrupulous users are well on their way toward finding a substitute.

While the length of six seconds was initially deemed by many critics not to be enough time to convey a coherent message, Vine's user base has largely disproven this theory. In fact, Vine provides an effective tool for making announcements, teasing lunch menus, or introducing new team uniforms.

Snapchat

Snapchat may be a small revolution in replicating face-to-face social interaction. However, it holds little value for schools and, in fact, may be one of the most potentially damaging and dangerous of the social media sites considered. The reason for that concern stems from the illusion that Snapchat creates. The promise of message deletion all the way to the server level causes some subscribers to engage in risky behavior, including the sending of inappropriate photos. Smartphones, however, can capture these photos with a screenshot feature. Once captured, photos that the original subscriber presumed to be temporary can then be sent to any number of other, perhaps permanent, social media sites. Snapchat has attempted to address this vulnerability by automatically notifying users when others have taken screenshots of their snaps.

As far as school benefits are concerned, all of them also carry great risk. It is unadvisable to permit teachers to have Snapchat accounts because of the risk involved with regard to the potential for inappropriate correspondence with students.

Tinder

The security risks with Tinder are based in a concept referred to as "geo-tagging." Users find people with whom they might possibly connect by allowing the application to use the smartphone's GPS to pinpoint their exact location. Individual users can set the radius within which other users can find them. If a subscriber selects a 15-mile radius, then all other users inside that same radius will likely find that subscriber's photo pop up in their timelines.

Sometimes online contact is harmless. Sometimes online contact is emotionally harmful. Most risks encountered with the aforementioned applications can be relegated purely to the emotional realm. When users begin to identify their exact location, however, physical risks come into play. Users can feel pressured into meeting up with individuals they just "met" on Tinder more so than on another application based solely on the open knowledge that each person is geographically close to the other. This pressure creates a completely new set of security risks.

YouTube

December 21, 2012 marked yet another milestone involving one billion when "Gangnam Style," the hit Korean pop song, garnered a billion views of its music video on YouTube. This music video now holds the distinction of being the first video ever to break the one billion milestone. Even more impressive, "Gangnam Style" had only been on YouTube for just over five months. That particular video aside, school administrators and staff members must be aware of the potential risks. As one of the most popular websites on the Internet, YouTube hosts millions of subscriber-uploaded videos that encompass virtually every activity known to man. Frequented by the bored, the curious, and everyone in between, YouTube stands as the largest video community in the world.

Before visiting YouTube simply for the sake of exploration, consider the following basic informational points.

- Individuals (above 13 years old) can create free accounts and upload their own videos along with links from almost anywhere.
- Anyone with an Internet connection, not just subscribers, can access any video as long as the video is published to a channel.
- Uploaded videos are not immediately filtered.

As with most social media forums, YouTube cannot monitor every single video a subscriber uploads prior to publishing. This potential delay allows users to post questionable items, such as inappropriate videos and copyrighted material. Most entertainment companies, such as Time-Warner, regularly monitor new YouTube uploads in an attempt to intercept and remove movies they have produced. Antipiracy efforts require time and resources. While copyrighted material is filtered out aggressively, sexually explicit content often manages to survive if it is not flagged as inappropriate by YouTube users. YouTube reviews the content of flagged videos and classifies them as 18+ or removes them entirely, if deemed to violate the site's community guidelines. For users attempting to access a video in the 18+ category—which usually involves nudity or violence—the site displays the message, "Content Warning — This video may be inappropriate for some users." YouTube controls automatically follow content warnings with a link stating, "Sign in to confirm your age." At that point, a user must sign in to his or her YouTube account, which contains his or her age information, or create a new account. Only viewers seeking to access videos in the 18+ category must have an account. Due to the incredible amount of video content uploaded daily, YouTube cannot possibly monitor everything perfectly.

YouTube does, however, provide multiple options for users to improve their security, including resources and information specifically for educators and parents. Some key resources follow.

- The ability to turn on and off safety mode under safety settings. This feature allows the user to block any videos that are in the 18+ category. It also provides the option of locking safety mode on permanently in your browser. As a result, parents/legal guardians can protect their children/dependents if they enable safety settings in those accounts. This feature is accessible through visiting "settings" in the Safety Center.
- The ability to access YouTube's Safety Center under the link "safety" at the bottom of its webpage. This Safety Center is a great tool for both educators and parents/legal guardians. Multiple links address various safety concerns, including teen safety, sexual abuse of minors, harassment, and cyberbullying. Each category provides information such as current laws about the topic, specific YouTube policies, advice for educators regarding YouTube, and advice for parents/legal guardians.

The Safety Center provides a convenient and useful way to understand the many options that are available for both preventing and managing social media situations.

We also suggest creating a school YouTube channel. Schools can post news stories, accomplishments, and upcoming events on the channel. They can also link the channel to many other online forums. If creation of a school YouTube channel sounds daunting, do not be afraid to recruit students for assistance. Involving students in the creative process will enhance the overall quality of the channel, shorten the faculty learning curve, and aid in establishing better connections with students.

Wiki Pages

There are numerous practical applications for wiki pages as social media. Any specialized group with a significant amount of knowledge about a particular subject or even a more generally concerned group can create, post, and manage content on a platform that encourages collaboration and democratic sharing of information. Teachers, for example, can set up wiki pages for their classes. This fosters an environment where students can interact in a dynamic and cutting-edge way. School administrators can creatively utilize wiki pages, as well. They can develop a school wiki page that can be accessed by parents to receive updates regarding areas such as sports teams and academic successes.

Although teachers and administrators may choose to use this service, they should be careful when setting up the wiki page and take into account its open-source platform. Depending on the settings for each individual wiki page, those that access the content may also be able to edit it. The consequences of the combination of totally open-sourced content and schemes hatched by immature teenagers late at night could range from minor to major depending on the situation. Therefore, as always, discretion is advised. Users should also possess an intimate knowledge of the functioning of wiki pages. Wiki page administrators can change the settings at inception in order to temper the open-source nature of the page. A balance must be struck that allows users to make edits, but keeps ultimate authority in the hands of the administrator. Administrators must retain the ability to review posts before they go live and reject changes if they are deemed inappropriate or incorrect. Wikipedia demonstrates this authority to a certain extent, but departs from it in that they review pages after the edits are already live. The Wikipedia process is probably not ideal for a schoolteacher or administrator, because without constant monitoring there is the potential that hours or days could go by without realizing that changes have been made to the page.

Overall, wiki pages represent a significant advance thanks in major part to the Internet and an increasingly globally minded and democratic world. This medium may not always be the right solution for administrators and teachers, but wiki pages remain a powerful resource with lots of untapped potential. The most important thing is to understand how to use this fascinating social media in order to harness its power and limit the risk associated with it.

Pinterest

As mentioned earlier, Pinterest is a website that serves as virtual pin boards on which individuals can engage in activities such as posting photos and videos, sharing designs, and viewing others' pin boards. It is especially popular among women as they typically upload and share more photos than men. While Pinterest provides a great way to organize and share images and thoughts, like most social media it is far from immune to security threats. In the digital age, it is difficult to regulate who has access to your information after it is posted on social media sites. It is also difficult to remove posts permanently after publishing them. With strangers having the ability to access personal information, users must understand the potential consequences that careless posts can carry with them. Make efforts to educate students and faculty regarding the appropriateness of posts, videos, and photos. It has become very common to capture underage individuals in possession of alcoholic beverages on photos. These situations can result in serious and lasting repercussions. Thanks to the advancement of mobile technology, such as smartphones, people are able to upload photos from virtually anywhere to anywhere. Yahoo estimated 880 billion photographs would be taken in 2014, most with a camera phone. Snapchat recently reported sharing 400 million snaps each day. Selfie, indeed![2] Emphasizing caution and explaining the risks associated with sites such as Pinterest can be an effective way to help students and faculty members avoid potential pitfalls.

Another way administrators can get involved with Pinterest is creating pin boards for the school. These pin boards can serve as virtual message boards or photo sharing sites. Unlike a Facebook page for schools, Pinterest is a customizable pin board that only the creator can edit. This prevents individuals from posting inappropriate content on the page and can be a nice tool for educating faculty, learning more about a specific program, and even demonstrating to students ways to avoid potentially damaging mistakes.

Dating Applications

In addition to the obvious risk of underage students attracting predators, dating applications also carry the possibility of placing school staff members at risk. Most of these sites and applications allow users to see who has viewed their profile. Imagine how quickly this scenario could turn sour. Suppose, for example, that an underage female student and an adult male teacher are both members of the same online dating site. The male teacher may stumble upon the student's profile by accident. The female student should not be there in the first place, but now discovers that the male teacher has viewed her profile. This scenario can only head in one direction.

Gaming Applications

There is one, overarching distinction among today's most popular game applications: some challenge the mind and some do not. Zynga games, such as Chess with Friends, Words with Friends (reminiscent of Scrabble), and Scramble with Friends (similar to Boggle), definitely challenge the mind. Other Zynga games, such as Farmville and Mafia Wars, do not necessarily challenge the mind in an educational way. Schools administrators and staff members do well when they identify and encourage students to take part in the gaming applications that will keep their minds sharp.

Law Enforcement and Social Networking

Administrators must understand the role of law enforcement as it applies to social networking. One of the more important lessons to learn is that most law enforcement officials are not specially trained in social networking, but are self-taught. Relying solely on law enforcement to handle technology threats is a passive approach that does not do enough to help students. As technology grows, new threats and issues arise for which law enforcement alone is unprepared. Being diligent in tracking new legislation regarding legal treatment of technology issues is necessary for maintaining preparedness should those issues arise. Keep in touch with local law enforcement in regards to technology safety. Close connections improve awareness. Involve law enforcement officials in the development of response plans. Ask educators to help inform law enforcement officials of potential threats.

Feeling hesitant? Intimidated? Overwhelmed? Improving your awareness and utilization of technology and social networking demands immersion.

Not long ago, the New York University Child Study Center estimated that approximately 40–75 percent of middle school students in America have cellular phones. That number has obviously grown significantly. Many of these students own smartphones. While this may sound alarming, especially when considering risks like sexting and the potential for cheating, we suggest focusing on the many safety benefits. For example, consider the possibility of storing ICE (In Case of Emergency) information in cellular phones. First responders rely on ICE to retrieve an individual's contact and relevant personal information when the individual is unable to do so. Store an emergency contact number in the contact list of a basic cellular phone under the heading ICE or download an ICE application from a smartphone appstore. Many such applications are free. These applications provide designated places to input emergency contact numbers. Emergency responders save valuable time in accessing this information. Most ICE applications also permit users to store important personal information, such as current medications, allergy warnings, organ donor information, and relevant medical history, which can assist responders in their treatment plans.

Numerous smartphone applications can positively affect safety. For example, personal panic buttons work with a smartphone's GPS to identify the location of someone in danger. Some of these panic applications automatically notify user-determined contacts at the touch of a button. Another application relies on GPS to generate a list of local sex offenders in a specific area when activated.

Students' cellular phone usage has proven helpful in any number of school emergencies. Whether contacting emergency responders or concerned parents, cellular phones can accomplish the task in a timely fashion. School incidents illustrate the benefits of peace of mind for parents who are able to maintain a lifeline of communications with children during a crisis. School administrators and security personnel should educate students and staff about the safety tools they often possess at their fingertips.

Web Filters

School web filters used to effectively govern access to Internet sites. Students and—sometimes to a lesser extent—staff were prohibited from surfing certain areas of the web. Technology departments blocked access to pornographic sites, gaming sites, and other dangerous places, like social networking sites. The reliance on web filters to control Internet access is dwindling with the advent of smartphones. A growing number of students no longer rely on the school's connection to access the Internet. Still possessing a certain amount of control, the following true story illustrates how some technologies can circumvent, if not overcome, other technologies.

A student walked into a computer lab at the local high school and sat down next to a friend. The friend was so engrossed in watching a compelling video on YouTube that he did not even notice the student's approach. The computer lab was hosting an extracurricular club and students were moving in and out of the area. Some participants were in the lab to begin working on rough drafts for an assigned presentation, but the allure of YouTube had been too tempting. The approaching student was surprised to find YouTube unblocked, excitedly watched the completion of the video, and quickly attempted to log onto the nearest computer. Having entered his information and typed www.youtube.com into the browser, he was dismayed to find that the website was blocked. He somberly opened Microsoft Word to begin his assignment. Suddenly, he began to wonder how his friend, sitting immediately next to him, was able to surf through video heaven on a school computer. He posited that either his friend had paid someone in the technology department to grant him access or something covert was happening. Considering his friend's uncanny ability to get out of detentions, both options seemed plausible. Demanding an explanation from his friend, he received a one word response: Ultrasurf. His friend explained that he was using a proxy program to access the inaccessible. Even more incredible, the program was free, and the friend was more than happy to share the love by copying the program onto the student's flashdrive. He soon found that Ultrasurf could essentially provide him with the solution to school boredom whenever and wherever he had access to a computer.

It was not enough for the student that he possessed the master key to the Internet; he had to tell other students about it. In short order, the secret of Ultrasurf swept through the student body. However, not a whisper of the proxy reached the staff. Similar to a prisoner mentality, students almost felt obligated to share it with other students that had long been restricted from accessing the real, outside world. In some ways, student consciences were relieved by the fact that Ultrasurf was neither illegal nor did it involve cost. In other words, possession and distribution of Ultrasurf was not technically a legal issue.

The only real problem with Ultrasurf from a school security perspective is the unmonitored browsing ability that it grants its users. Before delving into these potential security threats, however, it would make sense to explain first what Ultrasurf is and why it was created.

Ultrasurf falls under the banner of proxy technology. Tech-FAQ.com defines a proxy site as a webpage that allows users to browse any webpages that they choose, even if a content filter blocks the access to those websites. Ultrasurf is an elite, free proxy program. Its usage is continually growing, and the software keeps improving, as it has become one of the top proxy programs in the world. Originally released in 2002, Ultrasurf intended to help individuals in China access websites filtered by the Chinese government. Since then, it has expanded into more than 180 countries worldwide and has served as an outlet for many people in foreign countries facing censorship, allowing them access to online news and social media. At one point, Ultrasurf was receiving more than 800 million daily hits. Touting a slogan of "Privacy, Security, and Freedom," this remarkable program runs on a GIFT system platform that was able to crack the powerful Internet firewall in China and withstand multiple attempts by the Chinese government to take it down.

The software has the clever ability to hide your IP address, clear browsing history, and remove cookies to ensure anonymous browsing (privacy). It utilizes strong end-to-end encryption to prevent your data transfer from being seen by a third party (security).

And most importantly, Ultrasurf circumvents web-filtering programs to allow users unrestricted Internet access (freedom).

Translating this into the school setting, one cannot help but feel overwhelmed. While most proxy websites are blocked by the school's web filtering program, Ultrasurf is a program that launches its own proxy when opened. Unlike other proxies, its website cannot be blocked. Students have the unfettered ability to engage in gaming, social media, and pornographic material using a school computer. The most popular sites students are accessing, however, are gaming sites such as Armor Games and Addicting Games.

It only takes a flashdrive and a free program that downloads in seconds. To be clear, hacking the school's Internet feed simply involves plugging a flashdrive into a computer's USB port, opening up a folder to view the files, and selecting the Ultrasurf program. At that point, a web browser pops up and any investment the school has made to prevent students from viewing content deemed inappropriate is worthless. Attempts to track the IP address in order to find the hacker will be unsuccessful. Unless school staff members know that someone is using Ultrasurf, there is no way to tell that someone has or is. Searching the browsing history for red flags yields no information because the program clears browsing history and removes cookies. Hunting down users is next to impossible—even the Chinese government cannot do it. So with this in mind, how is this threat best handled?

Like most security concerns, raising awareness is the most effective deterrent. There are a few ways to know if students are using Ultrasurf. If you were to describe the program to faculty, the consensus would probably be that the best way to detect its usage would be to monitor student's screens. While this is definitely an option, it is complicated by the fact that when an Ultrasurf window is minimized it does not appear as a tab. It becomes a small gold padlock icon. If faculty members are unaware of this icon, it will not matter that they are monitoring computers, as they will not know what to look for. Additionally, unless every student's screen is monitored simultaneously (which is essentially impossible), tracking websites that students have visited is very difficult—demonstrating a gap in school Internet security.

While Ultrasurf usage in schools may not be extremely high, it still illustrates a point that schools should not ignore. There is no perfect solution to combating technology such as Ultrasurf. The easiest place to begin involves informing faculty about the program and explaining ways to identify it. While it might initially sound like an undetectable security breach, there are telltale signs, such as the golden padlock, that can be spotted simply by walking through a computer lab. Giving attention to new advances in technology and providing information about these types of programs is the best way to remove the anonymity from students. Educating staff via routine e-mail updates, discussing new technology in meetings, and actually demonstrating how these things work, can minimize risks.

Students today are at the core of technological advances and often love to talk about them. In order to tap into the greatest prevention resource available for technology safety, we recommend consulting students. Students are several steps ahead of adults in technology, and they know it. Ask students how they beat your security systems because most of them will be more than happy to share. Just as teachers enjoy demonstrating expertise, most students feel the same way.

Modern technology was intended to facilitate communication, not to monitor or regulate it. As technology rapidly changes and advances, it carries with it new potential for problems that demand new solutions. This does not mean a change in our security mindset, but rather improved awareness and new approaches. Think of it as a flu virus. The virus is dangerous when contracted, but deadly if ignored. The flu does not ever go away because it continually adapts to survive vaccines. Every year doctors prepare to counter it with a new vaccine in an effort to control it. While they are never sure of the form the virus will take, they are diligent and persistent in their attempts to minimize its damage. We do not know exactly what tomorrow's technology devices will look like or when the next big advance will arrive. All we know is that advances are coming and our responsibility is to prepare ourselves for changes, risks, and the formulation of response plans. Form student security teams to help keep up with new advancements. Build security awareness into the operational culture. Recruit tech-savvy students to help improve your existing technology presence and social media presence. Inform students and staff about the potential problems social media can cause.

Conclusion

Social media risks play a significant role in school security. Today's technological tidal wave is upon us. Some schools have already been hit and are wading through the resulting damage. Other schools know that is it only a matter of time before impact. Since students are the ones who are primarily involved, it makes sense to include them in the safety and security planning process. In fact, student inclusion is vital. With the help of students, school officials can acquire a basic understanding of social media, learn to use it safely, and positively influence those that use these services.

Remember, there is much at stake. From the prevention of cyberbullying and efforts to protect persons from predators to the appropriate sharing of information and emergency notification, schools must learn how to wield this two-edged sword effectively.

While the social media types mentioned in this chapter are far from exhaustive, they illustrate the pros and cons of behemoth social marketplaces and popular, self-contained products that are regularly being brought into these marketplaces. Along the way, we have also attempted to address related social media and technology issues.

Now is not the time to hide from the unknown and risk being left behind. Now is the time to be proactive. Now is the time to learn so that we can help others.

References

1. Aaron Smith, Laurie Segall and Stacy Cowley, "Facebook reaches one billion users," *CNN Money*, October 4, 2012, http://money.cnn.com/2012/10/04/technology/Facebook-billion-users/index.html.

2. http://techcrunch.com/2013/11/19/snapchat-reportedly-sees-more-daily-photos-than-facebook/

School Security Resources and Conclusion

Introduction

Occasionally I encounter someone who expresses a fatalistic view toward school security. That person might say something like, "If someone really wants to do something bad, there is no way to stop it." What does that mean? Should we cease in our attempts to protect students, staff, and visitors? Admittedly, there is no such thing as perfect security. A school can never reduce a risk level to zero. But any measure of risk reduction justifies efforts.

The tools and resources in this chapter have been selected to assist you in providing a more secure learning environment. While the list is extensive, it is not intended to be exhaustive. Do not wait until you have experienced a security incident or emergency situation to effectively address issues and vulnerabilities. You can significantly reduce your risk by taking a proactive approach and making use of these tools and resources now.

Chapter 3, "Developing A Plan" Resources

Threat Assessment in Schools: A Guide to Managing Threatening Situations and to Creating Safe School Climates — Created by the US Secret Service and the US Department of Education, this document (http://www.secretservice.gov/ntac/ssi_guide.pdf) provides revolutionary thinking on building a safer school environment through understanding the principles of the agencies' initial study, *The Safe School Initiative* (https://www2.ed.gov/admins/lead/safety/preventingattacksreport.pdf), and creating a threat assessment process. Furthermore, it assists the reader in understanding the meaning of a targeted threat or targeted violence. In collaboration with key district leadership, student services staff may use this design to draft a threat assessment process for identifying potential student risks and/or threats in their respective school environments. Note the last section (chapter 7), "Creating a Safe and Connected School Climate."

Chapter 4, "Securing Your Environment" Resources

Security Planning Team Stakeholders – Use the form in Figure 9.1 to identify internal and external stakeholders and organize a collaborative approach to security. Ideally, your security planning team should meet for 60 to 90 minutes each semester or trimester. The success of team meetings is determined by the ability of the facilitator to present a clear agenda and solicit input from the participants.

Security Planning Team   Date: _____

School: _____

Principal	_____
Asst. Principal	_____
Teacher	_____
Teacher	_____
Teacher	_____
Counselor/Social Worker	_____
Dean/Security Officer	_____
Technology Director	_____
Secretary	_____
Nurse	_____
Custodian	_____
Student	_____
Parent	_____
Police	_____
Fire/Medical	_____
Student Services (optional)	_____
Community Relations (optional)	_____
Transportation (optional)	_____
Other (optional)	_____

FIGURE 9.1

Incident Records – Security and discipline related incidents that occur in your school and among your students and staff should be documented and reviewed. Figure 9.2 provides a means to record such incidents for awareness and prevention purposes.

Student Safety Audit – Involving students in security initiatives has traditionally been avoided. Yet, students are more proficient than adults in regards to technology and often more aware of issues that are occurring or that may occur on campus. This anonymous survey (Figure 9.3) solicits important information from students.

Suspicious Mail or Package Poster – The US Postal Service has identified suspicious mail patterns and appropriate responses to protect those that handle mail.

SCHOOL: _____

Incident Records

It is important to note that this activity is designed to create a confidential, working document to be modified as appropriate, both to accommodate the needs of this school and to meet state requisites.

Indicate the number of incidents reported this past school year for the categories below.

INCIDENT TYPE	NO.		INCIDENT TYPE	NO.
Arson			Hate Crime	
Assaults (verbal)			Hostage Situations	
Assaults and Battery (physical)			Insubordination	
Bombs/Bomb Threats			Intrusion/Trespass	
Bullying/Mobbing			Kidnapping	
Bus/Transportation-related			Molesting	
Deaths: Accidental			Property Damage	
Suicide			Riots	
Homicides			Robberies	
Demonstrations			Shootings	
Drug/Narcotic/Alcohol			Theft	
Emergency Building Evacuations			Vandalism	
Fights			Weapons at School	
Gang related			Other:	
Graffiti				
Harassment: Physical				
Verbal				
Ethnic				
Sexual				

What have been the most common sources and times of recurring incidents at this school?

Incident Type	Source/Place	Time-Dates

Indicate the numbers for each of the following for this time period.

Suspensions	
Expulsions	
Transfers to other schools/agencies	

FIGURE 9.2

Student Safety Audit

School _____Grade _____ Gender_____

Ethnicity/Race_____

What kinds of problems are most likely to occur in this school?

Where are the places about the school that are least safe?

What types of things make students concerned in this school?

What should the school do to prevent violence and security problems?

Since students often are most aware of potential safety problems, how might the school encourage students to accept their responsibilities to prevent violence?

FIGURE 9.3

These are summarized in a poster available at http://about.usps.com/securing-the-mail/suspiciousmail.htm. The poster should be clearly displayed wherever mail is sorted. The website includes a link at the bottom of the page for printing your own full-sized poster in color.

School Security Resource Websites

This invaluable collection of resources will assist you in raising security awareness, preventing incidents, planning for emergencies, and funding related initiatives.

Funding Sources
- http://www.school-grants.org/
- http://www.grants.gov/
- http://www.eschoolnews.com/funding/

Community Oriented Policing Services Grants and Funding

* http://www.cops.usdoj.gov/Default.asp?Item=46

National Law Enforcement and Corrections Technology Center

* School Safety DVDs (http://srtbrc.org/2012/12/free-school-safety-resources/)

Transportation Security Administration

* School Transportation Security Awareness DVD (http://www.tsa.gov/stakeholders/school-transportation-security-awareness/)

Center to Prevent Youth Violence

* National anonymous school violence tip line: 866-SPEAK-UP
* http://www.cpyv.org/programs/what-is-speak-up-2/

National Crime Prevention Council Safe School Resources

* http://www.ncpc.org/topics/

Student Safety and Self-Assessment Audits

* http://www.isbe.net/sos/htmls/safe_at_school.htm

National Sex Offender Registry

* http://www.familywatchdog.us/

Crime Prevention Through Environmental Design (CPTED)

* http://www.cdc.gov/violenceprevention/youthviolence/cpted.html
* http://www.ncpc.org/resources/files/pdf/training/Best%20Practices%20in%20CPTED%20-2.pdf

School Safety News

* http://www.schoolsafetynews.com/

"Bomb Threat Response: An Interactive Planning Tool for Schools"

* http://www.threatplan.org/

School Safety and Security Periodicals

* Campus Safety (http://www.campussafetymagazine.com/)
* Security Management (http://www.securitymanagement.com/search/filter/94/347/Any/Any/sink_news/)
* School Planning & Management (http://webspm.com/Home.aspx)
* American School & University (http://www.asumag.com/)

Chapter 5 "Influencing Behavior" Resources

Center for the Prevention of School-Aged Violence

* http://goodwin.drexel.edu/cposav/

Bullying Prevention

Do not be discouraged by bullying prevention program implementation difficulties and restrictions. Strategic and creative thinking can turn formidable obstacles into feasible programs that are well worth the investment.

National School Safety Center — *Bullying in Schools: Fighting the Bullying Battle, Discussion Activities for School Communities* by Hilda Quiroz et al (http://www.dps.mo.gov/homelandsecurity/safeschools/documents/Discussion%20Activities%20for%20School%

20Communities.pdf). This is an outstanding resource that includes lesson plans and teacher and parent cheat sheets, and are easy documents to reproduce. They are comprehensive, yet concise.

Internet Crimes Against Children (ICAC) Task Force — helps state and local law enforcement agencies develop an effective response to cyberenticement and child pornography cases (https://www.icactaskforce.org./Pages/Home.aspx). This assistance encompasses forensic and investigative components, training and technical assistance, victim services, and community education. The program was developed in response to the increasing number of children and teenagers using the Internet, the proliferation of child pornography, and heightened online activity by predators seeking unsupervised contact with potential underage victims. The FY 1998 Justice Appropriations Act (Pub, L. No. 105–119) directed the Office of Juvenile Justice and Delinquency Prevention to create a national network of state and local law enforcement cyber units to investigate cases of child sexual exploitation.

The ICAC program is a national network of 61 coordinated task forces representing over 2,000 federal, state, and local law enforcement and prosecutorial agencies. In FY 2011, the ICAC program trained over 31,000 law enforcement personnel, over 2,800 prosecutors, and more than 11,000 other professional working in the ICAC field. In FY 2011, ICAC investigations led to more than 5,700 arrests and over 45,000 forensic examinations.

Kentucky Center for School Safety — An excellent resource for school leaders (http://www.kycss.org/index2.php). From classroom management to assessing a welcoming environment and all aspects of emergency preparedness, this is an easy-to-navigate website to have in your favorites list.

Olweus Bullying Prevention Program — A widely used and highly regarded antibullying program certified by the US government for schools. Its creator, Dan Olweus, is recognized as one of the foremost experts on bullying prevention. Numerous studies have demonstrated that his program is effective and beneficial for long-term bullying prevention, as well as improved peer interactions when used in schools. Over a dozen countries, including the United States, have used and are using the Olweus program. Thousands of schools across the country have employed it. The program is tailored specifically for elementary, middle, and high schools to address the age differences between students. More about the program and other bullying information can be found at http://www.Olweus.org/.

StopBullying.gov — A government-run website that addresses bullying concerns for schools and provides helpful information regarding bullying prevention (http://www.stopbullying.gov/). It is a great resource for finding out about anti-bullying efforts and ways to start dealing with bullying issues. The website provides links to evidence-based programs that the government endorses (studies must prove a program's effectiveness) so that schools can access credible programs. StopBullying.gov's Bullying Prevention Training Module resources have a new infographic with important facts and research on bullying. This infographic illustrates the many forms of bullying, the prevalence of bullying, and its impact on youth. Like the Bullying Prevention Training Module, it is designed to help community leaders raise awareness of bullying prevention efforts in their neighborhoods and schools.

StopBullyingNow.com — Stan and Julia Davis have written several texts that provide practical, inexpensive, research-based strategies for reducing bullying in schools. Highly esteemed as both authors and seminar leaders, their trainings integrate Stan's 40 years of experience as a therapist with well-founded research on bullying behaviors and skill building activities. He successfully guides the reader or audience member through a deeper understanding of what motivates a child to engage in what he has termed "peer mistreatment," a term he has coined as a contemporary alternative to broadening the understanding of what it means to be a bully (noun) and to bully (verb) another person. A critical text that is particularly helpful for school leaders is, *Schools Where Everyone Belongs, Practical Strategies for Reducing Bullying, 2nd Ed. (2007).* Find out more at http://www.stopbullyingnow.com/.

The following texts, websites and programs serve as key resources that also include information on cyberbullying:

- Beane, Allan L. *Protect Your Child from Bullying: Expert Advice to Help You Recognize, Prevent, and Stop Bullying Before Your Child Gets Hurt.* San Francisco, CA: Jossey-Bass, 2008.
- Center for the Study and Prevention of Violence (http://www.colorado.edu/cspv/blueprints/).
- Coloroso, Barbara. *The Bully, the Bullied, and the Bystander, From Preschool to High School: How Parents and Teachers Can Help Break the Cycle of Violence.* New York, NY: Harper Collins Publishing, 2008. Ms. Coloroso is an educator and internationally renowned expert on school discipline and bullying, among other topics; her website (http://www.kidsareworthit.com/) provides information on the services she offers to school districts and the four other texts she has penned.
- National Center for Mental Health and Juvenile Justice (http://www.ncmhjj.com/).
- Roberts, Walter B., Jr. *Working with Parents of Bullies and Victims.* Thousand Oaks, CA: Corwin Press, 2008. This is a must have text for your student services staff. *Working with Parents of Bullies and Victims* is a companion volume to Roberts's text, *Bullying from Both Sides: Strategic Interventions for Working with Bullies and Victims.* Thousand Oaks, CA: Corwin Press, 2006. Chapter examples in this text include "Every Parent's Nightmare—and Yours, Too!" which discusses the high cost of ignoring bullying problems, how to handle difficult dynamics with parents, and ways to guide parents through conversations with their children. Another chapter lists seven specific talking points for parents to cover with their children if they have been bullied. The text concludes with chapters on "Fair Expectations for Parents and Educators" and "The Courage to Act." The text also includes sample conversations,

checklists, case studies, behavior plans, and other helpful resources. An entire bullying program can be built into your district's wellness plan by implementing some of the strategies laid out in this text. At the very least, this is excellent staff development material.

- *Youth Violence: A Report of the Surgeon General* (http://www.surgeongeneral.gov/library/youthviolence/chapter5/sec3.htm). This report highlights effective and ineffective strategies. Programs are categorized as "model," "promising," or "does not work."

Dating Violence
- Association of Title IX Administrators: http://www.atixa.org/.
- Break the Cycle: http://www.BreakTheCycle.org/.
- California Coalition Against Sexual Assault: http://www.calcasa.org/.
- Conference On Crimes Against Women: http://www.conferencecaw.org
- Domestic Abuse Hotline for Men and Women: http://www.dahmw.org/ or (888) 746-5754.
- Domestic Violence, Sexual Assault, and Stalking Data Resource Center: http://www.jrsa.org/dvsa-drc/.
- FBI Victim Assistance: http://www.fbi.gov/stats-services/victim_assistance/.
- IACP Sexual Assault Incident Reports Investigative Strategies: http://www.theiacp.org/portals/0/pdfs/SexualAssaultGuidelines.pdf.
- Love Is Respect: http://www.loveisrespect.org/.
- Men Can Stop Rape: http://www.mencanstoprape.org/.
- National Crime Victims Center: http://www.ncvc.org/.
- National Dating Abuse Hotline: (866) 331-9474.
- National Sexual Violence Resource Center: http://www.nsvrc.org/.
- National Stalking Resource Center: http://www.ncvc.org/src/.
- National Victim Notification Network: http://www.vinelink.com/.
- OJP NIJ-Sexual Assault on Campus: http://www.nij.gov/topics/crime/rape-sexual-violence/campus/Pages/welcome.aspx.
- Rape, Abuse, and Incest National Network (RAINN): http://www.rainn.org/.
- Resources for Sexual Assault Response Teams (SART Toolkit): http://ovc.ncjrs.gov/sartkit/.
- Safe Horizon: http://www.safehorizon.org/.
- Start Strong: http://www.startstrongteens.org/.
- That's Not Cool: http://www.thatsnotcool.com/.
- A Thin Line: http://www.athinline.org/.
- Violence Prevention Coalition of Greater Los Angeles: http://www.vpcgla.org/.
- US Department of Justice, Office on Violence Against Women: http://www.ovw.usdoj.gov/.

Violence Prevention Resources: Mental Health

- National Association of School Psychologists: http://www.nasponline.org/advocacy/mhbrochure.aspx.
- Baltimore School Mental Health Technical Assistance and Training Initiative: http://www.schoolmentalhealth.org/

Chapter 7, "Managing Emergencies" Resources

Guide for Developing High-Quality School Emergency Operations Plans
- http://www2.ed.gov/about/offices/list/oese/oshs/rems-k-12-guide.pdf.

Federal Emergency Management Agency (FEMA)
- Multi-Hazard Emergency Planning for Schools: http://training.fema.gov/EMIWeb/IS/courseOverview.aspx?code=is-362.a.
- Introduction to the Incident Command System for Schools: http://training.fema.gov/EMIWeb/IS/courseOverview.aspx?code=IS-100.sca.

Lockdown Drill Evaluation Form – Many states now require lockdown drills, but evaluating their effectiveness can be difficult. Figure 9.4 permits you to know which aspects of lockdown are most important, establish benchmarks for continuous improvement, and identify issues that should be addressed.

Incident Command Structure – The National Incident Management System (NIMS) seeks to establish consistent patterns and common language to utilize during emergencies. An Incident Command Structure (see Figure 9.5) should be completed in order to comply with NIMS in becoming as prepared as possible for emergencies. Within this structure, key staff can be pre-assigned critical roles should an incident occur. Administrators should consider taking NIMS courses 100, 200, 700 and 800.

United States Department of Education Emergency Planning Resources
- http://www2.ed.gov/admins/lead/safety/emergencyplan/index.html.

Gallagher Bassett Services, "Tornado Preparedness for Schools"
- http://www.gallagherpost.com/cflms/f/modules/Tornado%20Preparedness%20for%20Schools/player.html.

Chapter Summary

The resources in this chapter are available to get you started building your baseline plan and to set benchmarks for growing a more comprehensive plan as you bring in new stakeholders to partner with you. We do not necessarily endorse these sources, but we have reviewed them and think that they may be of assistance.

Make a commitment to providing a safer learning environment. Undertake a collaborative effort. Get started today.

LOCKDOWN EVALUATION FORM

School: _____   Hallway/Wing: _____

Date: _____
Time of Day: _____

Time to Get into Lock Down: _____

Room	Unlocked	Noise	Visibility

Comments: _____

_____

_____

_____

_____

FIGURE 9.4

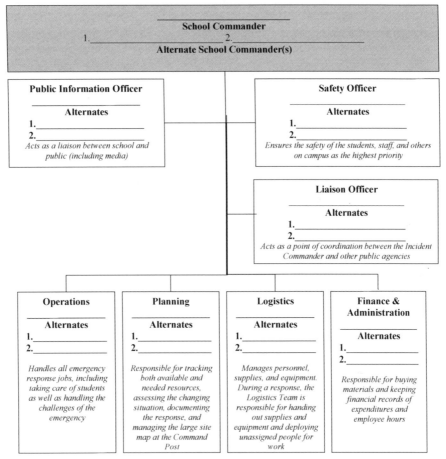

FIGURE 9.5

Book Conclusion

As a society, do we have priorities? What are they? We should, and they should be our children. Our children need to live and learn and prosper in safe and secure surroundings. It is our obligation to do everything we can to create that environment. We have learned through adversity that new awareness, preparedness, and communication can make a difference. Our future depends on our response.

Several years after the tragic events of 9/11, the former mayor of New York City, Rudy Giuliani, gave a keynote presentation at the annual ASIS International Seminar. I was among the thousands of attendees who waited with anticipation to learn what it was like to manage a crisis of that proportion.

Instead of describing the terrorist attack on the World Trade Center, however, Giuliani began by recounting what it was like to have presided over preparations for Y2K, or the Year 2000 problem. He considered the amount of time and money wasted on getting ready for something that never ultimately occurred to be the biggest blemish on the legacy of his administration. Until 9/11.

In the wake of a failed bombing attempt years prior, New York City had estimated that, if the towers ever fell victim to a real bombing at 9am on a weekday, they could expect over 12,000 fatalities. But there were only approximately 3000 deaths on 9/11. Giuliani explained to the attendees that the efforts that went into planning for Y2K unquestionably paid off on 9/11. Response agencies mitigated the crisis far more efficiently than they expected thanks to Y2K initiatives.

One week after the 9/11 tragedy, New York City faced the threat of anthrax poisoning. A few news stations and political officials received letters containing anthrax spores. Several people died and others were infected. The fear of widespread poisoning drove New York City officials to require hospitals to issue daily reports on how many individuals were being treated for flu-like symptoms, an indicator of anthrax poisoning.

Since the anthrax threat never materialized, the time and resources wasted on this reporting initiative might have felt like the Y2K experience. But, once again, a parallel benefit emerged. Reporting of flu-like symptoms aided New York City in identifying and successfully addressing the West Nile virus.

I refer to the lessons the former mayor shared as the "Giuliani principle." This principle states that whatever initiatives undertaken to improve security will pay off in the long run. In New York, Y2K preparation efforts paid off on 9/11. Anthrax preparedness measures paid off with the West Nile virus.

Apply the information in this book. Set collaborative decisions in motion. The school security initiatives you undertake will pay off in the long run. The Giuliani principle says so.

Index

Note: Page numbers with "f" and "b" denote figures and boxes, respectively.

Made in the USA
Middletown, DE
28 October 2017